To Bill —

River of God:

Where Religion Began and Why Grace and Love Will Triumph

by

Dr. Ron Boehme

Enjoy the "River"
of God's love & truth.

In Him —

4-6-21

DORRANCE
PUBLISHING CO
EST. 1920
PITTSBURGH, PENNSYLVANIA 15238

Dorrance Publishing Co
585 Alpha Drive
Pittsburgh, PA 15238
Visit our website at *www.dorrancebookstore.com*

ISBN: 978-1- 4809-5171- 6
eISBN: 978-1- 4809-5193- 8

Also by Ron Boehme:

Leadership for the 21st Century:
Changing Nations Through the Power of Serving

If God Has a Plan for My Life, Why Can't I Find It?
You Have a Destiny

Restoring America's Conscience

The Fourth Wave:
Taking Your Place in the New Era of Missions

"I highly recommend Ron Boehme and his mission and new book. He is a brilliant and gracious follower of Christ who dares to care and communicate his compassion with vigor. Everything he writes is worth reading."

Dr. Ted Baehr,
Chairman of the Christian Film & Television Commission

"Dr. Ron Boehme has written a powerful book that helps to answer the most important question a person can ask in their lifetime, *'Is there a God to whom I must answer?'* Echoing Jesus' poignant and penetrating question, *'Who do you say that I am?'* this book points all who are searching for truth to Jesus Christ, our Savior and King. *The River of God* is written with piercing clarity that will break through confusion and conflicts of choice. The love and grace of the 'Lord of All' shouts above the fray and draws the reader into a confident and settled understanding of the one true Way."

Dr. Glenn C. Burris, Jr.,
President, The Foursquare Church

"This is a book that is a must-read for at least three groups of readers: those who are religious, those who are not religious, and those who are not certain about religion. That seems to include most, if not all, of us. I cannot think of any person who would not profit from reading this remarkable book. Please do it!"

Dr. Paul Cedar,
Chairman. The Mission America Coalition

"Whatever your belief, you will find this book a challenge to your thinking to rise above the world and look down on five major worldviews. You will be forced to renew or make a new commitment. It will help you think globally and personally. That's quite a challenge."

Loren Cunningham,
founder, Youth With A Mission

"Ron Boehme is a man of wisdom. *River of God* is full of Ron's insightful way of looking at the world, at history, at the development of thought and its trajectory for our future. In this time of chaotic thought and multiplied outcomes of everyone doing what is right in their own eyes, Ron brings clarity and understanding. He crystallizes the plethora of religions into five worldview choices in the search for ultimate truth. What an invaluable tool for such a time as this."

Paul Fleischmann,
President Emeritus, National Network of Youth Ministries

"Dr. Ron Boehme's book *River of God* answers a deep and growing double need in our increasingly pluralistic world: First, how do we respect everyone without compromising the essential, eternal truths of the Gospel? Second, how can we effectually communicate the one true Gospel while overcoming the partial truths that have intensely captivated so many?

"In *River of God*, Dr. Boehme synthesizes his sincere compassion for benefitting all people and his profound passion for their receiving the transforming power of divine grace and ultimate truth for personal liberation. His very simple but accurate categorization of world religions empowers the reader to identify and diagnose the few variations of popular errors that we constantly encounter. The reader is also given a fresh telling of the liberating divine truth and grace that—in the awesome flow of the river of God—splendidly overcome those very popular errors that Dr. Boehme has exposed so well."

Dr. Paul de Vries,
President, Trinity Divinity School

"*River of God* is an open door for revelation and an invitation to an ever-deepening relationship with the only true God rooted in love and grace, requiring nothing but faith. Bring the longings of your heart to these pages, and open your mind to this journey of reason and faith, longing and hope. I assure you it will be a journey of joy."

Dick Eastman,
International President, Every Home for Christ

"Ron Boehme's *River of God* is the ideal guide for persons who are searching for answers to the great questions of life, but lack the time and resources needed to bury themselves in research. In the compass of one small volume, Boehme takes readers on a whirlwind tour of the history of the world's religions in which he supplies just enough information to enable readers intelligently to assess their spiritual options and choose the path they consider most likely to yield ultimate fulfillment."

Dennis W. Jowers, PhD,
Professor of Theology, Faith International University & Seminary

"My long-term co-worker in the Kingdom of God, Dr. Ron Boehme, has created a marvelous introduction to not only God's revelation of Himself and His truth in the Bible. In this book he explains to the beginner the basics of 'How we can know anything for certain?' and offers mental tools for evaluating one's perspective or 'grid' through which we see and judge all reality.

"Ron also offers valuable, clear definitions of the main competing worldviews and critiques them fairly in my estimation. I would hope all Christians could read this book if they are not already armed with a strong, Biblical introduction to the world of philosophy and have the tools for testing the differences between falsehood and reality."

Dr. Jay Grimstead,
Director, Coalition on Revival

"In a world full of more relativism and competing religious narratives, Dr. Ron Boehme's latest work, *River of God*, serves as a clear descriptive resource defining the 'other voices' while simultaneously proving that only one can occupy the pedestal of truth, eternal life, and grace."

Rev. Dr. Samuel Rodriguez,
President, NHCLC/CONELA, Hispanic Evangelical Association

"In the power of the Spirit, I believe a young generation can literally change the world. But we don't have years to let them slowly plod through scattered studies of worldviews and religions. Ron Boehme's new book represents the single most efficient way to give any believer a solid understanding of competing worldviews and the primacy of the God of the Bible. I recommend it without reservations."

Richard Ross, PhD,
professor of student ministry, Southwestern Seminary

"As soon as it arrives, I read Ron Boehme's 'Revive America' blog. Every time Ron has profound insights that either expand my understanding of the world around me, or take me deeper in my journey with Jesus. From exploring *River of God,* I can see this book doing for many what Ron's blog does for me—expanding understanding of the world and deepening intimacy with Jesus.

"For over 50 years I given my life to reach and disciple the younger generation. Nothing, from my perspective, will have more importance for the younger generation than answering Ron's two questions he raises in *Rive of God.* By answering the questions of 'Is there God to whom I must answer?' and 'If so, how do I come into a right relationship with God?' Ron addresses the two most significant needs of young people: *Perspective* from understanding the Truth in God's worldview and *Identity* that results from finding Life in Jesus. This book will have a considerable impact around the world and a deep influence on each person who reads it!"

Barry St. Clair,
President, Reach-Out Ministries

Contents

Foreword

You are holding in your hands a truly remarkable, thought-provoking book that I believe is particularly timely for the season now before the global Church as we prepare to gather in history's greatest harvest of lost humanity. For me personally, this message deeply touches the ministry I lead, Every Home for Christ, as our teams of tens of thousands of volunteers and field staff visit as many as 250,000 homes every day in 150 nations sharing a face-to-face presentation of the Good News of Jesus at every doorstep. Daily this army of volunteers and workers knock on these many thousands of doors and meet multitudes of people who are all asking life's biggest questions: Is there a God? Who is He? Who am I? How do I respond to God? What does God want from me?

In the pages that follow, Dr. Ron Boehme sets out to answer these central questions by taking a step back and looking at our history as humanity, considering all the ways we have developed answers to these questions and where we've found ourselves as a result. Ron probes the nature of truth, explores insightful comparisons, and ultimately leads us out of murky confusion and half-truths to the very shores of the *River of God*. Here you will find a vision for truth, for grace, for faith—for life in the fullness of an intimate relationship with the one, true God.

Ron's writing is, at once, deeply personal and widely relevant. Like an old friend, Ron opens his heart and invites us into his own story, taking us along on a search for truth that stretches back to creation and forward to the final restoration of the kingdom of God. We find here a compelling vision and a voice of reason, a quest that is as meaningful as it is honest.

Wherever you are on your journey of faith, I believe there is something here for you. This anointed book is a tool for believers to understand the hearts and minds of those they are called to "love into the Kingdom," as well as to find a deeper understanding of their own life's journey. It is a treasure for anyone asking life's central questions—and isn't that all of us?—a gentle guide to ask the right questions and search for answers in the right places. *River of God* is an open door for revelation and an invitation to an ever-deepening relationship with the only true God rooted in love and grace, requiring nothing but faith.

Bring the longings of your heart to these pages, and open your mind to this journey of reason and faith, longing and hope. I assure you it will be a journey of joy.

Dick Eastman
International President, Every Home for Christ

To Shirley,
my wonderful wife,
who personally taught me
most of what I know
about the gracious, loving God.

Introduction

I've tried to write the clearest book on religion that's ever been attempted. Why? Because the most important question a person will ever ask in life is "Is there a God to whom I must answer?" If the answer to that question is *yes* then the second most important question is "How do I come into right relationship with him?"

That's what religion is supposed to be about.

I personally began the search to answer those questions many years ago. My quest was wide-ranging—I looked at all I could. It was also selective—I was looking for answers that rested on solid principles and firm evidence. I'm a seeker of truth and continue to be. Maybe you are too. I read the Koran from cover to cover. I studied the philosophy of the Buddha and other eastern religions. I looked at the teachings of the Bible from Genesis to Revelation.

What I found was a River of God that satisfied my thirst and answered my biggest questions. The goal of this book is to make that search easier for you.

The proliferation of religious worldviews and the current trend toward global pluralism make it increasingly difficult for believers in God to hold to the uniqueness of their faith and defend its veracity in an increasingly post-modern (relativistic) world. As Terance L. Tiessen rightly states, "Spirituality is on the increase, and the religions of the world have become more rather that less prominent in our awareness."[12]

It is critical in today's diverse religious climate to understand the beliefs of the major religions, how they historically came into being, and whether all of them or one of them can lead us into proper alignment with the Almighty. Every person's salvation hinges on the answer to that final question.

When William Carey ushered in the modern era of Christian missions in the 1790s, relatively little was known about the religious beliefs of other cultures outside of their geographical regions. Carey's seminal work *An Enquiry into the Obligations of Christians to Use Means for the Conversion of the Heathens* contained 87 pages of statistics on the countries of the world in which, out of a then-global population of 731 million, Carey lamented that "420 million lie in pagan darkness."[3] That meant that two-thirds of the world's population, living in over one hundred nations, shared religious views that were unknown to most Westerners. The same was true of those who lived in Africa and much of the Far East.

Two hundred years later, we have a much better understanding as to what comprises the religions of the world. Exploration, the advance of civilization, and the explosion in knowledge fueled by the Information Age now give us a clearer picture of what earth's inhabitants believe.

According to David Barrett et al, editors of the *World Christian Encyclopedia: A Comparative Survey of Churches and Religions - A.D. 30 to 2000*, there are nineteen major world religions which are subdivided into a total of 270 large religious groups, and many smaller ones—numbering in the thousands.[4]

Surrounded by this sea of choices in religious worldviews, how is the average person to know which religion is true or false? In an age of many choices, this appears to be the most important question that most people will ask in their lifetime.

Furthermore, choices—especially religious ones—have serious consequences. For example, if you are a follower of Hinduism and believe that history goes in endless cycles that cannot be altered, you may do little to improve your state in life and live in abject poverty as do masses of people in India. If you are a Muslim jihadist, you might believe that violence is an acceptable means of securing worldwide submission to Islam. Witness the 9/11 bombers. You might commit despicable acts to obtain a reward of seventy virgins in heaven. That type of heaven may not exist.

If you are a follower of Jesus Christ, you will acknowledge that a loving and just God is directing the affairs of earth and will do your part to see His "will be done on earth as it is in heaven" (Matthew 6:10 NIV). This will include practicing the cultural mandate, belief in human rights and individual responsibility, promoting freedom and innovation, and working to improve the lives of people who are made in the image of the Creator. You will also do your part to share the Good News of God's forgiveness in Christ to the 14,000 people groups of the world with a goal of completing the Great Commission.

Religion matters—and affects nearly every area of our lives.

Yet, in this age of pluralism and varied religious beliefs, it appears that many people not only fail to understand the differences between the world's great religions, but they lack clear convictions about what they personally believe. Some confuse religion with their country of origin (i.e. "I was born in America so I must be a Christian" or "my family has been Islamic for centuries so I must be a Muslim."). Or they call themselves a follower of Christ, but engage in an immoral lifestyle that is contrary to the teachings of their faith.

If there was ever a time to be clear about one's religious beliefs—during a period when we have greater access to knowledge than any other time in history—that time must be today.

Why is understanding the historical background and essential beliefs of the world's great religions vital to every person? First, a universal concept and belief in a god or gods, found in nearly every culture of the world, points to some form of reality. And if there is such a thing as "the truth about God," then aligning yourself with that truth must bring benefits in this life. As Rodney Stark explains, "religion is everywhere because the needs it fulfills are everywhere."[5]

Second, if there is a God who is the final Judge of all people (a concept common to a number of world religions including Judaism, Christianity, and Islam), then knowing how to be in a right relationship with God is of supreme importance to every person and may determine the place you occupy in eternity.

Third, if you are a follower of Jesus Christ and believe that "there is salvation in no one else" (Acts 4:12 NLT)[6] then having firm convictions about your faith will make you effective in sharing and defending "the faith once delivered to the saints."[7]

This book will propose that truth does exist in the universe; that all roads do *not* lead to heaven or Nirvana; that, although there are thousands of religious faiths in the world, these beliefs can be boiled down to just *five* major concepts of God; and that the truth about God flows from one original source (the River of God) that was distorted in four directions over time, but remains the steady stream to human happiness and eternal life.

The advances of globalization and the explosion of knowledge in the twentieth and twenty-first centuries provide us unprecedented access to the religions of the world. This book, which presupposes that truth is a rational concept, will attempt to explain how thousands of religious expressions that exist globally can be condensed into five major concepts of God. Through comparing these five worldviews and analyzing their origins we will suggest that four of these religions are distortions of reality, and that only one of them can be true.

A Historical Perspective

The story of religion and man's conception of God are as ancient as the recorded history of mankind. Greek philosophers shared their concepts of deity and the proliferation of the gods before the advent of Christ (B.C.), but many of their writings were lost during the turmoil of the Middle Ages due to the collapse of the Roman Empire. European monks are credited with preserving a great deal of the literature of the West from the fifth through the tenth centuries A.D.[8]

Marco Polo's famous visit to China in 1275-1292 A.D. gave clearer understanding to the West of the religions of the East. His travels on the Silk Road and experiences in the court of Kublai Khan were widely read in Europe in *The Travels of Marco Polo*.[9] Earlier in the thirteenth century, St. Francis of Assisi dialogued with the Sultan Al-Kamil of Egypt on the differences between Christianity and the Muslim faith. Yet, for much of the past two thousand years, detailed interreligious understanding was not widespread. Most people had little access to the knowledge about religious beliefs in other cultures.

It was nineteenth–twenty-first century global travel and an increase in information that first led to books that chronicled and compared various religions and worldviews found in the nearly 200 countries of the world.

Acknowledgments

Dean Halverson's *Compact Guide to World Religions* (1996) proved invaluable as a concise starting point for me. Halverson and his contributors focused on seven world religions, providing a thorough comparison of their belief systems. Rodney Stark's excellent treatise *Discovering God: The Origins of the Great Religions and the Evolution of Belief* was helpful by offering its perspective on the various religious leaders of history and how each religion initially emerged in history. Stark is a respected sociologist of religion who writes from a Protestant Christian perspective.

Arvind Sharma's book *Our Religions* examines a different set of seven world religions—each written by a member of that particular faith. Terrance Tiessen's *Who Can Be Saved: Reassessing Salvation in Christ and World Religions* is another helpful guide to the possible similarities and links between different religious worldviews.

I also benefitted greatly from Dr. Stephen Whatley's twenty-six-hour series *Christian Encounter with World Religions* taught at Faith International University & Seminary, Tacoma, WA, in the summer of 2011. Dr. Whatley's comparisons of the strengths and weaknesses of the world's major religions were pivotal in my decision to pursue this course of study.

I am greatly indebted to Dennis Jowers, PhD, Professor of Theology at Faith International University & Seminary, who spent numerous hours editing and advising both the writing and theological content of the book.

Today there are many books and courses on the religions of the world—a topic much less discussed just one hundred years ago. I will attempt to add to the understanding of the world's religions through this study. Essentially, the case will be made that all concepts of God can be reduced to five; that these five share a common source; that four are distortions of the original; and that only one can be true.

Scope and Limitations

The scope of this study will be limited to analyzing and comparing the following five major views about God: 1) Biblical Faith— There is a triune loving God, 2) Polytheism—There are many gods, 3) Pantheism—Everything is God, 4) Islam—There is a single warring God, and 5) Atheism—There is no god (or man is god).

I will analyze these five concepts in their historical contexts. Time and space do not allow a comprehensive study of each of the world's major religions. These constraints have led me to focus on the emergence of each major religion in its historical context, the main teachings of each religion, and their comparison with one another.

I will suggest that biblical faith in a loving Creator was the first manifestation of God in the universe and grew in progressive revelation from man's creation (Yahwehism) to Judaism, and finally to trusting in Jesus Christ (The Way). I call this revelation the "The River of God " due to the life-giving, nourishing aspects of rivers and the use of this metaphor in the Bible. The biblical record begins with a river that went "out of Eden to water the garden" (Genesis 2:10 NKJV). Scripture concludes with a vision of heaven, which describes a "pure river of the water of life, clear as crystal proceeding from the throne of God and the Lamb" (Revelation 22:1). In these passages and many other places in Scripture, God's truth, presence and power are associated with the life-giving benefits of rivers.

My conclusion is that this River of God was the clearly manifested during man's beginning, but became distorted over time into four "false distributaries." All of these polluted streams are based on elements of the original truth. I will show how the four distortions are different in numerous ways, yet in matters of "salvation," are interestingly similar.

I believe that history is moving back toward a full manifestation of the River of God. Heaven will be the place of its final and eternal consummation. That River is full of truth. It is teeming with grace. It operates by love.

Methodology

I have used three different research methods to analyze the major religions of the world, their origins, beliefs, and the truthfulness of their views.

The first is historical. There is much that we can learn about religious worldviews by reviewing relevant histories and analyzing authoritative sources. A significant body of literature exists on this subject for which I am grateful. I will incorporate the writings of modern-day historians and academics who have written and lectured on the religious experience of mankind. As more has become known in the past one hundred years, numerous books have appeared on the subject of comparative religion.

My second method is conceptual. In my many years as a Christian missionary, I have traveled to over sixty nations around the world where a majority of the world religions exist. I am personally acquainted with their teachings and have shared my own faith with members of every major religious sect. My personal study and observations over past decades have produced a theoretical understanding of what religious worldviews have in common and when these points of commonality may have come into being.

I will present a conceptual paradigm that adheres to the belief that all people hold onto *one of five* primary beliefs regarding God. Suggesting that there are only five major views of God is not intended to limit the many religious expressions found in the world. However, this approach will make the comparison much easier to navigate as opposed to analyzing scores of major religions, each with numerous offshoots.

The third is the theological angle. Religious worldviews are a part of the "study of God" that theology encompasses. As a follower of Jesus, I will analyze and compare both the histories and theologies of the five major views of God through the lens of Holy Scripture.

The Bible is the world's mostly widely read and respected religious text. It contains a literal library of writings (sixty-six books), was written over thousands of years by some forty authors, and states unequivocally that it is the inspired word of God.[10] I believe the Holy Bible suggests that The River of God has nourished the world since its inception and continues to guide people of all nations into the truth. The theology of Scripture will be the backdrop of our conclusions about the world's great religions.

I will begin our discussion with a Prologue that sets the stage for our journey. It describes poetically the River of God as the only true reality in the beginning—and how the universe came to be. It ends with an introduction to one of history's most important characters, *the liar,* who is a major player in the history of man.

In the first section, Chapter One, we will expose the voluminous amount of lies that influence our daily lives. These falsehoods make it difficult to find the truth. Lies are not confined to the realm of religion. We meet them in our regular routines via government, the media, education, and other organs of culture. We find them in our history books and encounter them in our homes. We are deluged daily with lies about morality, life, justice, freedom, economics, and sexuality. Our world is drowning in half-truths and spurious claims.

Chapter Two will analyze the role of religious worldviews in trying to make sense of the many images we're forced to digest. A worldview is a "grid" through which one views reality (i.e. one's presuppositions about life.)[11] We will examine how every religion contains a worldview that addresses the basic questions about God, life, purpose, humanity, etc. I will use the word "worldview" as synonymous with religious philosophy. The universality of religion not only tips us off about the uniqueness of man, but also lends credence to the idea that truth exists and is worth pursuing.

My central thesis is that there are not hundreds or thousands of religions in the world. *There are only five.* Thus, religious experience might not be as vast as it seems. Five primary lenses exist through which to form a concept of God or absolute reality. That understanding might be helpful to you. I will propose that each of those five worldviews contains elements of the truth; that they all shared a common source we will call the River of God; and that four of them were distorted into half-or-partial truths that muddied the waters and led people astray.

In Chapter Three I will justify a belief most of us hold—that there is such a thing as truth. Truth is conformity with fact or reality, or exact accordance with that which is, has been, or shall be.[12] In an increasingly postmodern world, it is important to maintain an absolute belief in truth which can be verified through evidence.

In this study I will examine perceived truths about God through the evidence of history, literature, and personal experience. We will look at six different characteristics of truth that testify to its reality. Then we will explore some important questions that respectable worldviews must answer such as "Who's in charge?" "How did we get here?", "What's the basis of right and wrong?", and "Is there a future and hope?" If a worldview doesn't answer life's basic questions, it is worthless for the purpose of directing our lives.

We will explore in Chapter Four some reliable sources truth that we possess. I believe there are three. One is invisible, but half of the world pursues it daily. Another made the pursuit of truth fashionable—then it was lost for hundreds of years until some industrious monks resurrected it. The final source of truth is simply the River of God.

In Section Two we will take a detailed look at the world's five major religions in the order in which they appeared in history. In Chapters Five I will discuss biblical faith in a Loving God which most books on world religions call "Christianity." But that word is not found in its Scriptures (The Bible) and the followers of Jesus Christ preferred to be known as the people of "The Way."[13] For the sake of this study, I will consider biblical faith the progressive revelation of God as found in both the Old and New Testaments. Thus biblical faith in a Loving God includes faith/redemption from the time of Adam and Eve to Abraham, believers in the Hebrew nation and the followers of Jesus Christ.

Chapter Six will propose how the next religious worldview—polytheism—appeared on the scene of human history. Polytheism is belief in or worship of a plurality of gods—from the Greek words "many gods."[14] This view was prevalent in many ancient civilizations such as Egypt, Greece, and the Roman Empire. Currently, polytheism is practiced in numerous modern religions such as Hinduism and Buddhism and many animistic folk religions.

Chapter Seven will take a look at pantheism which is closely tied to polytheism—especially in India. Pantheism is a doctrine that equates God with the forces and laws of the universe. It is also called monism which is an "impersonal oneness."[15] Pantheism is a main feature in Hinduism, Buddhism, Sikhism, and the New Age Movement. The Gaia Theory or Principle is a quasi-scientific expression of pantheism.

Next we will discuss in Chapter Eight the rise of atheism/secularism. Atheists claim that they do not believe in a deity. Atheism has some ancient expressions as in Chinese Confucianism and Buddhism, but most of its adherents come from the modern world of secular humanism, Marxism, and Fascism. The atheist's rejection of God oftentimes leads to the worship of man or an all-powerful state (as in communism).

We will conclude our tour of the world's major religions with the history and beliefs of Islam and its meteoric rise in the seventh century A.D. The term Islam means "submission" to the will of God and the person who submits is this ideology is generally called a "Muslim." Islam was founded by an Arabian named Mohammed in the city of Mecca in 622 A.D. Muslims make up nearly one-fourth of the people in the world.[16]

In the final section of the book, beginning in Chapter Ten, we will compare the five worldview choices that the seeker of the truth must confront. Which worldview makes the most sense? Which conforms to conscience and an innate sense of duty? Interestingly enough, I will propose that four of the world's religions are the same in their motivation and call for human behavior. Only one champions the power of *grace* and *faith*. This one worldview appears to answer best the questions of life and possesses all of the characteristics that truth must display. Thus, I will propose that only one of the perspectives on God can be true—and should be chosen by both individuals and nations that are seeking freedom and salvation.

Chapter Eleven will explore the worldview battles that are taking place around the globe today. The "Western War" is a titanic struggle between secularism and biblical faith. The Eastern Front is a four-way tug-of-war between the ideologies of pantheism, polytheism, secularism, and biblical faith. And on a global scale, there is a third war of "jihad" being fought between Islam and the world. We will predict the outcome of these worldview wars.

Finally, in Chapter Twelve we will discuss the triumph of truth in the world of ideas. In the beginning there was only the River of God. In the end, that river will once again become all-in-all. We will discover that this cosmic, nourishing fountain is centered in a Person who will be the focus of eternity. I will encourage all seekers to "wade in the water" until their thirst is completely quenched.

The Epilogue will transport us to the end of time where we find two different bodies of water, a river of life and a lake of fire. We will discover the destiny of *the liar* and all who believe his lies. And more importantly, we will learn where the truth will lead us if we are willing to believe.

Thank you for taking this journey with me from the River of God to the religions of the world.

Here's how it all began, and how it turned from truth to lies.

Prologue

Once upon a time there was the River of God. The River was a part of God and a perfect expression of his heart and nature. All things were made through the River, who set in motion all that is and is to be. The stars, the planets, the galaxies all shouted with joy over the life-giving aspects of the River which nourished and sustained all things.

The River was pure; the River was true; the River gave definition to everything that encountered its generating and refreshing waters.

The River of God watered the earth where men and women came to dwell. Man and woman drank of its rich abundance and experienced the fruits of its bounty. Everything was good because the River was truly a fountain of life.

Then *the liar* appeared. He had once been a part of the River, enjoying its healing powers and extending its expansive dominion.

But *the liar* turned against the River of God. He plotted to pollute its bountiful streams and muddy its pristine passages. *The liar* desired to destroy the River—or keep its grateful inhabitants from quenching their thirst in its sweet and limitless reservoirs.

The liar had a plan.

Section One

THE SEARCH FOR WATER

Chapter One

Lies

"When the Liar speaks, he makes it up out of his lying nature and fills the world with lies."

(John 8:44—The Message)

My life was changed by a lie. It was a big lie that tore my family apart and took my father from me for three years.

That lie also motivated me to be a seeker of the truth.

I will never forget one memorable childhood event. I was a ninth grader at Marcus Whitman Junior High School in Port Orchard, Washington—a picturesque little town of 4,000 people in the center of Puget Sound and a ferry ride away from the Emerald City of Seattle. Physical Education (P.E.) class was breezing along when my teacher and football coach, Bob Ames (who once a tried out with the Green Bay Packers), yelled my name and asked me to follow him to his office. He looked troubled.

"Whatcha need?" I asked as I plopped down on a chair amidst the clutter of Mr. Ames combination office/locker room/equipment storage area. Bob Ames was big and strong—an old-fashioned football coach who was always in control of everything and everyone—including his carefully concealed feelings.

Not today. With moisture brimming in his eyes and his pupils glancing nervously at the floor, he said the words that would change the trajectory of my life:

"Ronnie, I'm sorry to have to tell you this, but your dad was convicted this afternoon and is going to prison." He looked painfully away as if he was going to puke.

The words hit me like a jarring thud. Going to prison—my dad? I'd already lost my mom to complications from meningitis five years earlier. In the years since, Dad had re-married, and my brother and I were working on a new relationship with our stepmother.

Now my father was also being taken from me?

In that moment my world went dark. In a fog of uncertainty and grief, I left school early and went home to be with my family. Some weeks later, we celebrated Christmas on December 22; three days before most normal kids opened their presents.

We had no choice. Dad would be in prison by December 25.

I remember getting many expensive gifts that day—it was Dad's generous way of softening our goodbye. But the main thing that sticks in my mind is that we cried all day long.

All of this happened because of a lie.

FRONT PAGE NEWS

Dad's imprisonment had been coming for years—but my brother and I were mostly shielded from it by the distractions and limitations of youth and a protective family clan. My father, Robert Boehme, was a successful family doctor in our hometown who had moved his parents and four siblings from Akron, Ohio to the west coast following graduation from medical school. He'd started his first practice in Port Orchard and met my mother while giving student vaccinations at the local high school. Greg was born a year later, and I followed in eighteen months. Soon, our family of four was living

4

happily in a nice middle class home overlooking Sinclair Inlet and the Olympic Mountains. Picture *Leave It to Beaver* or *Father Knows Best*. Little did we know that disaster lay ahead.

My dad was a fervent advocate of lower medical prices and better service. He partnered with a Portland, Oregon, entrepreneur who had invented a new way to do mass blood tests through innovative mechanization. The upstart business was called United Medical Labs. Blood tests could be done faster and cheaper.

Together, my father and his friend set out to change the medical world.

But big medicine didn't like their profits being slashed, so the medical hierarchy came after them with a vengeance. I was too young to comprehend what was going on, but over a period of six years, the medical establishment and their political cronies viciously came after United Medical Labs to put them out of business.

Three different trials on trumped up and unrelated charges were leveled at my father. My mom died during the first trial. My dad was acquitted. After re-marrying, more charges were leveled at him—but again he was acquitted.

My parents were doing repairs on our boathouse at the Port Orchard Marina when a beam fell and hit my stepmom—now adopted mother—in the head. She landed in the hospital for some time but fully recovered. But the powers we were fighting saw another opportunity and mercilessly went to work. They accused my father of attempted murder—not because of the falling beam—but that he tried to *poison* my mother while she was recuperating in hospital.

The case went to court and during that year; the "Boehme Attempted Murder Trial" was the third most common front-page story in our local newspaper (next to the Vietnam War etc.). Everyone in town knew that Dad was innocent—and that the fight was politically and economically motivated.

Why was Dad taken from us and sent to prison?

A lab technician lied on the witness stand that he found poison in my mother's system. It was his word versus ours. The jury ruled in favor of the medic. Some months later the lab tech "committed suicide."

But the lie had accomplished its purpose. My dad went to prison for three years; United Medical Labs was discredited and forced to close its doors; our family lost everything except our home; Mom worked nights to pay the bills and keep the family together.

And I began a search for truth—not just about my dad's injustice, but about the meaning of life, whether there was a God out there, how we got into this crazy, lying world, and how I could personally overcome it.

WHAT'S IN A LIE?

According to a favorite dictionary, a *lie* is: "to utter falsehood with an intention to deceive, or with an immoral design. To exhibit a false representation; to say or do that which deceives another when he has a right to know the truth, or when morality requires a just representation."[17]

A lie is an *intended deception*. It might contain elements of truth, and often this is the power of the falsehood—it is a *half*-truth. Nonetheless, lies are used by moral agents (those who possess intelligence and intentions) to fool others with a specific design to hurt or destroy them.

The first recorded lie in historic literature is found in the Bible, in Genesis 3:1-5:

> Now the serpent was the shrewdest of all the creatures the Lord God had made. "Really?" he asked the woman. "Did God really say you must not eat any fruit of the garden?" "Of course we may eat it," the woman told him. "It's only the fruit from the tree at the center of the garden that we are not allowed to eat. God says we must not eat it or even touch it, or we will die." "You won't die!" the serpent hissed. "God knows that your eyes will be opened when you eat it. You will become just like God, knowing everything both good and evil" (Genesis 3:1-5).

Let's note some of the characteristics of lying that are found in this early exchange. First, an intended deception is designed to get you to doubt something you know to be true. "'Really?'" said the deceiver." "Did God really say?" Sowing seeds of doubt is the first trick of the lie. The goal is to move you from faith to a degree of unbelief. It is only when you stand on shaky ground that's you're able to be toppled.

Secondly, the original liar told the woman a half-truth: "'You won't die!' the serpent hissed." That clever statement was both true and not true. It was *true* that the man and woman would not die instantly. That would happen later. But it was *false* because they immediately died "spiritually" (became separately from their Creator) and eventually died physically. This half-truth was the power behind the deception. Keep this in mind as we analyze the world religions in coming chapters. Much of their power is found in half-truths that sound good and are partially right—but still intend to deceive and manipulate the hearer.

The final twist of the original lie came with these deceptive words: "God knows . . . .your eyes will be opened . . . You will become like God . . . " This is heady stuff. First, "God-language" was used to sanction this act of disobedience. Second, they were told that their eyes would be opened—and yes, that was true, but not in a beneficial way. Third, they were encouraged to pursue god-like stature. Who wouldn't want to believe such lofty promises?

But it was a lie—based on intentional deception, using doubt and half-truths to generate a confused spiritual pride. Matthew Henry comments, "Satan teaches men first to doubt, and then to deny. Satan ruined himself by desiring to be like the Most High; therefore, he sought to infect our first parents with the same desire, that he might ruin them too."[18]

That is the purpose of lying—to hurt or cause ruin to the hearer. Think of the millions of falsehoods that have been and are being told in the world. No wonder the average person finds it difficult to find the truth in many areas of life.

A WORLD OF LIES (AND FAKE NEWS)

It is important to comprehend the vast ocean of lies that confront us every day. I can't begin to scratch the surface, but five examples will help to paint the picture. Elevating our view of the prevalence of lies in our world should give us greater understanding as to why people seek for truth and comfort in the realm of religion.

Lies about Origins

By the time I graduated from high school, evolutionary theory had been around for over a century and was firmly established in educational circles. When I studied evolution at both the high school and college level, I was not opposed to the theory that there was no God and that everything had simply evolved from nothing. That might be possible. But there were other ideas that seemed more plausible to my inquisitive mind.

However, none of those theories were allowed in the schoolroom—especially anything that mentioned God or a Creator. When the theory of Intelligent Design came along and seemed to explain some of the problems with evolution—especially the concept of "irreducible complexity" being seen in molecular biology, there was a huge backlash from the educational world that virtually banned the idea from every university in America.[19]

Michael Behe, a professor of Biochemistry at Lehigh University in his book *Darwin's Black Box*, clearly said that he was not using his research to point to a Creator God. "The inference to design can be held with all the firmness that is possible in this world, without knowing anything about the designer."[20] Yet Behe and other intelligent design proponents were marginalized by the scientific community and told to keep their ideas to themselves. Apparently evolution held a monopoly on truth in the "origins" arena.

Yet, the more I studied macro-evolution (the theory of common descent of all living things over millions of years), the more difficulties I saw with the theory. Where did the original matter come from? Didn't the Second Law of Thermodynamics—the principle of entropy—point toward the breakdown of natural processes, not their improvement? What about the lack of transitional life forms in the fossil record, or, for example, the fact that "the Piltdown bones were the object of deliberate forgery" in the early twentieth century?[21]

Charles Darwin, whose 1858 book *The Origin of the Species* brought evolutionary theory into vogue, had his own doubts about evolutionary theory, and especially the contrary evidence that is found in the fossil record. He says there is a "a crowd of difficulties" related to fossil evidence and laments, "I can hardly reflect on them without being in some degree staggered. If species have descended from other species by fine gradations, why do we not everywhere see innumerable transition forms?"[22]

Good question, Charles. Were you open to any other ideas?

These and many other questions makes we wonder whether we might be lying to ourselves about man's origins because of secular scientists' opposition to creationism and disdain for alternative ideas. At the least, the deck is stacked against other theories of our beginnings. At the worst, we are hiding behind a lie that is keeping many people from finding ultimate meaning and personal destiny for their lives.

If Darwinian evolution is true, then you and I are merely accidents in a meaningless world of survival of the fittest. I hear an echo of deception in that very depressing scenario.

Lies about History

Winston Churchill is reported to have said that "history is normally written by the victors." But that doesn't mean the facts should be excluded from their presentation. I will use two illustrations, one personal and another current, to illustrate how human history can be manipulated by lying about reality.

During my late twenties I served as a coordinator for one of the largest prayer gatherings in American history. Washington for Jesus (WFJ), on April 29, 1980, took place in Washington, D.C., when thousands of believers from all fifty states arrived in the capital city for a twelve-hour assembly of repentance and prayer. I worked on the event for a year; the day of the gathering we bought out the entire city subway system to transport the crowds to the Washington Mall. We knew that WFJ would be one of the largest gatherings of people in American history and were excited about its impact in the nation and its story being told to the world.[23]

On the appointed day, over 700,000 people showed up—a number confirmed by the Washington, D.C., Capitol police (the official crowd counters). Yet, when I saw the evening newspaper, the Washington Post reported only 100,000 participants, and their lead story on Page One focused on "ten people" who were involved in a "sit-in" at National Airport.

Why the false reporting (what is currently labeled "Fake News")? The secular media found Washington for Jesus to be politically incorrect. Ten protesters took priority over 700,000 intercessors in the daily news cycle.

The Park Police told us that day that our event brought the second largest crowd ever assembled on the Mall. The largest, an anti-Vietnam War rally held in the late sixties, drew one million people to the capital according to official police count. However, the media also chose to under report that event because it didn't fit their current political agenda.

So, both of Washington, D.C.,'s largest people gatherings (up until that time) were never reported in the history books. Selective history reporting withheld the truth.

Remember, any *intended deception* is a lie.

One of the most brazen examples of lying about history was the propaganda of Iran's President Mahmoud Ahmadinejad, denying the Jewish Holocaust. On December 14, 2005, the BBC (British Broadcasting Corporation) first reported that the Iranian dictator said in a speech in Tehran: "They have created a myth today that they call the massacre of Jews and they consider it a principle above God, religions and the prophets."[24]

This preposterous lie has been re-stated many times since including during a march in Iran on September 18, 2009. According to CBN News, "During the march Ahmadinejad addressed government supporters saying that 'confronting the Zionist regime is a national and religious duty,' and that Israel 'has no future.' And in a move likely to draw the ire of both Israel and the West, [he] once again dismissed the holocaust as myth - saying it was merely "a false pretext to create Israel."[25]

Tell that to the Jewish survivors who lost loved ones in the concentration camps; tell it to the liberating Allied forces who saw firsthand the wretched gas chambers, wept over the mass graves, and struggled to bury the mountains of skeletons left by Nazi genocide.

One of the most moving historical museums in the world is the Holocaust Museum in Washington, D.C., I have visited it many times and left in tears after viewing the carnage displayed in the photos, newsreels, and artifacts from that dark period of the mid-twentieth century. It reminds me of a personal visit to Dachau—a Germany concentration camp in 1974. These words are emblazoned at the entrance to the facility: *Never Again.*

That desire will not be achieved if tyrants keep lying about history.

It would be impossible to enumerate the vast amount of lying that has occurred in the reporting of history. I simply encourage you to read your books and newspapers with discernment. Do your homework well; yet don't look for conspiracies under every bush. I believe that history will be seen in truth one day. Until then, be watchful to spot the obvious lies.

Lies about Sexual Morality
I was a child of the 1960s and '70s and witnessed the sexual revolution first-hand. It was a time of questioning authority and casting off cultural restraints, especially in the area of sexuality. We were encouraged to "make love and not war" and that "free sex" was the new order of the day. The casting off of long held sexual mores was celebrated through events like "Woodstock" on August 15-18, 1969, and in many other venues. The accompanying sexual revolution—in essence, a fabrication about morality—has created devastating consequences ever since.

Sex is not "free." Separated from marriage and healthy human restraint, it produces a vast array of social problems and ills. One is an explosion of sexually transmitted diseases. In the 1960s gonorrhea and syphilis were the only well-known sexually transmitted diseases (STDs), and both of these could be treated with penicillin.[26] Today there are over twenty-five different STDs, and some of the most common ones are without cures.[27]

For example, a venereal disease outbreak in Rockdale County, Georgia, in 1996 left local officials desperately looking for answers. Here's what they found:

> It was not uncommon when all the young people would get together, to engage in group sex. There was group sex going on in terms of one guy having sex with one of the girls, and then the next guy having sex with the same girl. There was group sex going on in terms of one girl having sex with multiple male partners at the same time, multiple females having sex with each other at the same time . . . Registered nurse Cynthia Noel, who was among those who discovered the epidemic, referred to 14-year old girls with 20, 30, 40, 50 or 100 sex partners . . . And they said they were watching the Playboy Channel in the girl's bedroom. And there would be 10 or 12 of them up there . . . One young boy said 'you have to imitate what the Playboy people are doing.' Another commented, 'It doesn't matter if you're two guys or two girls or a guy and a girl. It doesn't matter. You just have to do what they're doing.' [28]

Where did this generation and the one that preceded them learn to "just do what others are doing?" Noted twentieth century philosopher Francis Schaeffer reveals one source—the famous Kinsey Reports—*Sexual Behavior of the Human Male* (1948) and *Sexual Behavior of the Human Female* (1953) in which Kinsey changed what was "right" about sex into a matter of "statistics." "Many people read his books because at that date they were far more titillating than other books accepted as respectable. However, their real impact was the underlying conception that sexual right and wrong depend only on what most people are doing sexually at a given moment in history. This has become the generally accepted sexual standard in the years since."[29]

Unfortunately, another result of this change in morality was the explosion of pornography which is far more titillating and destructive than anything Kinsey ever dreamed. In 2006 porn sales generated 97.6 billion dollars worldwide, more than the revenues of Microsoft, Google, Amazon, eBay, Yahoo!, Apple, Netflix, and EarthLink *combined*.[30]

The modern idea that sex should not be protected by a committed married relationship—and that morality is simply "what other people are doing"—has caused the marriage institution to be abandoned by some Western nations, driven up divorce rates, put more children into poverty, and greatly encouraged once unthinkable sexual acts such as incest, pedophilia, homosexuality, and bestiality. [31]

Two of my close friends died of AIDS. They had fallen for a "free sex" lie that contributed greatly to their premature deaths. I don't want it to happen to others. We need to reject the "easy sex" lies of the sexual revolution and return to the ancient wisdom that says there is no true sexual freedom without wholesome self-restraint.

Lies about Health

I received the following personalized e-mail recently.

> Dear Ron,
>
> Let me be a blunt Texan. There are a lot of dumb and dangerous medical myths out there. The worst myths are the ones that so many people believe. Myths like: The quickest fix for heart disease is a $50,000 bypass surgery. Nonsense! The quickest fix is this $14 mineral. Glucosamine and other expensive supplements are the best solutions for arthritis and joint pain. Nonsense! The quickest fix is FREE and you can make it from last night's dinner! Every

man must subject himself to an annual PSA test. Nonsense! Even the M.D. who pioneered the PSA test now says it is not only unreliable, it is utterly useless.

The truth is, there's not much truth out there anymore. I'm sending you this letter because I believe you're looking for truthful, inexpensive health solutions that work. I've uncovered the 50 most important medical answers to life-threatening health issues in my book, *Library of Medical Lies*. Your free report has the answers to the top three that everyone needs to know NOW. I'd like to share them with you. Save your life and your life savings with the medical answers that matter most.

Sincerely, _____

I'm sure you've received some messages like this. In the past they came in the mail. Now they appear on your computer. One of my childhood favorites touted "Injun Joe's Kickapoo Joy Juice." It promised to cure everything from cold sores to hemorrhoids (which was a big word I didn't understand). I didn't believe them then and I don't believe them now. When it comes to your health, there are just too many charlatans (people who tell lies) out there.

My parents were both medical professionals. Some years ago my dad went through quintuple-bypass surgery after suffering a heart attack. While recovering, he read a book called *The New Nuts among the Berries: How Nutrition Nonsense Captured America* by Ronald Deutsch to help our entire family learn the secrets to good heart health.

The book opened with the story of Daisie Adelle Davis Sielinger—popularly known as Adelle Davis—probably "America's most celebrated nutritionist."[32] Adelle did all the correct things, ate all the right foods, played tennis five days a week, cleansed her colon regularly, and said she'd never get cancer.[33] Deutsch commented, "Indeed, in all of history, probably no other person has been so closely identified . . . with the gospel of food and health." She also made quite a bit of money dishing out her medical-nutritional advice.[34]

Then the unthinkable happened. Adelle Davis, at the age of sixty-six, came down with *multiple myeloma cancer*. She was dead by the age of seventy. Deutsch points out in the book that most "medical cures" or "miracle nutritional ideas" can be innocently or fraudulently peddled by people because according to an AMA study, when most physical problems are left untreated, "perhaps as many as 80 percent of human illnesses are healed by normal bodily processes."[35]

There are many half-truths and bold fabrications floating around our world related to medicine, health, nutrition, and prevention. Save your hard-earned money, talk to a trusted physician, and don't order any "Injun Joe's Kickapoo Joy Juice." The saying "there is a sucker born every minute"[36] only applies when we make ourselves accessible to the lies.

Lies about Freedom

One of the titanic struggles in our world, and certainly a battle that has been fought in various forms throughout the ages, is the human struggle for freedom. With this struggle come many counterfeit forms or definitions of freedom that are tantamount to lies.

Abraham Lincoln, in the context of the nineteenth-century battle over slavery, tells us there are different definitions of freedom that are diametrically opposed to each other:

> We all declare for liberty; but in using the same word we do not all mean the same thing. With some the word liberty may mean for each man to do as he pleases with himself, and the product of his labor; while with others, the same word may mean for some men to do as they please with other men, and the product of other men's labor. Here are

two, not only different, but incompatible things, called by
the same name—liberty. And it follows that each of the
things is, by the respective parties, called by two different
and incompatible names—liberty and tyranny.[37]

In Lincoln's statement, the issue pertains to one person's freedom in relation to another. We probably agree today that slavery was tyranny and emancipation is liberty.

But there are other definitions of freedom that go beyond inter-personal relationships. One touches the nature of human liberty itself. The other applies this understanding to the rights of people in human societies (civil government). We need to understand the nature of true freedom so that we can resist the lies about it that bombard us daily. If, as according to the U.S. Declaration of Independence, God has given every person a right to "life, liberty, and the pursuit of happiness," then it critically important to understand what real freedom entails.

Let's begin with individual freedom. Personal liberty must be understood as the power and wisdom to do what you *ought,* not the ability to do what you *want*. Jesus said nearly two thousand years ago, "Everyone who sins is a slave of sin. A slave is not a permanent member of the family, but a son is a part of the family forever. So if the Son sets you free, you will be free indeed" (John 8:34-36).

According to those words, real liberty starts in the human heart and is freedom from destructive actions, not from God or morality. This means that true freedom is always in proportion to wholesome restraint. The more you control yourself, the more liberty you will enjoy in your life and relationships. Doug Simpson, the author of the excellent book *Looking for America: Rediscovering the Meaning of Freedom* rightly says, "Liberty always grows out of a people's understanding that true liberty is liberty from sin. Liberty from sin is the first step of freedom." [38]

This concept of freedom makes sense on a personal level. We know that we can use our wills to make choices that enslave us. This is what an alcoholic experiences when he or she becomes addicted to alcohol, or a drug addict to cocaine. They think their "freedom" is in the choosing, but the wrong choice brings them under the power of another. The person who engages in immoral sex might believe they were "free" in choosing a prostitute, but once they come down with a venereal disease, even AIDS, they learn that their lack of self-restraint actually takes away their freedom—possibly their life.

True personal freedom comes from right choosing, and right choices assume a necessary moral order. The moral order provides boundaries that keep the person "free" from becoming enslaved to selfish actions. Constitutional lawyer Mark Levin, who has written two excellent books on freedom (*Liberty and Tyranny* and *Ameritopia*), puts it this way: ""[Each individual] is a unique, spiritual being with a soul and a conscience. He is free to discover his own potential and pursue his legitimate interests, tempered, however, by a moral order that has its foundation in faith."[39]

The principle that necessary boundaries create real freedom applies to our physical existence as well. What allows us to "move around" freely in our homes? It is the fact that physical laws keep the walls from moving, the floor from dropping out, or objects floating around and hitting us in the face. The physical "boundaries" allow us to move freely from one room to another. If the physical laws (like gravity) were not in place, your "freedom" would be smothered by chaos.

The same is true in the moral realm. "You shall not steal, kill, lie, commit adultery" etc. are helpful boundaries to keep us *free* from destroying others and ourselves. When we choose wisely and "do what we ought," the result is true freedom. When we disregard the boundaries and simply choose to "do what we want" the result is negative (hurt, addiction, disease, guilt, bondage etc.).

A favorite cartoon of mine shows a man in scene one with a sledgehammer about to strike a replica of the Ten Commandments. The caption reads, "Some men think they can break God's law . . . " In scene two you see the result: The Ten Commandments haven't budged, but the man and his sledgehammer have broken into a thousand pieces. The caption reads, "But they only break themselves on it."[40]

How true. Don't believe the lie that "I'm really free to do anything I want." Understand what you *ought* to do and experience real personal freedom through wise self-control.

Levin mentions the role of "faith" in producing freedom. He is alluding to the American (biblical) concept of liberty that over the past two centuries helped create the freest nation in the history of the world. The American "experiment in liberty" was based on three important building blocks: *Faith* (in God) producing morality, and *morality* (virtuous character) leading to *freedom* both in individuals and the nation as a whole.

The main role of governments is to protect that individual freedom. Levin states that: "Religious freedom is the very basis—and the only basis—for true liberty. Freedom and liberty are synonymous . . . Therefore it is the job of government to guard liberty—individual liberty. That is the only real job of government." [41]

Freedom for entire nations is at stake in today's world. If we fail to understand that governments exist to protect individual freedom (including property), then civil governments just might lie to us about the nature of liberty and remove those freedoms from us. This is a battle facing many societies in the twenty-first century. It is a clash of worldviews between democracy and socialism—liberty and tyranny.

One of the finest books ever written on the subject of liberty (in nations) is Austrian economist Friedrich Hayek's *The Road to Serfdom.* Hayek understood the nature of freedom and how lies (change of definitions) would be used to try to enslave nations in the modern world. He wrote:

> Democracy and socialism have nothing in common but one word: equality. But notice the difference: while democracy seeks equality in liberty, socialism seeks equality in restraint and servitude. To allay these suspicions and to harness to its cart the strongest of all political motives—

the craving for freedom—socialists began increasingly to make use of the promise of a 'new freedom.' Socialism was to bring "economic freedom," without which political freedom was not worth having. To make this argument sound plausible, the word 'freedom' was subjected to a subtle change in meaning. The word had formerly meant freedom from coercion, from the arbitrary power of other men. Now it was made to mean freedom from necessity . . . The demand for the new freedom was thus only another name for the old demand for a redistribution of wealth.[42]

One of the more serious lies of our time is the historic change of meaning of the concept of freedom in nations. For hundreds of years liberty meant "freedom of opportunity" where people could succeed or not succeed based on their own choices and motivations. Hayek calls this "freedom from coercion." In our history it's been labeled individualism. Karl Popper writes, "This individualism, united with altruism, has become the basis of western civilization. It is the central doctrine of Christianity ('love your neighbor,' says the Scriptures, not 'love your tribe')."[43]

But recently, as nations in the West have abandoned faith—and the morality it produces—civil governments have increased their reach through force (increased taxation and re-distribution) and a desire to create an "equality of outcomes" for various classes of people. "Equality" becomes the new rallying cry, but as Mark Levin points out, it is really "equality in *misery*—that is, equality of result or conformity is advanced as a just, fair, and virtuous undertaking. Liberty, therefore, is inherently immoral, except where it avails equality."[44]

Thus a wonderful and freeing concept such as individual liberty can be turned on its head in the name of equality. Think North Korea and its starving masses. Think all the communist nations of the twentieth century—all formed in the name of "freedom and equality."

And think the post-modern and post-Christian West which is drowning under bloated bureaucracies, staggering national debt-loads, and shrinking personal liberties where every aspect of life is being regulated and funded by a voracious monster Mark Levin calls "statism."

Welcome to the "new freedoms" of the twenty-first century. Too bad it is all based on a lie.

DROWNING IN A SEA OF LIES

Lies about origins, history, sex, health, freedom, and numerous other subjects seem to be the order of the day. We find them at every turn, and may even (unwittingly) promote a few ourselves. Our world is drowning in a sea of lies. It has always been this way—but modern communications certainly amplify the sound.

As I mentioned at the beginning of this chapter, my own family was the victim of a very cruel lie. The awful effects prompted me to look passionately for meaning in life and for answers to my questions. I began a deliberate search for truth.

Thousands of years ago, other humans were also drowning in the falsehoods and confusion of their eras and made the same choice. They wanted to know the truth about life.

Their search led them to religion.

Chapter Two

Religion

"Man is a religious being; He will worship."[45]

Dr. James B. Walker

Religion as a concept brings starkly different images to people. To some, it conjures up warm thoughts of devotion to God or worship. To others, it connotes something negative that can be legalistic and hollow, especially when compared to having a *relationship* to a loving Deity. For still others, it ignites horrible memories of torture or slaughter in the name of a higher power.

Even so, religion remains a universal feature of human cultures that has thrived in every era of time.[46] You find it everywhere in the world. The only species on earth that practices religion is human beings. Animals don't pray or worship. Only human beings do. That's why James Walker states, "Man is a religious being; He will worship."[47]

Today, however, many different explanations tell us *why*.

In the past two hundred years, numerous social scientists and anthropologists have studied the ethnologies of world religions—both ancient practices and current religious faiths— and have come up with some diverse conclusions on what religion entails.

In this chapter, I discuss the meaning of "religion" and why it is vital in our lives in the twenty-first century. The battles of our time will be fought over religion.

Before I share my own thoughts on this subject, it might be helpful to analyze some of the concepts about religion that have arisen in modern times. Some are helpful, and others are fairly bizarre.

A "STARK" LOOK AT RELIGION

To aid his study, I am grateful to American sociologist Rodney Stark and his compelling book *Discovering God: The Origins of the World Religions and the Evolution of Belief*. Stark's literary goal was similar to my own, but with a few significant differences. He begins his research with these questions:

> Does God exist? That is, have we discovered God? Or have we invented Him? Are there so many similarities among the great religions because God is really the product of universal wish fulfillment? Did humans everywhere create supernatural beings out of their need for comfort in the face of existential tragedy and to find purpose and significance in life? Or have people in many places, to a greater and lesser degree, actually gained glimpses of God? [48]

I add the following question: Do human beings innately search for God or the supernatural because there *is a* River that he wants each of us to discover so we may escape the world of lies and enjoy relationship with him?

Rodney Stark is a university professor who has penned twenty-seven books on the history and sociology of religion. In *Discovering God*, Stark attempts to narrate how world religions developed over time and to analyze what he calls the key religious innovators who influenced their growth.[49] His most interesting insight reveals that some of the great religious founders were contemporaries in the sixth century B.C. (Buddha,

Confucius, Lao-Tzu (Taoism), Zoroaster, Mahavira (Jainism), Pythagoras, and the biblical prophets Jeremiah and Ezekiel. Stark poses the question, "Have people in many places, to a greater or lesser degree, actually gained glimpses of God?"[50]

Stark answers "yes" to the rhetorical question, but he doesn't clarify how they are related and especially how *different* religious ideas emerged from this time period. As we will see later on, the Buddha's ideas taught an eastern form of atheism, Confucius' concepts of morality pointed toward civic duty and social cohesion, and the teachings of the biblical prophets were accepted as inspired revelations from a loving God.

How are these polar-opposite views related? I suggest that rather than being similar communications from God, they further distorted the River of God's true revelation.

But let's return to Stark's historical analysis. His four hundred-page treatise begins with a discussion about primitive religions, including their belief in a High God, why temple religions arose, and how they were eventually replaced with the marketplace of religious ideas that permeated Rome. In the second half of the book, he discusses polytheism, the re-emergence of monotheism, the birth of various religions in India and China, and concludes with the rise of Christianity and Islam.

Human Beings are Religious

I believe Stark is right when he suggests that there is a progression in the development of human religious experience. He calls this theory, "Divine Accommodation," which holds that God's revelations are always limited to the current capacity of humans to comprehend.[51] This is significant, but I'm especially interested in his analysis of what ancient peoples appear to have believed about God, and what anthropologists say this tells us about religion.

As Stark scans the evidence for early human expressions of religion, he observes, " . . . as to where God was during primitive times, I shall raise the possibility that he was there all along, revealing himself within the very limited capacities of humans to understand.[52] In fact, he says that the evidence suggests that until about 3000 years ago, everybody heard from God.[53]

Early human beings voraciously practiced religion.

How do we know? Evidence exists in numerous ancient cultural ruins where scientists have found burial objects which indicate a belief in life after death. In some places archeologists discovered caves with altars, and in pre-historic sites such as Catalhoyuk in Turkey there is evidence of bull sacrifice and the worship of a mother goddess.[54] These finds pre-date the dawn of recorded civilization (10,000—4000 B.C.). So evidence remains scarce.

Yet they tell us a significant fact: *Religion stands as a universal feature of human cultures* although the first primitive expressions found were fairly crude.[55] The most fascinating aspect of the universal prevalence of religious faith is the incredibly diverse interpretations by various social scientists regarding the very same evidence!

Yes, people have their biases about religion. The following list of personalities and their various theories confirm that fact.

Muddying the Waters—What Religion is Not

Max Muller (1823–900) served as a German scholar of comparative language and religion and spent most of his adult life as a professor at Oxford. Muller coined the term "Naturism" which states that religions have their origins in the personification of natural forces and objects and the "myths" that arise from these personifications. [56] Muller taught that humans gain a sense of the divine from natural phenomena: sun, moon, star, mountains, rivers, thunder and lightning, storms, seasons, animals and plants. When applied to classical mythology, this perspective turned to word games and stories about the gods that were simply a disease of language and untrue.[57]

To Muller, religion was a *myth*.

Edward Burnett Tyler (1832–1917), an English anthropologist and critic of Muller, coined the term "Animism" to distinguish primitive religion from more advanced forms. Animism consists of the belief that literally everything is inhabited by a spirit, not only animate things, but inanimate ones as well.[58] Tyler, along with other early anthropologists, defined religion as the "belief in Spiritual Beings." But Tyler viewed these tribes as low on the scale of humanity whose world was a childish one cluttered with invisible spirits.

Tyler believed that religion was *superstitious*.[59]

Herbert Spencer (1820–1903), a near hermit and severe critic of Muller, supported Tyler and wrote an entire bookshelf of works on social and cultural evolution. Spencer went a step further than Tyler and asked the question: *Why* do primitive people believe they are surrounded by spirits? His answer, which became known as "Ghost Theory," hypothesized that primitive people, lacking proper awareness of their own mental powers, were puzzled by the difference between the living and the dead, and between when they are dreaming and awake, especially when they dream about the dead.[60] This led to a concept of two different realities, one of which was inhabited by a spirit. When one died, this duality became permanent and also gave rise to ancestral worship, and eventually led to the invention of Gods and the formation of religious organizations.

To Spencer, religious primitives were *morons* (a commonly held view at the time).[61]

W. Robertson Smith, (1846–1894), brought into vogue the fourth perspective on primitive religion which became known at "Totemism." Smith believed that all religions originated in the practice of each collective tribe, or of each clan within a tribe, identifying with a particular animal species (totem) that was held to be sacred and not to be harmed. He said that the origin of all rites and practices associated with sacrifice, especially of blood sacrifices, came from these humble beginnings then produced more advanced religions.[62] Smith went so far as to say that Jewish sacrifices originated from the totemic tribes, but many dismissed his claims as fantasy because in all the ethnographic literature there was only *one* example of any group actually sacrificing and eating its totemic animal.[63]

Smith traced all religious belief to *animal identification and sacrifice.*

Following these four basic theories, a single volume of work by Emile Durkheim (1858–1917) dominated the sociology of religion. Durkheim worked as a professor at Sorbonne in Paris where he wrote *The Elementary Forms of Religious Life.* Durkheim said that God wasn't important in religion (How's that for a bias?), but that "all religious rites constitute society worshipping itself in order to sustain social solidarity."[64] Durkheim studied the literature of the Australian aborigines and concluded that they practiced a modern form of the ancient totem religions where the centrality of religious rites and practices arouse deep emotions of belonging to something far greater than the individual, and this reality is the society."[65]

Other scholars pointed out that Australian Aboriginals actually worshipped a rather sophisticated form of God, but Durkheim scoffed at those theories or rationalized them away. Durkheim concluded that that religion was a "united system of beliefs and practices relative to sacred things . . . which unite into a single moral community."[66]

To Durkheim, religion was simply a convenient *social construct.*

Enter Sigmund Freud (1856-1939), the well-known psychoanalyst who made Totemism world famous by concocting a theory that the earliest humans lived in small groups where all young males where driven off by the father who monopolized the women. Freud said that some of the young males, consumed by lust for the women (their mothers), combined against their father, killed him and ate men in totemic style, and then possessed the women.[67]

Freud also claimed that "God" was to blame and that in Christianity, the totemic sacrifice of Christ atoned for this bloodguilt. He said, "The Christian communion . . . is essentially a fresh elimination of the father, a repetition of the guilty deed."[68] Freud's conclusion is bizarre—but remained an accepted theory on religion until Freud was later discredited for many of his views' fraud.[69]

Freud believed that religion was linked to *sexual lust and guilt.*

A few others deserve "honorable mention." They come from the evolutionary theory/atheist side of the isle. Pascal Boyer labored as an anthropology professor who wrote a book called *Religion Explained: The*

Evolutionary Origins of Religious Thought. Boyer believed that our brains are hardwired to *mistakenly* believe in supernatural beings. To him, "Religion is thus a 'parasitic rider' on valuable mental circuitry that evolved for valid reasons, but has the unfortunate 'side affect' of prompting supernatural beliefs which involve the 'sleep of reason' since religion is, of course, 'an illusion.'"[70]

British biologist Richard Dawkins concocted a similar rationale to Boyer through his well-known books *The God Delusion* and *The Selfish Gene.* Dawkins gave atheists something to cheer about when he theorized that cultural "memes" are passed from one human being to another "just as genes propagate themselves in the gene pool by leaping from body to body by sperm or eggs, so memes propagate themselves in the meme pool by leaping from brain to brain in a process, which, in the broad sense of the term, can be called imitation."[71] To Dawkins, religion acts as a mind parasite that is highly contagious. In fact, he scoffs that "faith is one of the world's great evils, comparable to the smallpox virus but harder to eradicate."[72]

So, according to Boyer, Dawkins, and a stream of other ardent atheists, religion is simply a *chemical illusion of the brain.*

At this point it should be helpful to summarize Stark's findings from this broad group of illustrious scholars. They believe that religion is: *A myth, superstitious, moronic, related to animal sacrifice, a selfish social construct, driven by sexual guilt, and ultimately a brain delusion.*

Well, at least they were creative! But all these bizarre explanations seem to fly in the face of the universal God-consciousness that human beings possessed from the beginning of time.

Which leads me to the following conclusion: If it's true that men act so free that they have the ability to deny their own freedom, it seems equally true that human beings remain so innately religious that they can manufacture myriads of reasons to explain away their religiosity.

I propose a more plausible explanation: *Human beings are religious because God made them that way.* This conclusion follows simple logic, just like objects fall to the ground because gravity exists. We will explore the evidence for God—the River— in the remaining chapters of the book.

A UNIVERSAL REVELATION OF GOD

We conclude our journey of "definitions of religion" with the very interesting discovery that anthropologists today frequently believe "the many similarities of religions around the world are *not* evidence that they are human inventions but reflect a 'universal revelation' dating from earliest times."[73]

Do they refer to a universal revelation of God? Did the earliest peoples on earth share a similar concept of Deity?

The first scholar to promote this momentous discovery is Scottish anthropologist Andrew Lang, (1844–1912), who did a superb translation of Homer's *Iliad* and the *Odyssey,* and broke with Tyler's animistic theory when he wrote *The Making of Religion.* Lang sifted through much of current ethnographic accounts of religion in primitive societies and came to the conclusion that most of the early peoples believed in the existence of High Gods that were "moral, all-seeing, directors of things and of men . . . eternal beings who made the world and watch over morality."[74] He didn't find full-blown monotheism, because subordinate gods were allowed—but the focus centered on the High or primary God.

Many of Lang's contemporaries dismissed his ideas due to their bias that both man and religion had culturally evolved—hence it was impossible for early peoples to have a "sophisticated" concept of Deity. Yet, Lang filled the 355 pages of his book with numerous examples of the "High Gods of Low Races."

One example tells the story of the Adaman Islanders (Indian Ocean) who believed in a "High God named Puluga who was never born, is invisible, and is immortal. Puluga created everything . . . is regarded as omniscient . . . knowing even the thoughts of the heart. He is angered by the commission of certain sins . . . He is the Judge from whom each soul receives its sentence after death."[75] What makes this story believable is that the Adamanese were an isolated tribe who could not have been influenced by missionaries.[76] Stark says that this and numerous other examples gave credibility to the idea that "many of the most primitive peoples known to anthropologists had High Gods."[77]

One hundred years ago, this was a significant find.

Further twentieth century research confirmed Lang's analysis of universal belief in High Gods. In 1924 well-known American cultural folklorist Paul Radin published *Monotheism Among Primitive Peoples* which fully corroborated the theory that early peoples held a belief in a Supreme Creator. This was followed by University of Chicago professor Mircea Eliade's research on Australian primitives:

> There is a general belief among the Australians that the world, man, and the various animals were created by certain Supernatural Beings . . . Baiame, the supreme deity of the tribes of South East Australia . . . dwells in the sky, beside a great stream of water (the Milky Way), and receives the souls of the innocent. He sits on a crystal throne . . . Baiame is self-created and created everything from nothing . . . He sees and hears everything.[78]

Eliade went on to identify High Gods all across South America at the same time that other scholars were coming to similar discoveries among the early cultures of Africa. Ninian Smart reported: "In most, if not all, of the indigenous cultures of Africa, there is a belief in a Supreme Spirit ruling over or informing lesser spirits and gods. He governs natural forces, dwells on high, is inexplicable, create souls, men, and things."[79] High Gods were also common among the religions of North American tribes.[80]

Discovering the River of God

Quantifying early peoples' belief in a High or Creator God became the pursuit of George Peter Murdock, (1897–1985), who scientifically organized the available ethnographic literature in 1967 where he coded 427 past and present cultures on dozens of variables. One measured the prevalence of High Gods.

His results stunned anthropologists:

Of gathering clans, 43 percent believed in a High God.

Of nomadic people groups, 64 percent believed in an active or inactive High God.

And, of the agricultural tribes, 67 percent believed in a High God.[81]

But the best analysis about early peoples' nearly universal faith in God was left to Wilhelm Schmidt (1868-1954), a Jesuit scholar at the University of Vienna. Schmidt served as a master of the ethnographic literature and a voluminous author whose works included an epic twelve volume series called *The Origen of the Idea of God (Ursprung der Gottesidea)*. He was thirty years old when Lang's book appeared (*The Making of Religion*) and he instantly recognized its importance. He soon announced to the world, "The Supreme Being of the primitive culture is really the God of monotheism."[82]

Rodney Stark summarizes Schmidt's amazingly simple conclusion:

> The many similarities of religions around the world are not evidence that they all are human inventions, but reflect a 'universal revelation' dating from earliest times. Schmidt proposed that at the dawn of humanity all religions were alike; everyone knew the same God. It is the variations from one religion to another that reveal the insertion of human inventions, of misunderstanding, and of faulty transmissions across generations . . . In this way Schmidt showed how snugly the huge ethnographic literature of primitive religions fits with the account in *Genesis* of the Creation and the Fall.[83]

> Schmidt really discovered what I propose is the River of God.

So forget myths, superstitions, animal sacrifices, sexual guilt, or mental delusions. At least according to the earliest cultures of mankind, religion entailed the worship of and search for the High Creator God. We'll give Professor Stark the last word on this subject:

> Today it is fashionable to deny any validity of religion. Rodney Needham in *Science and Civilization* says there is basically no such thing as religious belief but that all religious activity is just socio-emotional expression. It requires a great deal of sophisticated social-scientific training for a person to accept such nonsense. People pray to something! To something above and beyond the material world.[84]

Yes, people *do* pray to something or someone. Julian Jaynes is correct when he suggested that until about 3,000 years ago, everybody heard God's voice and responded back.[85]

That brings us to the true meaning of religion.

NOAH WEBSTER WAS RIGHT

It is amazing how human beings can educate themselves away from common sense. The concept of religion is simple—yet we contort our brains into such knots that we move a galaxy away from the nearest star.

Let's return to a favorite dictionary, (Noah Webster's 1838 American classic), for a straightforward definition of the meaning of religion. I'll share Webster's four main points and offer some summary comment.[86]

RELIGION, *n.* from the Latin *religio,* from *religo* to "bind anew." This word seems to have originally signified an oath or vow to the gods, or the obligation of such an oath or vow, which was held very sacred by the Romans. Comment: *Religion is something to which we are strongly and personally bound.*

1. Religion, in its most comprehensive sense, includes a belief in the being and perfections of God, in the revelation of his will to man, in man's obligations to obey his commands, in a state of reward and punishment, and in man's accountableness to God. Comment: *Religion exemplifies a belief in God and accepts his demands on our lives.*

2. Religion, as distinct from theology, is godliness or real piety in practice, consisting in the form of all known duties to God and our fellow men, in obedience to divine command, or from love of God and his law. Comment: *Religion requires a lifestyle of obedience and love.*

3. Religion, as distinct from virtue or morality, consists in the performance of the duties we owe directly to God, from a principle of obedience to his will. Hence we often speak of religion and virtue as different branches of one system. (Webster then shares a famous quote from George Washington: "Let us with caution indulge the supposition that morality can be maintained without religion.") Comment: *Religion produces morality.*

4. Any system of faith and worship. In this sense, religion comprehends the belief and worship of pagans and [Muslims} as well as Christians; any religion consisting in the belief of a superior power or powers governing the world, and in the worship of such power or powers. Thus we speak of the religion of the Turks, of the Hindus, of the Indians etc. as well of as the Christian religion. We speak of false religion as well as true religion. Comment: *The word "religion" can include any system of worship, of which some are true and others are false.*

I appreciate Webster's simplicity and clarity on mankind's universal desire to worship God. First, he explains that the root meaning "religion" means to be "bound"—to take an oath of loyalty to God or the gods. Religion involves a willful commitment to what one believes about God. It is not casual or purely intellectual. Religion acts as a willing slave to someone in whom you see greater value or position than yourself.

Secondly, Webster stresses the importance of accountability to God and others in a lifestyle of loving devotion. Next he mentions that religion produces moral goodness that is linked to relationship with the divine. Finally, Noah Webster suggests that the word "religion" applies to whatever "binding" system a person believes in. But he rightly qualifies this belief: *Your religion can be true or false.*

Not all roads lead to heaven or the real God.

This definition squares with other modern understandings of religion. Terrance L. Tiessen, in his insightful book *Who Can Be Saved?,* quotes missionary theologian Lesslie Newbigin who says "the term *religion* refers to all those commitments that, in the intention of the adherents, have an overriding authority over all other commitments and provide the framework within which all experience is grasped and all ideas are judged . . . From this perspective, no one is without a religion."[87]

Newbigin argues that religion is a binding commitment to an "overriding authority." It creates a "framework" through which to seek reality. And, because all people are bound to something, all people are religious. Tiessen agrees. "Everyone has a sense of deity, a religious consciousness. This is the basis of human religion."[88] Theologian Wayne House lists fifteen different definitions of religion that agree with this concept.[89]

Paul Hiebert, Daniel Shaw, and Tite Tienou also confirm man's innate religiosity and make this observation:

> Because humans are creatures in the image of God, we are invincibly religious, a point noted by Paul in his lecture to the 'extremely religious' Athenians (Acts 17:22, 26-28). Consequently, it is often difficult to distinguish a people's religion from their culture, especially in situations where secularism has little or no impact. This being the case, anthropologists now define *religion* as beliefs

about the ultimate nature of things, as deep feelings and motivations, and as fundamental values and alliances.[90]

Let's summarize the clear, historical, universal understanding of religion—without the clutter of bias or false interpretation. *Religion is belief in God or a substitute for God that answers life's ultimate questions and shapes our thoughts and behavior.* It provides a "framework" through which we seek reality—to help us navigate through a world of confusion and lies. That framework can also be called a *worldview.*

Religions are Worldviews

I never remember hearing the word "worldview" until I began to look for the truth about life—and it was twentieth-century philosopher Francis Schaeffer who first defined the term for me. In his influential book *How Should We Then Live?* Schaeffer (with whom I personally became acquainted during the 1980s) analyzes how worldviews impact and create human culture as seen in the following perspective:

> People have presuppositions, and they live more consistently on the basis of these presuppositions than even they themselves may realize. By presuppositions we mean the basic way an individual looks at life, his basic worldview, the grid through which he sees the world. Presuppositions rest upon that which a person considers to be the truth of what exists . . . Their presuppositions also provide the basis of their values and therefore the basis of their decisions.[91]

Schaeffer taught what Abraham Kuyper described a generation earlier—that every person lived by a *weltanschauung*—a worldview—that touched every aspect of their life. Kuyper labored as a tireless Reformed theologian, prime minister of the Netherlands (1901–1905), and founder of the Free University in Amsterdam. His *Stone Lectures* laid the foundation for

Schaeffer's belief that 1) Every person had a set of assumptions about life—what is "true" and important to them, 2) These presuppositions form a life system of thoughts and actions, 3) This worldview forms the "grid" through which each person views reality, and 4) Your personal worldview displays your "life beliefs."[92]

I adhere to the belief that *all religions are worldviews.* Worldviews don't consist of isolated thoughts about deity or duty. Whether consciously reasoned out or not, they are commitments to a "grid" of reality through which each person views and lives out their life. Vishal Mangalwadi, considered by some to be "India's Francis Schaeffer" says, "Knowledge of God is not an abstract, otherworldly luxury. It is the starting point of drawing a map of reality—developing a worldview that explains reality—making it possible to live as we were meant to live."[93]

The greatest battles of the twenty-first century will be waged in the arena of religion or worldview. For many years, I believed myriads of religious worldviews littered the world. I've changed my mind. There are only five religions or worldviews from which all human beings must choose.

And not all of them can be true.

Chapter Three

Truth

"What is truth?" —Pontius Pilate

The dirtiest, bumpiest van ride of my life took place some years ago when I took a missions team to the nation of Mongolia. Our youngest sons, Ryan (15) and Jason (13), joined me along with other American and Mongolian friends. For nearly a decade I'd been working in Mongolia with local churches to help this poverty-stricken-but-beautiful country between China and Russia emerge from communism into the blessings of freedom.

This particular day we were scheduled to work at the worst maximum-security prison in the nation—an isolated penal colony called Darhiin Shoron—a four-hour drive from the capital of Ulaanbaatar. Our hosts didn't tell us that in a developed nation the trip would probably take ninety minutes. But in this part of Mongolia, where the prison had been strategically located far away from the rest of humanity, the terrain was very difficult and the "commute" would be akin to riding a bucking bronco.

Hour after hour we gyrated, wove, and swerved through riverbeds, barren pastures, and crossed swollen streams to get to our destination. The van's door had a one-inch crack along the floor allowing dust to pour in from every direction. Most of the team members held clothing over their mouths to prevent dust particles from being inhaled. When we arrived at the prison, beaten up and tired, our faces were covered with brown soot. I thought we might scare away even the most hardened criminals!

After cleaning up a bit, we performed drama presentations and skits in the prison courtyard with the convicts watching from a distance. Then we made our way into an auditorium where we got our first close look at this rough crowd of murderers, rapists, and thieves. We weren't afraid. We had good news to share with them.

That particular afternoon, I spoke for the first time on the subject of the "Five Views of God." The convicts listened respectfully and responded warmly at the end of the presentation. Our Mongol teammates also paid close attention. In particular, the message deeply touched a Mongol young man who was one of our interpreters.

Our new friend grew up in an alcoholic home filled with violence, poverty, and constant disappointment. After contemplating suicide during his teenage years, he regained hope through one of our teams in 1998 and began a journey toward God. As I shared the message in 2007 on the five worldviews about God—his spiritual eyes opened. When I mentioned that one religious founder had said "I am still looking for the truth" and another boldly declared, "I *am* the truth," the penny dropped for him.

He had found the truth. The lies of his past life melted away and the future became filled with hope. As I look back now, that dirty, bumpy ride was well worth it. Today, our Mongol friend serves a pastor in his native land and remains a changed and radiant individual who helps other people all over the world.

The truth set him free.

Pontius Pilate, in his famous encounter with Jesus of Nazareth nearly two thousand years ago, asked one of the most important questions of the ages: "*What is truth?*" (John 8:38). In other words, does truth really exist? Can it be known or is all of life relative? I asked the same question for years in my own life. Then the question was answered.

In this chapter I propose that truth is real and can be known—*especially* as it relates to religion. I also suggest that in order for something to be true, it must live up to six necessary characteristics that validate its claims. Finally, I will discuss the essential questions about reality that truth must answer in order to be believable.

But first let us examine the five major concepts of God.

FIVE VIEWS OF GOD

I once believed that hundreds of religions, or even thousands or millions of different expressions of those ideologies existed. Eventually I discovered at least nineteen major world religions exist which can be subdivided into a total of 270 large religious groups, with smaller ones—numbering in the thousands.[94]

Yet, the more I pondered this immense religious landscape, the more it became apparent that this vast array of religious expression could ultimately be boiled down to five views. Let's list them below and state the central view of God or deity that is at the heart of each worldview. They will be examined in detail in coming chapters. My theory is that every person on earth is "bound" to one of these views (remember the basic definition of "religion"). I list them in the order in which they appeared in history and also the general percentage of global population they represent.

1. *Loving God.* (Biblical faith)—Most books on religion use the term "Christianity," but that word doesn't appear in its source book, the Bible, and, more importantly, many people of biblical faith lived *prior* to the time of Jesus Christ. Since Judaism came about as an Old Testament expression of belief, I also include it here. The central fact of biblical faith states that there is a loving triune God who created and rules the universe. One-third of the global population holds to one of the expressions of biblical faith.[95]

2. *Many Gods.* (Polytheism)—This religion contends that there are many gods that either created the world or impact our lives on

earth. Polytheism has shown itself in many forms in history. Today it boasts expressions in Hinduism, Buddhism, animism and folk religions, religious Taoism and Shintoism. Polytheists make up 16 percent of the world[96] (animism is also practiced as a "technique" in other religions, so this total could rise to 40 percent of global population).[97]

3. *Everything is God.* (Pantheism)—It also goes by the name "monism" and teaches the Oneness of all of life without duality or differentiation. Pantheism displays two primary forms in the modern world in Hinduism and the New Age Movement including Gaia theory. Sikhism holds essentially pantheistic beliefs. Pantheism's central belief says that everything is God. Pantheists make up approximately 15 percent of world population (living mainly in India).[98]

4. *No God.* (Atheism)—Though some atheists existed in earlier times, atheism and its more common term, "secularism," developed most rapidly in the past two hundred years. Atheists believe there is no God. The practical effect of this belief as seen in humanism, communism, fascism, and secular governments produces powerful dictators and tyrannical states who become the gods of the culture. Philosophical Taoism, Theravada Buddhism and Confucianism demonstrate atheistic tenets. Atheism's adherents make up over one-tenth of the world and growing.[99]

5 *Warring God* (Islam)—This world religion began in the seventh century A.D. and controls much of the Middle East, northern Africa and parts of central and East Asia. Islam considers itself the final installment in monotheistic revelation. Muslims believe there is a warring God who created and rules the world. Muslims makes up over one quarter of global population.[100]

In the center section of the book, I trace the history of each of the five religious worldviews or concepts of God, analyze their teachings and practices, and suggest why they came into being. All of them, in a variety of ways, purport to be true.

THE TRUTH TEST

How do we determine truthfulness or error regarding different worldviews? First, I suggest a *six-fold truth test* that helps us discern the degree of truth found in each religion. Harold Netland is correct when he suggests that there are elements of truth in all worldviews and that our "encounters with other religions should build upon the 'precious fragments of truth' contained within them."[101]

But some contain more truth than others. The truth test I've developed helps us do a more thorough and honest evaluation of each point of view. Plus, the necessary characteristics of truth apply not only to religion, but to our daily lives as well. Keeping the truth test principles in mind just might help us live a wiser and better life.

Second, we probe a little deeper and look at ten different questions that a serious religion or worldview must answer. By combining the necessary characteristics of truth with the ten questions a worldview must tackle, I hope to introduce a helpful measuring stick for evaluating the five different concepts of God.

For our purposes, six (truth tests) plus ten (answers to questions) = the truth.

Or at least the closest we mortals come to such a lofty assignment.

Necessary Characteristics of Truth

The six-fold truth test contains a number of elements that most of us rarely think about—yet probably assume in our decision-making as we navigate the myriads of lies or the choices we make each day.

For example, all of us "believe" some things are true. I believe it's *true* that I'm typing words on a computer keyboard right now. I also believe it's *true* that my wife loves me. I believe it's *true* that today is a cloudy day (it usually is in the Pacific Northwest!). I also believe in the *truth* of electricity.

I see its effects all around me. And I believe it's the *truth* that the earth is a sphere, and that it revolves around the sun.

Furthermore, I believe the *truth* about the Holocaust and reject the anti-Semitic propaganda. I believe it's *true* that Abraham Lincoln served as one of the greatest U.S. presidents—and that John Wilkes Booth cruelly assassinated him. I believe it's *true* that I shouldn't kill innocent people or steal from my neighbors. And I believe it's a *truth* there's life after death.[102]

The list could go on. All of us make judgments every day—some of them are possibly life and death decisions (think of a heart surgeon or policeman)—all because we've decided some things are inherently true.

So how do we determine the truthfulness of something—especially something as important as a worldview or religion? At least six things should be considered:

Test One—*Truth is often clear and simple*
Though the world we live in remains complex beyond our imagination, most of us accept the idea that truth in its basic form possesses a wonderful degree of clarity and simplicity. In fact, sometimes we search for difficult or complex answers . . . and then it finally dawns on us: the answer to this problem is *simple*.

I remember praying years ago for the young people in our youth club. I worked with some great kids, but they sometimes fought and were divided, and some messy relationship problems plagued the group. For weeks I tried to figure out what to do. Should I launch some special training? Should I use skating or pizza parties to build stronger friendships? The problems seemed very complex, and I didn't know where to begin.

One night I was thinking and praying about the problem and a simple question came to my mind: "What is the one thing that divides people?" I pondered the question and answered in my heart: *I don't think personality or style divides us. It must be selfish attitudes or actions (sin).* Then the next question came: "If selfishness divides people, then what unites them?" I mumbled the obvious answer under my breath: *Removing the selfishness (repentance).*

At that moment, a light bulb went on. Yes, human relationships display complexity, but only sin divides us (including tensions and wars between nations), so only the removal of selfish attitudes or actions unites us. A Scripture came to mind to back up the truth: "Confess your faults one to another, and pray one for another, that you may be healed" (James 5: 16).

I knew what I needed to do.

For the next few weeks I spoke on the problem of selfish attitudes and actions to the youth group. Soon, people began to confess their sins to each other and relationships started to change. After a few months, we experienced a growing unity and love in the association, and it grew dramatically—from thirty, to fifty, to one hundred, to one hundred and fifty—and made a significant impact in our community and in other parts of the world.

The youth revival exploded because of a simple truth about unity.

This is one reason why most cultures have wise sayings or proverbs that state the corporate truths of the group. The book of Proverbs in the Holy Bible takes complex subjects and reduce them to simple and clear axioms such as: "The fear of the Lord is the beginning of knowledge" (Proverbs 1:7) or "Birds of a feather flock together." Real truth often rings simple and clear—even in the most complex subject areas.

One of my favorite concepts from the complex world of science is the principle known as *Ockham's razor* (in Latin, *lex parsimoniae* (the law of parsimony, economy or succinctness). Its theory states that among competing hypotheses, choosing the one that makes the fewest new assumptions usually proves the correct one. It says that the simplest explanation remains the most plausible until other evidence proves it false.

In the realm of religious worldviews, we need to apply this same metric. Does this particular view of God ring true with simplicity and clarity? Or is it so convoluted that it does not bear the signature of truth?

Test Two—*Truth is usually reasonable*

Truth also makes sense. When we understand or learn a "truth," we usually describe a rational thought process that creates meaning in the mind such as "2 + 2 = 4." When the mind sees the rightness of the idea, it says to itself: "This must be true!"

One factor contributing to the growth of biblical faith in the Western World has been its central focus on reason. Rodney Stark explains, "Jews and Christians have always assumed that the application of reason can yield an increasingly more accurate understanding of God." [103] This was a key to my own spiritual pursuit. For many years I grappled with various questions about life, history, religion etc. The universe didn't make sense to me. Religion appeared unreasonable.

Then I responded to God's invitation in Isaiah 1:18—"'Come, let us reason together,' says the Lord." Over a number of years, I presented my questions to God in prayer and searched for understanding that made *sense*—that rang of truth. God eventually answered all my major religious questions I had posed as I "reasoned them out" with him.

This focus on human reason uniquely produced the primary ideologies of the Western World. From the Greek philosophers of the ancient world to the Christian scholastics, professors, inventors, and eventually scientists of the Middle Ages—Western civilization owes much of its success to the use of reason that served as a "gift" from a reasonable God. Here's the "reason": God made people in his image with the power of rational thought. The mind could thus be used to develop the earth (the dominion mandate), through business, technology, science, and the arts to improve the plight of people for the "glory of God."[104]

Indian thinker Vishal Mangalwadi agrees that reason was the catalyst for the development of Western civilization. In his excellent book, *Truth and Transformation: A Manifesto for Ailing Nations*, he notes that European peoples are not smarter than Asian peoples. Human beings are human beings. The difference— which allowed European and American civilization to develop at a much quicker pace than that of other cultures—was the use of faith and reason in those societies. Foundational premises were based on "truth" and were *mined* with the tools provided by reason.

Mangalwadi notes in describing the industrious monasteries of Medieval Europe:

> The human mind was different from the animal brain; it was made in God's image . . . They (the monks) believed that the human mind can know God, goodness and beauty; that human words can communicate truth because God made our minds in his image; and that God gave us the gift of language so that he might communicate with us, his children. These schools of piety created a uniquely *rational* religious man who became capable of developing complex theories. These theories created capitalistic economy and institutions that produced civil societies.[105]

Mangalwadi devotes an entire chapter in his book to the truth-producing power of "Rationality" that has brought prosperity to so many Western nations. He calls the power of human reason under God "the forgotten force behind Western technology."[106] He explains that many Asian peoples, due to inferior worldviews, fell behind the Western knowledge explosion that came from applying reason. He asks, "Why did Buddhist monks not develop technology?: [Because] transcendental meditation is not to know truth but to empty one's mind of all rational thought." He then explains, "a word (logos) is a sound *with* sense; a mantra is a sound separated from sense."[107]

In his enlightening book *What's So Great About Christianity*, Dinesh D'Souza affirms that science blossomed in the Western world because of Christianity's emphasis on the importance of reason.[108] He notes that the discipline of theology produced strong, rational minds which led to men unlocking some of the mysteries of the universe. D'Souza concludes: "The kind of reasoning about God that we see in Augustine, Aquinas, and Anselm is typical of Christianity. There is very little of this in any other religion. Out of such reasoning, remarkably enough, modern science was born."[109]

Most of us intuitively accept the idea that truth makes sense. Truth is reasonable, it is logical, and it can be found by those who diligently seek it.

Test Three—*Truth is based on evidence*

Our modern-day law courts—born of the biblical faith that champions reason—base their ideas on the principle that truth can be determined through analyzing evidence. If the preponderance of the evidence in a case points in one direction, then that conclusion should be accepted as true. In the case of a felony charge such as murder, the burden of the evidence must often reach the threshold of being "beyond a reasonable doubt." In other words, the weight of the evidence must be so strong that it nears the 100 percent threshold.

Modern scientific theory operates by the same principle. The Scientific Method refers to a series of techniques used to investigate the laws of nature, acquire information, or update and integrate previous knowledge. In order for something to be considered a scientific conclusion, the experiment must gather empirical and measurable evidence that conforms to standards of reason. The Oxford English Dictionary says that the scientific method contains: "a method or procedure that has characterized natural science since the seventh century, consisting in systematic observation, measurement, and experiment, and the formulation, testing, and modification of hypotheses."[110]

English philosopher, jurist, and pioneer of the scientific method Francis Bacon (1561-1626) taught the inductive use of knowledge, "the method of reasoning from particulars to generals, or the inferring of one general proposition from several particular ones."[111] In other words, collect the evidence (particulars) and arrive at the truth (general proposition). He believed that all scientific discoveries must be verified by observation, experiments, and analysis—the evidence being the critical component to eliminate wrong ideas and move closer to the truth.

One of the strengths of the scientific method is that objective scientists let reality speak for itself, even if the evidence contradicts a previously held position. This principle is known as *falsifiability*. Terance L. Tiessen calls this method "critical realism." He says about the pursuit of truth, "I believe that truth exists and that it can be known, but I also realize that no one seeks this truth . . . without presuppositions that significantly shape what we hear . . . For a statement to be true, there must be some appropriate correspondence between true statements and actual features of the world." [112]

For something to be true, the facts of reality must point to it.

So what type of evidence do we look for in determining whether a religion or worldview is true, either in totality or in part? I would suggest a number of categories:

- Historical Evidence—Does strong proof exist from history, that personalities, events, or ideas are based on historical realities, or is the historical evidence vague or in question? Charles Sanders in *Introduction to Research in English Literary History* contends there are three important historical tests: 1) Bibliographical—is the religious text or historical reality (person or event) quoted or mentioned in other works? 2) Internal Evidence—is the book or event consistent with its own teachings, and 3) External Evidence—do other outside "witnesses" such as archaeology satisfy the claim to truth.[113] Religious worldviews must pass the historical evidence test. And where there are controversial findings or interpretations of fact, they must be satisfied if possible to determine what is more likely the truth.

- Supernatural Evidence—With the exception of atheism, religion deals with a subject that presupposes the supernatural in the form of angels, demons, or Deity. Since these beings are by definition outside of the natural world, one would expect evidence of supernatural phenomena that gives credence to the truth claim. In *Evidence That Demands a Verdict*, Josh McDowell tells a story of encountering a student at the University of Uruguay who asked him: "Professor McDowell, why can't you refute Christianity?" McDowell replied, "For a very simple reason. I am not able to explain away an event in history—the resurrection of Jesus Christ."[114] The book then chronicles eighty-five pages of proofs for a supernatural event called the Resurrection and ends the discussion with these words: "The decision is now yours to make; the evidence speaks for itself. It says very clearly that Christ is risen indeed."[115] If you make a supernatural claim, you'd better be able to back it up with evidence.

- Transformational Evidence—You would also expect the realm of religion to produce a highly transformational effect upon its practitioners since one of the basic definitions of religion relates to impacting our thoughts and behavior. If a religion professes to be true, it should have a clear trail of changed lives that gives meaningful credibility to its claims. Paul Little, discussing the transforming power of Jesus of Nazareth on his followers, poses the question: "Are these men, who helped transform the moral structures of society, consummate liars or deluded madmen? These alternatives are harder to believe than the fact of the Resurrection, and there is no shred of evidence to support them." [116] If God is real, then his presence in the lives of his follows must be transformational. This is an important subjective measure of the truth of any religious worldview.

Test Four—*Truth resonates in our conscience*

Human conscience also plays the role of a "witness" in the trial for truth. J.M. Gundry-Volf states that, "Conscience is an inner tribunal which determines whether behavior (in the broad sense, including thinking, willing, speaking, and acting) agrees with the moral norms and requirements affirmed by the mind and which testifies of this verdict to the subject."[117] Conscience helps us find truth and reject error. So what constitutes the human conscience?

The conscience fulfills a crucial part of human personality. Closely related to the will and emotions, it gives the mind the ability to confirm moral beliefs and put them into practice. Romans 2:15 describes the human conscience this way: "in their hearts they know right from wrong. God's laws are written within them— their own conscience accuses them, or sometimes excuses them" (Living Bible).

Conscience provides a God-given sense of right and wrong for every heart. The ability of conscience points us to what's true, supplying right feeling toward obedience and wrong feeling toward disobedience. This ability to confirm and encourage right behavior is a precious gift from God. Without it, we would drift along in a world of confusing options. A mind without a conscience would be like a body without nerves. If you smashed your finger with a hammer, without the feeling of pain, you might continue hitting your finger, not knowing the severe damage you were doing.

The conscience does the same thing and more. It not only pains you when you choose to go against it, but it tells you the right thing to do before you do the smashing. It guides before you choose and registers approval or disapproval after the action. That's pretty amazing!

But the human conscience can also be extremely perverted or darkened. It can be "bent" to acknowledge the wrong things or deadened to hear nothing at all. Chuck Colson, the famous convert of Watergate, says it this way: "So, where does conscience come from? It's something God gives us at birth, but it has to be cultivated." This divinely planted sense of right and wrong is easily warped or perverted. When we do right, we feel approval and encouragement. But when we do wrong, our conscience "frowns" upon our wrong choice and we feel guilty, confused, dirty, or wrong.

In some ways, your conscience acts like a stereo speaker. If the speaker is well built, with wires properly connected to the sound system, the sound that is produced will be clear and understandable. But if you abuse the speaker or the wires get frayed, then the music sounds fuzzy, faint, or fails to get through at all. When this happens, the sound system is not at fault.

Its pitch and clarity have not changed. The problem is the speaker not receiving the clear signal.

If we do not protect and cherish our God-given conscience, then the truth about what's right and wrong becomes fuzzy, barely discernible, or completely silent. God's beam of truth hasn't changed. His signal remains as clear as it has always been. But our speaker—the human conscience—has been abused in a way that does not allow it to function properly.

It is crucial to listen to your conscience. The more you disobey it, the harder it is to hear. If you disobey your conscience often enough, its inherent moral compass won't direct you in the right way, but will become clouded by deception. Conversely, if you let your God-given conscience guide you, the arrow will consistently point you in the right direction. Freedom and success will be yours.

Five hundred years ago the great Swiss Reformer John Calvin stated that God had revealed himself via the human conscience. He remarked, "From this light the rays are diffused over all mankind . . . For we know that men have this particular excellence which raises them above other animals, that they are endowed with reason and intelligence, and that they carry the distinction of right and wrong engraved on their conscience. There is no man, therefore, whom some perception of *eternal light* does not reach."[118]

Truth Five—*Truth is eternal.*
All religious worldviews, with the exception of atheism, seem to agree that truth possesses a timeless quality—it lasts forever. This means that since religious truth reveals the pathway to God, then that path was equally available five thousand years ago, during the Middle Ages and today. If truth doesn't apply to all human history, then it doesn't pass the "longevity test." Truth is timeless. Its essentials do not change.

Truth's timeless veracity contains another important idea. Contemporary American novelist Madaleine L'Engle describes it this way in her book *An Acceptable Time*, when she states, "Truth is eternal, knowledge is changeable. It is disastrous to confuse them."[119]

I agree we invite disaster when we miss eternal truth through incorrect knowledge. A number of religions teach that our life in eternity, (e.g. human beings are immortal beings), hinges upon the choices we make in this one. For example, an Islamic idea that purports to be the truth teaches that if you wage jihad in the Name of Allah, such as the 9-11 hijackers did in killing 3,000 innocent people on September 11, 2001, you are rewarded with virgins in heaven to ravish forever.

Buddhism holds out the hope that if you reach the final stage of "enlightenment" you enter into eternal nothingness—forever. Hope is also not the same as truth. And biblical faith states as "truth" that "God so loved the world that he gave his one and only Son, that whoever believes in him shall not perish but have eternal life" (John 3:16).

All three rewards profess to last forever—but with substantially different outcomes. Human beings agree that truth must stand the test of time—it lasts forever (Psalm 119:160). But it remains absolutely crucial to discover *which of these beliefs* is *really true*. Why? Because whatever the real destiny of jihadists, transcendental meditationists or followers of Jesus, their fate lasts forever. In religion, it is crucial to make the correct choice—for eternal reasons.

Test Six—*Truth is universal*
There remains one final test. Our rational mind tells us that for something to be true, its veracity must not only be timeless, but it must also apply universally to every person and nation. In matters of religion, it must not be isolated to just Asia, Europe, or Africa. If God and truth exist, his ways must apply to all. This idea led me to consider the biblical faith worldview.

I am a missionary who has traveled to sixty nations around the world. I've heard many common stories about man's origins or ancient history that are preserved in various cultures and am amazed at their similarity. The following story illustrates the universality of truth.

Bob and Cecilia Brown served as missionaries during the 1990s among the Saluan people in the jungles of Sulawesi, Indonesia. The Saluans regularly recited a traditional story of "the Snake and the Man" that was eerily similar to the Genesis creation story:

> "The-One-Who-Formed-Our-Fingers had made a beautiful place. When he made the man and the woman he told them that they could live in that beautiful place. So they lived there, and their fire never went out, and their water flasks never went dry. The-One-Who-Formed-Our-Fingers said that he was going away and that they must not eat the fruit of one tree while he was gone. Then he left. While he was gone, the snake came. Now, the man and the snake were brothers. The snake told the man that the fruit was so good and that he should try some. The man did eat the fruit. The He was afraid of The-One-Who-Formed-Our Fingers. When the One-Who-Formed-Our-Fingers returned, he knew right away what had happened. He chased the man away from the beautiful place and said, 'From now on the water won't come by itself, and the firewood won't come by itself, and the food won't come by itself. The sweat will drip off your jaw and your fingernails won't get long because you will have to work to get food."[120]

The Saluan tribe knew nothing else about The-One-Who-Formed-Our-Fingers other than another story about a flood that covered the mountains. Of course the story of an ancient universal flood recorded in Genesis 6-8 is found in many nations of the world. Is this just a coincidence? I don't think so. The worldwide evidence of common stories is too immense to explain. The universal nature of the story actually inspires a high degree of confidence that it is true. No other explanation comes close.

The creation account inspires similar confidence. The Saluan story above—orally passed down by generations in the islands of Indonesia—is remarkably close to the Genesis 1-3 creation details written down some

10,000 miles away in the Middle East. Many other religious traditions contain creation accounts—and though some of the stories are embellished or even downright weird—they point back to an original reality.

If something is true, you would expect this type of universal (historical) confirmation.

Don Richardson points out in his ground-breaking book, *Eternity in Their Hearts,* that as we saw in the previous chapter, a universal concept of a High God exists in many cultures. He documents the work of nineteenth century Scandinavian missionaries working among the Santal people of northwest India. They held to an ancient tradition concerning Thakir Jiu, the "Genuine God" Thakir Jiu told the Santals that people would come one day to give them understanding of the way of salvation. When Christian missionaries arrived, large people movements to Christ erupted.[121]

Richardson goes on to say that in other nations, "This benign, omnipotent 'skygod' of mankind's many folk religions has a propensity to identify Himself with the God of Christianity. For "sky god," though regarded in most folk religions as remote or more or less unreachable, tends to draw near and speak to folk religionists whenever—unknown to themselves—they are about to meet emissaries of the Christian God!"[122]

Stories like this one only confirm that if God exists, his ways must be universal and he must have a plan for all the peoples of the earth. This amazing message is being distributed and received all over the world.

So to summarize: Truth contains unique and wonderful qualities. It often displays clarity, simplicity and reasonableness. Truth rest on valuable evidence and includes a witness of conscience. It remains true for all-time (eternal) and it applies to everybody (universal).

Now let's conclude our discussion of truth with the problems it must solve.

QUESTIONS TRUTH MUST ANSWER

Rabbi Daniel Lapin believes that there are three paramount questions about life. 1) Where did we come from, 2) where are we going, and 3) what are we supposed to do in between? [123]I agree with the rabbi's assessment and contend that a truthful worldview must supply meaningful answers to these and other questions. If its answers are vague, it also fails the truth test.

I expand those three basic questions into the following top-ten:

1. God—*"Who's in Charge?"* The essence of every religion flows from its concept of God. How is God defined? What constitutes the nature and character of Deity? For a worldview/religion to have credibility it must answer questions relating to who made and sustains the universe and what is his current role in it. We all recognize authorities in life. Who or what is the supreme authority over the universe?

2. Source—*"What's its source of information?"* An idea or theory can only be as good as its source. Is the source credible? Can its veracity be verified or confirmed in history? Most religions have texts from which we learn about their leaders and teachings. How reliable is the religion's sourcebook? Which particular religious worldviews have the most credible or compelling guidebooks?

3. Origins—*"How did we get here?"* A credible worldview must be able to answer the question of the origins of the universe and man. Does the story make sense? Does it align with the reality that we see around us? If a religion gives no clarity on how we got here, how can it be trusted to take us into the future?

4. Organization—*"How does life on earth and in the cosmos operate?"* The universe and all that is in it displays amazing order, precision, and complexity. Not only must there be an authority or sovereign in control, but there must be social organization of some type. Large companies have structure and order. Does a particular religion define the organization of the universe in a way that makes sense?

5. Human Beings—*"What is the nature of human beings and why are we here?"* A credible worldview must give us answers about the nature of human beings. Are we simply physical beings, or do we

have a spirit or soul? Are we immortal, or does existence end when we die? What kind of beings are we, and why are we here? If a religious worldview cannot compellingly explain the nature and destiny of man, should we trust it to explain the concept of God?

6. Morality—*"What's the basis of right and wrong?"* Most religions have a moral code of prescribed duties. Which one makes the most sense? Where do our concepts of right and wrong originate? Do our moral choices have a bearing on eternity? If a religion can't give a clear explanation of its moral compass, it probably won't lead us to the right concept of God.

7. Sin—*"Why's the world so messed up?"* We all seem to recognize that there's something wrong with human beings on the earth. Why do we struggle with personal behavior and relationships? Why are there wars and tension between nations? If a religion can accurately define the problem, then we might be able to trust in its solution.

8. Salvation—*"How can the world be made right?"* Every religion teaches a way that we can be made right with God, the universe, or ourselves. Which one makes the most sense? Where does the power come from to bring change? Are all roads to God or heaven the same? Is human redemption or improvement just for this life or is it applicable for eternity?

9. Earth—*"How should human beings look at the earth?* Are we simply passengers on a journey, or do we play a role in the stewardship of our environment? We live on a beautiful planet—unique in our solar system and possibly in the universe. Why were we placed here? What is our duty or destiny toward planet earth? A legitimate worldview should guide us to a proper approach toward the place in which we live.

10. Heaven—*"Is there a future and a hope?"* And finally, where is everything headed? Do we possess real reasons for hope, or is that just an illusion? Does life after death exist, and if it does, is there a hell to avoid and a heaven to enjoy? What is the ultimate future

of my own life, mankind, the earth and the entire universe? If a religion can't provide hope, then we probably shouldn't believe it.

For thousands of years, human beings have sought answers to the biggest questions of life in the realm of religion. Before we analyze the five religions and the answers they provide, there is one more question to ponder.

It has been said that up until three thousand years ago, everyone heard the voice of God.[124] What about since that time? What voices or sources of truth actually exist in the world?

And which one of them should we listen to and believe?

Chapter Four

Sources

"The world is a spiritual battle zone, which is why it looks that way."[125]

Gregory Boyd

A basic premise of honest journalism is: *check your sources*. Information is only as good as the source or person from which it came. There's another way to describe it: "Be careful what voices you listen to."

I learned a big lesson about "voices" in when I was young. I was spending a college year in New Zealand with three friends who joined me in a search for God and adventure. One October afternoon, I hopped on my bicycle and sped quickly through the quaint streets of Auckland, New Zealand, to the home of a spiritual mentor named Blythe Harper. I was troubled about some areas of my life and wanted to get some advice from a man I'd grown to trust.

Blythe was a successful businessman with a twinkle in his eye and a gentle demeanor. He possessed a spiritual depth in his life that I found very attractive—which highly motivated me to seek his advice. He graciously invited me to spend the afternoon at his modest but comfortable Mt. Roskill home.

After welcoming me into his study, we shared some small talk over biscuits and tea. Then I opened up about the bitterness I held in my heart and a struggle I faced in my thought life. "Blythe," I said almost wearily, "I just can't seem to control the hurt and resentment that I carry. I have many bad thoughts, and I know they are wrong, but they seem to hinder my spiritual walk and I want to be free of their influence."

"When do these thoughts come to you," he asked probingly. I explained they came when I obsessed on past hurts. I had experienced a season of rejection in my life, and then struggled with my thoughts and feelings from time to time after that. Blythe continued to gently ask questions, and I poured out my heart as best I could.

I was bitter and confused—and my head was spinning.

After an hour or so, Blythe stopped the questioning and shared his perspective. He said he was sorry for what I'd experienced and believed I needed to be "set free." He explained that bitterness was like a poison, and that the voices in my mind were certainly not the voice of God who wanted to comfort me and free me from the bad memories.

Then he prayed. His words were soothing, life giving, and powerful. At a point in time, he raised his voice and declared, "Satan, I bind you in the Name of Jesus and command you to take away those lying words and get out of Ron's life." As he spoke, totally beyond my own human volition, my hands contorted as if a power was struggling within me. As Blythe continued to pray, the contortions became more obvious and firmer to the point where my hands were like hooks and nearly clenched together.

Struggling against an unseen power, I confessed the sin of bitterness and asked God to take control of my life. I thanked him that he loved me and had power over the forces coming against me. The prayer session lasted for hours with Blythe continually praying and speaking words of encouragement to me. By late afternoon, my hands completely loosened, a surge of relief swept over me, and the voices of bitterness vanished.

Bicycling home at full speed, I sensed for the first time I was FREE! Really FREE!

This exhilarating and life-changing experience formed a crucial foundation for me. I learned a great lesson about "voices" or sources of truth. For, in my meeting with Blythe Harper, it had become clear to me that there were *three* voices I need to differentiate between in my life: *The voice of men, the voice of demons, and the voice of God.*

These three form the primary sources of "truth" (information) in our world. Before we analyze the world's five major religions, we must understand where all ideas originate—including religious ones. Here's a simple starting point—they come from moral beings that can think, feel and act.[126] That leaves us three realistic options: 1) Human beings who possess these attributes of personality, 2) Satan and his fallen angels (demons) who use these abilities in the invisible realm, and 3) God (and his holy angels who are an extension of his Kingdom).

If you're a secularist, you probably don't believe in God or angels, but you might add one other category of moral agency—*space aliens*. For the purposes of this chapter, we will leave "Star Wars" alone and focus on the first three. I actually believe demonic forces perpetrate the space alien myth. But that's another story.

VOICES OF PHILOSOPHY—
PEOPLE SEEK FOR MEANING AND GOD

Human beings "create" via ideas. In the historical record, the first voices we hear of man's search for truth (or God) came from the ancient Greek philosophers whose ideas contributed to Western civilization. Desiring to move beyond their polytheistic culture, beginning in the sixth century B.C., they crafted an approach to knowledge based on reason and evidence. They sought after God while attempting to explain him as a single underlying principle in nature.[127] Their primitive scientific ideas proved overly general and none achieved wide consensus, but they succeeded in partially switching the debate away from a High God or gods to the "love of wisdom" (philosophy) which focused on metaphysics (concepts of being), epistemology (the theory of knowledge), and ethics (right and wrong).[128]

One of the earliest to achieve fame was Socrates from Athens (469-399 B.C.E.). Whereas the early philosophers focused on the physical world, Socrates made the thoughts and opinions of people his starting-point. His reasoning style became known in debating as the Socratic Method (critical thinking). Socrates was a popular figure, but also had many enemies. Contemporary authorities eventually executed him for "corrupting the youth of Athens" by allegedly turning them away from their polytheistic gods. His martyrdom made him a humanistic hero.[129]

We primarily know about Socrates because of his pupil, Plato, who wrote about his famous mentor in works such as *Apology* (in which Socrates' defends his teachings), *Crito* (when Socrates was in prison and refused to escape), and in *Phaedo* (where he describes the immortality of the soul.) Plato's main contribution to philosophy, which was now advancing the idea that "man is the measure of all things,"[130] remains the threefold division of philosophy into dialectic, ethics, and physics.

Plato originated the theory of "forms." The highest form of being is the "Good," which stands out as "the ultimate basis of the rest, and the first cause of being and knowledge."[131] Mark Levin believes that the idea of the "Good" is similar to the biblical concept of God or ultimate truth.[132] I suggest that, over time, it led to a greater acceptance of atheism that elevated man's reason above the revelation of God.

Levin devotes an entire chapter in his book to Plato's classic *Republic* in which the philosopher invents an ideal city/state where childbirth is regulated, eugenics encouraged, and the nuclear family abolished. In Plato's *Republic*, education is state centered, an elite group of men govern the populace, and Plato boasts, "Just as the philosopher is best and happiest of men, so the aristocratic State is the best and happiest of states."[133]

Mark Levin points out that the *Republic* laid the groundwork for future humanistic models such as Thomas More's *Utopia*, Thomas Hobbe's *Leviathan,* and even Karl Marx's *Communist Manifesto*.[134] The twentieth century saw other utopian models put to practice in the Soviet Union, China, North Korea, and Cuba. But these "dictatorships of the proletariat" ultimately made political tyrants and tyrannical governments the "gods" of the people—and the "Good" became whatever powerful men wanted it to be.

Aristotle of Stagira (384-322 B.C.) emerged as the last major figure in the trinity of Greek philosophers. Whereas Plato spoke of the ethereal forms of the Good, Aristotle preferred to start with facts given to us by experience. To him, philosophy meant science, and its aim was to discover the purpose of all things through moving from a number of facts to a universal. In a series of writings called *Organon,* Aristotle set forth the laws by which the human reason reaches conclusions from particulars to the Big Idea.

Some theologians believe the propositions of the Greek philosophers somewhat paralleled God's revelations in history. Clement of Alexandria spoke of the Old Testament and Greek philosophy as "two tributaries of one great river." He noted, "To the Jews belonged the Law and to the Greeks Philosophy, until the Advent (the coming of Christ); and after that the universal call to be a particular people of righteousness . . . brought together by one Lord, the only God of both Greeks and barbarians, or rather of the whole race of men."[135] Justin Martyr believed that "When the philosophers, such as Plato, wrote about the immortality of the soul, or punishments after death, or contemplation of things heavenly, they had received such suggestions from the prophets. There seem to be seeds of truth among all men." [136]

But there remains a troubling difference. Lacking clear understanding of a High Creator God, and lacking access to the Old Testament Torah, the Greek philosophers focused their attention on a man-centered search that ended up elevating man's reason and sowing the seeds of secular humanism (a philosophy that espouses reason, ethics, and justice, and specifically rejects the supernatural and religion).

One thousand years later, the man-centered ideas of the Greeks philosophers found fruitful soil in the European Enlightenment which arose in Europe to challenge its religious foundations and change the face of the continent. Enlightenment thinkers Rene Descartes, Rousseau and Voltaire, and David Hume carried, in a variety of ways, the torch for human reasoning that brought massive societal upheaval and change. Some of the consequences the Enlightenment created were ugly—such as the blood bath of the French Revolution.

But the greatest impact of philosophy was enlarging a man-centered orientation toward knowledge. Francis Schaeffer warned us: "Renaissance humanism steadily evolved toward modern humanism—a value system rooted in the belief that man is his own measure—that man is autonomous, totally independent."[137] This fifteen-hundred-year march by ancient and modern philosophers created one of the five religious worldviews—atheism. It proposed that man use his mind alone to seek for truth. This view often produces governmental tyranny.[138]

We need to use care when listening to the "voice" of men. They contain many elements of truth we need to hear, but oftentimes their voice rings incomplete or agonizingly wrong.

Despite the atheistic tendencies, many early Greek philosophers didn't totally reject the supernatural—including the realm of fallen angels and the demonic. Terance L. Tiessen reminds us that "Plato simply assumed that the cosmos is inhabited by good and evil demons (*daimons*). He and his colleagues assumed that these "middle creatures," being free, were capable of harming human beings. For instance, it is common knowledge that Socrates credited his personal *daimon* with leading him and instructing him throughout his life."[139]

Many Greek philosophers *did* believe there was another realm of moral beings who influenced life on earth. They reveal the next "voice" that we must learn to recognize.

VOICES OF DECEPTION—
FALLEN ANGELS SEEK TO DESTROY PEOPLE.

Human beings create ideas about God and truth, but does the evidence suggest that another group of moral beings also busy themselves by influencing human thought and behavior? Many of the world's peoples think so. They call these entities fallen angels, spirits, demons, devils, and even deceased ancestors. I call them the voices of *deception*.

Belief in a devil and his fallen angels stands as one of the most universally accepted truths in the world. The secular West plays down or rationalizes the concept, but the remainder of the world accepts it as a *fact* in their daily life experience. Why do most people believe in a devil, demons, or fallen spirits? The evidence shouts out everywhere that they exist.[140] (Remember the fourth truth test?)

Gregory Boyd in his books *God at War* and *Satan and the Problem of Evil* makes a compelling case for the reality of demonic beings and the spiritual warfare taking place between them and righteous angels who serve God's Kingdom. He says,

> It was apparently self-evident to the vast majority of ancient people, and still is to primitive people today, that the world is not all physical, not even primarily physical, and certainly not right. It was, rather, a world that was populated with influential spiritual beings, some of whom were evil, and most of them were at war with one another . . . This worldview is that perspective on reality which centers on the conviction that the good and the evil, fortunate or unfortunate, aspects of life are to be interpreted largely as a result of good and evil, friendly or hostile, spirits warring against each other and against us.[141]

Boyd calls this perspective of the cosmos a *warfare worldview*. Dean Sherman shares the same idea in his popular work *Spiritual Warfare for Every Christian*.[142] I agree with both men that a spiritual war exists on planet earth. I experienced firsthand it in my own life.

Satan at War & *The Screwtape Letters*
Boyd's fills his weighty volumes with numerous examples of demonic voices and activities in the lives of people—from the jungles of Indonesia to red-light district of Amsterdam. He says that Jesus and his disciples recognized

their reality and cast them out almost daily.[143] Though God created them as good, "these cosmic forces made themselves evil."[144] Boyd summarizes the demonic reality this way: "The world is caught up in a cosmic battle and thus is saturated with horrifying suffering and diabolical evil. *That* is the final explanation for evil."[145]

The Bible certainly backs up the warfare worldview and its portrayal of the demonic. In Genesis, we find the devil (Satan), in the form of a serpent lying to and tempting Adam and Eve (Genesis 3); The book of Job paints a clear picture of Satan's tactics and purposes; Daniel learns of the spiritual warfare battle while engaged in intercessory prayer (Daniel 10); Jesus speaks to and hears from demons while casting them out (Mark 5:1-20), and faces Satan directly in the wilderness; Finally, Revelation concludes with the devil and his angels being banished to a lake of fire (Revelation 20:10).

Nothing in these stories indicates that fallen angels are symbolic or allegorical. They are real moral beings that terrorize the human race.

C.S. Lewis's best-selling book *The Screwtape Letters* provides a fictional look into the demonic realm. It presents an imaginary dialogue between demon master (Screwtape) to his lowly apprentice (Wormwood), who is learning to tempt and enslave human beings. The demon master uses the letters to reveal many of Satan's strategies and tactics in a gripping narrative that comes very close to home. Listening to this demonic "chat" is like hearing an echo of scenes from your own life.

Lewis states his belief clearly: "I believe in devils. I do. That is to say, I believe in angels, and I believe that some of these, by the abuse of their free will, have become enemies to God, and, as a corollary, to us. These we may call devils. They do not differ in nature from good angels, but their nature is depraved. *Devil* is the opposite of *angel* only as Bad man is the opposite of Good Man. Satan, the leader or dictator of devils, is the opposite, not of God, but of Michael."[146]

And what should be our posture toward these malevolent beings? Lewis gives some good advice: "There are two equal and opposite errors into which our race can fall about devils. One is to disbelieve in their existence. The other is to believe, and to feel an excessive and unhealthy interest in them. They themselves are equally pleased with both errors, and hail a materialist or a magician with the same delight." [147]

In other words, don't doubt their existence or look for them under every bush.

Most cultures find it easy to believe in demonic forces because they encounter them regularly in their thought lives, rituals, relational struggles or even tribal wars. Western people, inoculated by skeptical atheism, find it more difficult to believe in the existence of a devil and his minions though that belief is extremely helpful in figuring out Charles Manson, Adolph Hitler, and why many men are so strongly tempted to surf the Internet for pornography.

A Celt and a Canadian

To enlighten our Western unbelief, I share both an ancient and modern example of Satan and his demons at work. The first is an ancient description of Celtic warfare that can only be described as demon possession. The portrait is taken from Thomas Cahill's *How the Irish Saved Civilization.* Would you like to fight a warrior like this?

> The Irish, like all the Celts, stripped before battle and rushed their enemies naked . . . The Romans, in their first encounters with these exposed warriors, were shocked and frightened. Not only were the men naked, they were howling and, it seemed, possessed by demons, so outrageous were their strength and verse . . . The Irish heroes were aware that they became possessed when confronted by the enemy and that their appearances would alter considerably, and they called this phenomenon the warp spasm . . . This is how it appears, 'The warp-spasm seized a man and made him into a monstrous thing, hideous and shapeless,

unheard of. His shanks and his joints, every knuckle and
angle and organ from head to foot, shook like a tree in
the flood or a reed in the stream. His body made a furious
twist inside his skin . . . His face and features became a
red bowl . . . His mouth weirdly distorted: his cheek
peeled back from his jaws until the gullet appeared, his
lungs and liver flapped in his mouth and throat, his lower
jaw struck the upper a lion-killing blow . . . In this great
carnage he slew one hundred and thirty kings, as well as
an uncountable horde of dogs and horses, women and
boys and children and the rabble of all kinds. Not one
man in three escaped . . . [148]

Cahill's story takes up three pages, but I spared you the length. I think
you get the picture. Fallen spirits empowered these human warriors in such
gruesome fashion even Stoic Roman soldiers shivered in their boots. Out-
of-this-world power always trumps unbelieving humans. No wonder the
Roman Empire fell. Demonic hordes overran it.

A modern-day story strikes closer to home. It also took place in the
West, not with armies in conflict, but between a Canadian man and an un-
wanted nighttime guest:

In 1984 Robert Wheeler of Abbotsford, British Colum-
bia had had little contact with the church in the first
thirty-eight years of his life. Some neighbors led his wife
to faith in Christ which bothered him when she began to
pray for him. One Saturday night several weeks after her
conversion he had what he described as a battle with an
evil creature while he was trying to sleep. Its face re-
sembled a human face without skin, and it frightened
him. He tried to fight off this creature but he was not
successful. Just off to his right stood a man wearing a

white sackcloth robe with a sash around his waist. Robin never did see above the shoulders of the second person, but he considers it to have been Jesus. Robin tried to tie up the creature with the sash from Jesus, and as he did so, Jesus disappeared . . . Robin's wife was with him when these struggles were taking place. She told me that he levitated for long periods of time that coincided with the struggles, and seemed to go in and out of consciousness. She says that Robin floated in midair in a horizontal position above the bed. His body was in a perfectly rigid position, and all the veins in his body were bulging. His head was bent so far back, she says, she thought it would break. Although she did not see the figures that appeared to him, she could ask him what was happening, and he would describe the events taking place. She estimates that the various struggles occurred over a six hour period, but he had no sense of the passing of time. When a fight sequence came to an end, his body would drop back onto the bed, and he would relax until a new struggle began . . . The struggles finally ended when Robin found that his efforts to tie up the monster did not succeed and he requested help from Jesus who bound the monster for him. Robin considers this to be symbolic of his own inability to restrain the powers of evil that tired to envelop him. The next day Robin decided to become a Christian.[149]

The previous two examples may be unusual in their severity, but they represent a truth that modern man should consider. A large body of historical and experiential evidence indicates we are not alone in the universe. Fallen spiritual beings wage war with human life and seek to tempt, deceive, and destroy us.

Demonic Impostors

Sometimes, demonic beings imitate non-existent "gods" to confuse us about religion. Terance Tiessen warns, "The gods worshipped by other nations are not real and are unable to save; in fact, the worship of these gods might be stirred up by demonic forces as a means to hold people in spiritual bondage."[150] He concludes that false religions are not ordinarily stepping stones to Christ, but more often, they are paths to hell.[151] These religions often contain rays of truth or half-truths (as the serpent expressed in the Garden), but as J.N.D. Anderson comments, the best explanation for them might be that "even Satan himself can and does sometimes appear as an angel of light (2 Corinthians 11:14)."[152]

I learned a long time ago that Satan and his demons exist. The majority of people in ancient and modern times agree. These fallen beings want to mess with our minds and ultimately destroy our lives. This is why the Bible tells us that "we are not fighting against flesh-and-blood enemies, but against evil rulers and authorities of the unseen world, against mighty powers in this dark world, and against evil spirits in the heavenly places" (Ephesians 6:12, New Living Translation).

We need to resist them. Otherwise, the advice from demon master Screwtape to his apprentice Wormwood just might come true: "Keep everything hazy in his mind now, and you will have all eternity wherein to amuse yourself by producing in him the peculiar form of clarity which Hell affords." [153]

Both human reason and demonic deceptions can be presented to our minds as "truth." But another moral being exists in the universe that communicates with man—the God who is there and he is not silent.

VOICE OF REVELATION—GOD SPEAKS TO REDEEM PEOPLE

We have shown that human reason via philosophy and fallen angels through deception are two "channels of information" about what is true in our world. Human philosophy purports to be man's search for truth or God. Satan uses demonic deception to hunt down and destroy human beings. Human reason sometimes "gets it right"—and devils are clever in telling half-truths.

But the greatest and purest source of truth that exists in time and space is the River of God that flows from a just and loving Deity *who looks for people to save them.* He is the ultimate source of all truth and wants to reveal it to us. That leads us to the following question: How do we know that we know? Put another way, "Where does knowledge begin?"

American philosopher Francis Schaeffer made "the coin drop" for me in the area of epistemology—"how we know that we know." I questioned for some time whether *I* initiate knowledge by thinking a thought or engaging a concept. Does knowledge begin with *me and my perceptions,* or can knowledge originate elsewhere? Believing that "knowledge started with me" seemed a scary or risky idea.

Schaeffer intellectually answered my doubt. He taught the *validity* of the presupposition that knowledge originates with man. But he trumpeted another equally valid premise: Knowledge begins with the *revelation of God.*

Here's how Schaeffer stated the idea in *He is There and Is Not Silent:* "[God] is not silent. This is the reason we know. It is because he has spoken . . . he has told us the truth about himself—and because he has told us true truth about himself—that he is the infinite, personal, triune God—we have the answer to existence . . . at the point of metaphysics—of being, of existence—general and special revelation speak with one voice."[154]

Schaeffer's first book on this subject, *The God Who Is There* placed the center of metaphysics (the nature of being) in the existence of God. He exists; he created the world, including us; he controls all things and has purposes and plans for everyone. The most basic intuitive fact of reality is that *God is there.* This defines building block one.

His follow-up book explained the epistemological question of knowing. It presented building block two. Because *God is there, he is not silent.* He is a communicator; he communicates in many ways in the world; he exists as the *logos,* the "word" from which all truth flows. Schaeffer explains:

> Christianity has a different set of presuppositions. It begins
> with a God who is there, who is the infinite-personal God,

who has made man in his own image. He has made man to be the verbalizer in the area of propositions in his horizontal communication to other men. Even secular anthropologists say that somehow or other, they do not know why man is the verbalizer. You have something different in man. The Bible says, and the Christian position says, 'I can tell you why: God is a personal-infinite God. There has always been communication, before the creation of all else, in the Trinity."[155]

So how does God speak to a world he made and deeply loves? Theologians categorize the logos (communication) of God in two different ways. One they call *general* revelation—broad ways God has revealed himself to all people. The other is termed *special* revelation—where he has made himself known in greater clarity and precise detail. Let's first discuss two areas of general revelation that are sources of truth for all human beings.

God Speaks Through Creation
We learn much about the character and ways of God by looking at and studying his creation—the entire cosmos (through telescopes, satellites, and spacecraft) and the wonderful world in which we live (by experience and experimentation). Regardless of your view on *how* God created it all, the grandeur of the cosmos and beauty and provisions of the earth tells us many things about the Creator God.

No wonder the Psalmist explains with excitement:

The heavens tell of the glory of God.
The skies display his marvelous craftsmanship.
Day after day they continue to speak;
Night after night they make him known.
They speak without a sound or word;
Their voice is silent in the skies;

Yet their message has gone out to all the earth,
And their words to all the world.

(Psalm 19:1-4 New Living Translation).

The incredible design and majesty of the world point to an Amazing De-signer who is wise, powerful, knowledgeable, and creative. Studying the features of a flower gives us a sense of his gentleness and beauty. Analyzing the galaxies through an instrument such as the Hubble telescope creates awe and wonder at his power. Romans 1: 19-20 explains, "For the truth about God is known to them instinctively. God has put this knowledge in their hearts. From the time the world was created, people have seen the earth and sky and all that God made. They can clearly see his invisible qualities—his eternal power and divine nature. So they have no excuse whatsoever for not knowing God."

Honest eyes see God in creation. No other explanation makes sense.

I recently watched a moving presentation of God's amazing creation called "How Great is Our God" by youth specialist Louis Giglio. Louis skillfully portrays the unfathomable size of the universe and various stars we've been able to see and name—and then concludes by describing how the seventy trillion celled human body is a microcosm of the Milky Way Galaxy.[156] Amazing! No wonder King David exclaimed in Psalm 139:13-14:

"Oh, yes, you shaped me first inside and out;
You formed me in my mother's womb.
I thank you High God—you're breathtaking!
Body and soul, I am marvelously made!
I worship in adoration—what a creation!" (The Message).

Ancient peoples, undistracted by modern technologies and amenities, gazed at creation and worshipped the High God. They saw God's power, his provision, and his presence in the magnificent world around them. And they worshipped. Those with "eyes to see" do the same thing today.

God Speaks Through Conscience

We've already discussed human conscience as a vital truth test (Truth Test #3). Man exists on earth as the only moral agent that possesses "judgment of right and wrong, or the faculty, power or principles within us, which decides on the lawfulness of our own actions and affections and instantly approves or condemns them. Conscience is called by some writers the moral sense."[157]

This ability of conscience was entrusted to human beings as a guide to lead us into truth—truth that has been revealed within. James Walker states, "Both faith and conscience look to God for authority; and until faith sees God in truth, conscience will not convict the soul of guilt for disobedience. Hence in the moral culture of the soul, everything depends on the *revealment* of truth . . . Without revealed truth, reason has no data, faith is false and conscience is corrupt."[158]

What do we learn about God from our conscience? We learn of his character and values—that he is just, fair, good, and especially *loving*. Because he exists, we learn from our conscience that we *ought* to love him in return. Because other human beings exist, we're often convicted by our God-given conscience that we *ought* to love other people as much as we love ourselves.

Most moral codes, and especially the more developed ones such as the Ten Commandments (Exodus 20:1-17) and two great commands of Jesus (Luke 10:27), center on the revelation of conscience that God has given to all people. We can pervert the "messages" of conscience, but only rarely extinguish them.

God reveals important aspects of his character and standards by way of universal conscience. We'd be much happier if we listened to the voice of conscience.

Now let's conclude our "God-source" analysis by touching on two aspects of God's revelation that are different from general revelation. Important truth about God can be seen in creation and imparted to our consciences. But God didn't stop there. He chose at least two other ways to share with us the truth about life. We call this area *special* revelation.

God Speaks Through Scripture

Vital things can be learned about the High God by studying the natural world and paying attention to the voice of conscience within. But that knowledge only takes us so far. Apparently, the wise God knew we needed further revelation if we were to know him in complete truth. He decided to give us his *graphe*—a written communication.

We call this written word, Scripture (sacred writings), or the Bible (the books), which houses the Old and New Testaments. It contains an amazingly specific revelation of God.

There are many religious texts in the world. We will discuss them in later chapters as we look at the five major religions. But the Bible stands above the others as absolutely unique: [159]

1. It stands unique in its *continuity*—Written over a 1600-year span (60 generations) by forty-plus authors from every walk of life. (The Koran had one author recording "recitations" over a period of three weeks—written forty years after his death.)

2. It stands unique in its *circulation*—It has been read by more people and published in more languages than any other book. The first major book to be "published" was the Latin Vulgate (Old Testament). The first book published on the Gutenberg Press was the entire Bible (Old and New Testaments).

3. It stands unique in its *translation*—It was the first book translated (Septuagint c. third century B.C.) The Bible has been translated, retranslated and paraphrased more than any book in existence. Plans are underway to put it into the language of every people group on earth by the year 2020.[160]

4. It stands unique in its *survival*—Bernard Ramm says, "There are over thirteen thousand manuscripts, complete and incomplete, in

Greek and other languages that have survived from antiquity. No other work from classical antiquity has such attestation."[161]

5. It stands unique in its *prophecies,* its accuracy about *history*, and its influence on other forms of *literature*. It also contains some of the most beautiful poetry every written. (Think Psalm 23 and the Song of Solomon).

But the Bible makes the most unique contribution of all history in the New Testament by telling us how God came to earth in the Person of Jesus Christ to reveal his heart and to redeem human beings from their sin. The most known verse of the world's most known book says, "For God so loved the world that he gave his one and only Son, that whoever believes in him shall not perish but have eternal life" (John 3:16).

No greater revelation can be made than by *coming in person*. Maria-susai Dhavamony reminds us, "God has left traces of himself and of his salvific plan in the other religious traditions. They have some insight into God, truth [and] spiritual riches but only partly rather than wholly. Hence Christ fulfills them and brings them to perfection."[162] We will discuss the uniqueness of Jesus Christ in greater depth later as we come to fuller understanding of the River.

Francis Schaeffer agrees to the Bible's importance in revealing God when he says, "Man can know both truth about God and truth about the things of creation because in the Bible God has revealed himself and has given man the key to understanding God's world." [163] Scripture is a very special communication from the one who desires "none to perish" (2 Peter 3:9).

God pursues human beings out of love. The Bible shares his story.

God Speaks to You and Me
There is another way God communicates *especially* to men and women on earth—through direct, personal communication. You would expect a personal God to do so. Creation—though awesome—comes up an incomplete teacher. Conscience provides necessary guidance for right and wrong be-

havior, but it can be tarnished through disobedience or neglect. The Bible serves us well as a vital a moral compass of who God is and where history is headed.

But many people have never seen the Bible, and the other sources remain incomplete. How can they know him in a personal and intimate way? Here's a fascinating proposal: *by listening to him*. From the human side of the veil we call it "prayer." From God's standpoint, his *rhema* word comes to us (an "utterance," or God "speaking" in our hearts.)[164]

For many years I didn't believe God spoke personally to people—at least not today. I'd read many stories about it in the Bible, such as David asking God for guidance and God personally giving his answer (e.g. 1 Samuel 8:8-10, 23:2). Then there was the "conversation" God enjoyed with Job at the end of his time of suffering (Job 39-41). Many examples in Jesus' life showed him listening to the Father and acting on what he heard (Luke 3:22, John 5:19-20).

But we're not David, Job, or Jesus. Does God speak to ordinary people like you and me? The answer from history and personal experience is a resounding yes! The author of communication personally talks with those he has created. He is there—and he is not silent.

Youth With A Mission built its global missions outreach on the ability of each individual to hear the voice of God.[165] Loren Cunningham, the founder of YWAM, tells the story of our mission in his book *Is That Really You, God? Hearing the Voice of God.* As the title implies, the book brims with fascinating stories of how Loren and his wife, Darlene, and many YWAM missionaries built one world's largest Christian missionary societies by hearing God speak and obeying his words. The back of the book contains "Twelve Points to Remember" about hearing God's voice. They include submission to his will, having a clean heart, aligning his *rhema* with Scripture, humility, being aware of counterfeits (man's reason or demonic deception), and God's words being confirmed by others.[166]

The Creator of the universe speaks personally to us in myriads of ways. These include a "still small voice" within, or words, pictures or impressions in our mind. He can use dreams or visions (as he did with Daniel, and some modern-day Muslims who are coming to Jesus).[167] He also uses spiritual leaders, teachers, counselors, training, worship, devotional times, almost anything—to share his thoughts with us. In ancient times he even used a "donkey" when the donkey's master wasn't paying attention. (Numbers 22:21-35).

God's words share no limits. We simply must learn to *listen*. One personal story will illustrate the point.

Is That Really You, God?

Some years ago I flew to a small town in Pennsylvania to speak for a week at a Bible school. The Sunday before the training began, I attended a potluck at the sponsoring church. I knew nobody at the church—except my host. When I walked into the fellowship hall, I noticed two teenagers holding hands and acting very "friendly." Without prompting, the voice of God spoke to my heart: "See those two young people over there? They are involved in sexual sin and I want to warn them from me to turn away from it."

I gulped as the words sank in. I immediately began to practice my YWAM heritage by asking over and over again in my mind, "Is this really you, God?" "Was that message from you?" After a long inner debate, and finally discerning this was a *rhema* from him, I walked over to the young couple and spoke these words: "You don't know me from the man in the moon, but I believe when I saw you, God spoke to me that you are involved in sexual sin and need to repent and get right with God."

I thought they would respond positively and revival would break out. But I was greatly disappointed. Instead of repenting, they gave me an angry look and walked away. After dinner, my host took me home, and later the phone began ringing off the hook. "Who was the visitor who accused the youth pastor's daughter and her boyfriend of immorality?" "That took a lot of nerve!"

Wow. This could be trouble.

The following evening the pastor of the church, his youth pastor and wife, and the daughter and her boyfriend and I met together to discuss my "word." I humbly told my story and relayed what I believed God spoke to me. Again, toward the end of the meeting, no revival ensued, but a number of people dropped their heads and prayed tearfully for the youth group. I took note, but wasn't satisfied. The remainder of the week I spoke at the Bible school and then flew home.

The day after I returned, my Pennsylvania host called. Excitedly he said, "Ron, you'll never believe what has happened. After you shared your words we found out that the youth pastor had been involved in incest, his daughter was sleeping with her boyfriend, and our youth group was filled with sexual sin. This week it was all exposed and people are getting right with God."

The revival came after all. All because God *spoke* some very personal words to those whom he loved.

TURNING TO THE RIVER

To summarize, three different sources of "truth" (information) exist because three types of moral beings occupy the world. Men use human reasoning to search for the truth; Demonic beings deceive and hurt us through distorting the truth; Finally, God lovingly communicates his truth through creation, conscience, the Bible, and personally.

Francis Schaeffer reminds us, "In the Judeo-Christian position, we find that there is someone there to speak, and that he has told us about two areas. He has spoken first about himself, not exhaustively but truly; and second he has spoken about history and the cosmos, not exhaustively but truly . . . Rationalism could not find an answer, but God speaking, gives the unity needed for the nature and grace dilemma (natural vs. supernatural explanations)."[168]

Now we are prepared to examine the five religious worldviews that make up our world. Every human being believes one of the five because each of us is religious.[169] All of these worldviews purport to be "the way" or "a way" to understanding the universe and our place in it. Which one is correct? Do all roads lead to heaven, or do all lead nowhere?

Each of us must choose, consciously or not. I hope the following pages help you to make an informed decision. We begin with the River of God itself, revealing a loving Creator and Redeemer who calls all people to faith in his provision for sin.

But first, we must once again hear from the *liar*.

Section Two

THE RIVER OF GOD AND ITS FOUR FALSE DISTRIBUTARIES

From his high vantage point in the unseen realm, the *liar* gazed on the beautiful earth the Creator had fashioned. The earth teemed with animals. The waters brimmed with amazing sea creatures who frolicked in their underworld serenity. The face of the ground sported luxuriant trees large and small, lush grasses and meadows.

The *liar* peered over the mountaintops and saw the vast river systems that flowed from their peaks and watered the ground. He knew that the Creator, his Enemy, loved the miracle substance of water. In all of the cosmos, earth reigned supreme as the water kingdom. Its vast blue oceans, the mist that moistened the ground, and the life-giving waterways all nurtured the beauty and growth of life on this remarkable planet. Even the newly created human beings—vermin to the *liar*—were mostly composed of water.

He hated the thought—despised all of them with every fiber of his twisted being. Yes, he had convinced other Enemy subjects to join his rebellion against Heaven. This gave him a perverted sense of power. He possessed legions to command! But that wasn't enough. He desired to vent his fury against everything God made—especially the unsuspecting humans. But how could he succeed?

As he leered at the Garden below and agonized over the River that nourished it, his demented mind concocted a plan. *I know what must be done,* thought the master of evil. *I will trick them into disbelieving the words of the Enemy. I will puff up their pride, open their eyes to evil, and draw them into the rebellion.*

His strategy emerged that moment. He would take the form of an animal and draw them downward into animal-like behavior. *Yes, that was it.* He fiendishly grinned. Polluting the River of God would be his mission—his ravenous passion—and his eternal legacy.

Chapter Five

Loving God

There is a triune loving God
"I have loved you with an everlasting love; Therefore with loving kindness I have drawn you" (Jeremiah 31:3 NKJV).
"For God so loved the world that he gave his only Son . . . " (John 3:16).
"God gave his approval to people in days of old because of their faith" (Hebrews 11:2).

From start to finish, the biblical narrative exudes a *love story*—the greatest one ever told. God—the maker of heaven and earth—is a loving being in his very essence (1 John 4:8). In fact, we learn from the scriptural narrative that the Godhead, amazingly, consists of three Persons in One Essence who love each other deeply and created human beings to share in their love.

The triune God is the perfect example of healthy and loving relationships.[170]

We were created in God's image—to love and be loved in return. For example, it hurt deeply when my mother passed away young or when my father went to prison. Love *died*. Decades of married love to my wife,

Shirley, forms my greatest gift on earth—love *blossomed.* We care for our children and delight in close relationship to them—love *multiplied* through their addition to our family. No wonder the vast majority of human songs ever written speak glowingly or hauntingly of love—either its joyous fulfillment or its devastating loss.

We yearn to love and be loved. Why is this so? It is because God created us for loving friendship—with him and with other human beings. But something broke that loving relationship. It needed to be restored—which God took the initiative to do. This is the Bible's consuming message. All God required from us was *faith* in return.

BIBLICAL FAITH IN A GOD OF LOVE

We begin the analysis of the world's religious worldviews with both oldest and the largest of the five—what I term *biblical faith.* It ranks as "oldest" because its recorded origins and ancient stories propel us back to the beginning of time when the world was created and human beings first lived on earth. It remains the world's "largest" religion due to its longevity, global impact, and evangelizing faith.[171]

Most books on world religions call biblical faith by the name "Christianity."[172] But the belief system of the "followers of Jesus Christ" shares a much longer history. People of faith populated the planet for thousands of years before the coming of Jesus. Thus, our understanding of biblical faith must include the progressive revelation of God as found in both the Old and New Testaments to be accurate in its scope. It includes redemption of human beings from ancient times, to Abraham and the children of Israel, to believers in the Hebrew nation, and finally to its largest expression through the followers of Jesus Christ.

I also prefer the term "biblical faith" over "Christianity" because we don't find the latter word in the Bible. The term "Christian" appears a few times in the book of Acts, but not the elongated form of the word. The followers of Jesus Christ originally preferred to be known as the people of "The Way," a reference to Jesus' amazing and unique claim found in John

14:6 ("I am the Way, the Truth and the Life"). But it also carries the connotation of the way of salvation or the way of *faith*.

Another reason for preferring biblical faith to Christianity includes the reality that some extremely horrible acts have been committed in Christianity's name. Think of the medieval Crusades, the Spanish Inquisition, and the atrocities of the Thirty Years War—to name a few. I don't believe Jesus' followers exhibited "biblical faith" during these and other periods when evil people perverted religious truth. On the contrary, the people of historical faith take their delight in a *triune, loving God* who has demonstrated his righteousness and mercy to the world for thousands of years.

I call this progressive revelation of love the River of God. Before I recount the "Story of the River," let's take a quick look at the role that physical rivers play in our lives on earth. Without them, life would cease to exist.

THE IMPORTANCE OF RIVERS

Although rivers makes up less than two-tenths of a percent of all the fresh water on earth, they play a crucial role acting like "roads" that transport water, organisms, and important gases and nutrients to every nation on earth. They also help drain excess rainwater and provide fertile habitats for many plants and animals. As they make their way to the sea, rivers change their channels—helping shape the features of the earth.

Rivers are extremely dynamic. The shape, size, and content of a river are constantly changing, forming a close bond between the river and the land through which it flows. On its way, a river may carve through majestic mountain ranges and create deep gorges and canyons while watering tranquil valleys, lush meadows, and sprawling plains. Over time a river may change from a powerful, overflowing torrent in the spring, to a frozen underworld in the winter.

Four of the world's great civilizations—those born in China, India, Egypt, and Mesopotamia—depended upon the life-nourishing aspects of the great rivers that served them. Interestingly, most of the world's major religions emerged from these vast river valleys. Rivers not only provided water for peoples' domestic needs and agricultural purposes, but also transported human beings from place to place. The distribution of goods and the contacts of people between different parts of the same river promoted cultural/religious exchanges. Rivers helped to spread civilization.[173]

Modern travel has diminished our understanding and appreciation of rivers. We cross mighty rivers effortlessly on high suspension bridges and fly high above them unaware of their topographical boundaries. Yet, rivers are to the earth what the circulatory system is to the human body. They provide the flow of *life*. The River (of God) just might be their ultimate inspiration.

THE STORY OF THE RIVER

Scene One: Beginnings

Our love story begins in a garden called Eden (Delightful) in a region known as Mesopotamia (Middle of the Rivers) or the Fertile Crescent. One magnificent river flowed from the Garden of Eden (Genesis 2:10) then divided into four branches: The Pishon, Gihon, and the more famous Tigris and Euphrates rivers (Genesis 2:11-14). Bruce Feiler reminds us in his book *Where God Was Born* (2005) that the Garden of Eden was most likely in Iraq, and that even today, thousands of years since our human beginnings, the Euphrates River ("Sweetwater") remains the twenty-eighth largest river in the world at 1,740 miles long.[174]

The original Garden was beautiful beyond description—a "paradise" where human beings and their Creator could share intimate, loving friendship. According to the Bible, God created Adam (Man) in "our image" (Genesis 1:26)—an early reference to the Godhead's multiple nature—and placed him in the garden to "tend and care for it" (Genesis 2:15). God later created Eve ("To Give Life") as a perfect companion for him. Together, Adam and Eve walked in close friendship with their Creator (Genesis 2:19, 3:8). Apparently, this loving paradise was created for *all* of us to enjoy.

In "Delightful" Eden, Scripture reveals that Adam and Eve shared a trusting, holy friendship with God (Elohim) until the devil, impersonating a serpent, tempted both to rebel and abandon their trusting relationship

(Genesis 3:1-13). (I discussed the devil's "half-truth" lies in Chapter One.) Their "sin" brought a curse to the earth, a changed relationship with each other, and separation from God. Elohim "atoned for" their foolish act by an animal sacrifice, and "covered" their nakedness with the skins—his first act of redeeming love. (Genesis 3:21).

Many foundational principles leap from this story. We learn the origin of man, of marriage, and restoration of relationship with God through forgiveness, sacrifice and faith/obedience. We encounter spiritual warfare, a devil, temptation, and sin. We see God's holy nature revealed and his first acts of grace. We helplessly watch as selfishness pollutes the River of God for the first time—but hope also blossoms that the relationship can be restored.

God is love—and his river of love, in pursuing sinful man, is just beginning.

Following these staggering events and man's exile from the Garden, we meet Abel who enjoyed a loving faith-relationship with God (Hebrews 11:4). Next we encounter Enoch, a third descendant of Adam and Eve, living such a demonstrably faith-filled life that he didn't experience sin's penalty—death—but was taken to heaven miraculously (Genesis 6:23, 24).

The rest of humankind fared differently. After watching sin corrupt the majority of the burgeoning human race, God's heart was broken over man's rebellion, and he decided to start over (Genesis 6:5, 6). God destroyed the world through a once-in-history global flood—so impacting in the memory of earth's inhabitants that it remains one of the most commonly told stories of human folklore.[175] Only Noah and his family continued to walk by faith in response to God's love (Genesis 6:9, 10, Hebrews 11:7). After the earth returned to normal, Noah's descendents (Shem, Ham, and Japheth) repopulated the Fertile Crescent and, after Babel, were scattered all over the earth.

Scene Two: Abraham—the Father of Faith
Scene Two brings God's next step for rescuing fallen people because of his great love. The main actor in this story is Abram from Ur—a larger-than-life figure later known as Abraham, the father of *faith* (Galatians 3:7). Feiler

reminds us "that all monotheistic religions claim him as their father (Judaism, Islam, and Christianity)."[176] As I describe in *The Fourth Wave*:

> The Lord called (Abram) out of his ancestral country to go to a new land (Palestine), taught him faith and friendship, and severely tested him. When he passed the test, God changed his name to Abraham and promised, "Because you have obeyed me and have not withheld even your own son, I swear by my own name that I will certainly bless you. I will multiply your descendants beyond number, like the stars in the sky and the sand on the seashore. Your descendants will conquer the cities of their enemies. And through your descendants, all the nations of the earth will be blessed (Genesis 22:16-18).[177]

Notice Abraham's destiny in the narrative: God intended to bless the entire world through his faith. But that faith must be developed. During the famous encounter with God describing the near sacrifice of his son, Isaac, we glimpse biblical salvation in action. Abraham exercised humble faith, the loving God accepted his heart obedience, and provided a wild ram to "atone" for his sin. The equation remains the same throughout the ages, God loves people and provides atonement for them through substituted suffering (e.g. 1 Corinthians 13:13) and they, in turn, are restored to relationship with him by faith in his grace.

Trusting in God's love is the timeless "current" of the River of God.

Abraham then imparted his faith in his son, Isaac, and Isaac, to his offspring, Jacob. After a four hundred sojourn in the Nile River valley in Egypt, the stage was set for scene three of God's pursuing love.

Scene Three—A Covenant Nation
It was necessary for God to use a man—Abraham—to re-kindle friendship with God through faith following the flood. But God's larger plan centered

on igniting an entire nation to love and trust him. Enter Moses (his name means "Drawn Out of the River"), the next character in our love story, whom God used to birth the *people of Israel* and bring biblical faith to a growing nation. The added feature was a written expression of the God-man love relationship. We call this national "marriage agreement"—the Mosaic Covenant—the beginning of Judaism.

The Old Covenant or Testament contained three parts. The ceremonial laws taught God's character (holiness), the sacrificial laws provided atonement for sin, and moral laws expounded how love to God (Yahweh) and others must be lived out. As to the moral law, rabbis estimate that the 613 commandments given to Moses contained 365 prohibitions and 248 positive ones.[178]

Through writing down the principles of the "Law of Love," Yahweh showed a great desire to elevate the Jewish nation out of the idolatry of the time to take his message to the ends of the earth: Here's the mandate expressed: "Let the whole earth sing to the Lord! Each day proclaim good news that he saves. Publish his glorious deeds among the nations. Tell everyone about the amazing things he does" (1 Chronicles 16:24). The nation of Israel possessed a calling: love and trust Yahweh and take his salvation to the nations.

Judaism didn't change biblical faith. It *explained it* in greater detail. As James B. Walker reminds us, "Knowledge, as the mind is constituted, can be communicated in no other way than progressively."[179] The establishment of the nation of Israel displayed Yahweh's next step in his loving progressive revelation. Covenant relationship blossomed. Lewis and Travis explain:

> Since a covenant by definition describes a particular set of
> relationships that embody mutual obligations, the parties
> to a covenant need to act faithfully. Faithfulness (or the
> lack of it) is a recurring theme in Israel's history. God, for
> his part, undertook to provide for the people and to estab-
> lish an enduring relationship with them. For their part, the

people were to carry out consistently the beliefs and practices given at Sinai, from motives of faithfulness and love . . . The people of Israel were to be 'a kingdom of priests and a holy nation.'"[180]

Notice once again the essence of biblical faith. Yahweh, in his love, desired to rescue his people from their sinful rebellion. A covenant of loving friendship ratified the relationship by *faith showing itself in obedience*. The tabernacle-based sacrificial system provided atonement that added a further stage to God's revelation, but didn't alter what had always been true.

For hundreds of years following the exodus, the nation of Israel experienced numerous ups and downs as God's covenant people. David united the kingdom through his brave leadership and his son, Solomon, built a permanent temple for worship and sacrifice. During the time of the kings and prophets, the Israelites periodically walked by faith (e.g. during the reigns of Asa, Jehoshaphat, Hezekiah, and Josiah), and during other seasons they disbelieved and disobeyed (e.g. under Jereboam, Omri, Ahab, and Manasseh).

In 722 B.C. God regretfully dispersed the northern kingdom for their unbelief (Hosea 11:8) and the southern kingdom of Judah followed into exile in Babylon in 587/6 B.C. Seventy years later, as promised by the prophet Jeremiah (Jeremiah 29:10), the Jews returned to the land, eventually rebuilt the destroyed temple—but never really recovered their national glory.

Throughout the entire period of ancient history covered by the Old Testament, numerous other individuals and even nations encountered the loving God through humble faith in his atoning sacrifices. Terance Tiessen gives us a partial listing:

Among those in the Old Testament who were saved but came from outside the covenant people, I would include the following: Abel, Enoch, Noah, Job, Melchizedek, Lot, Jethro, Naaman, Rahab, Ruth, Bathsheba and Ebed-melech (a pagan Ethiopian eunuch in the court of the evil king Zedekiah who rescued Jeremiah from the pit and was saved by Yahweh because 'he trusted in him' (Jer.39:15-18). Possibly, we can include some of the Ninevites who responded well to Jonah's call for repentance. And perhaps some of the foreigners were saved—those whose prayers Solomon asked God to answer when they were offered toward the temple "so that all the peoples of the earth may know your name and fear you, as do your people Israel" (1 Kings 8:41-43)[181]

God's salvation came through Abraham, Isaac, Jacob, Moses, and the nation of Israel. But many before them and others after them also came into relationship with God through biblical faith. By the end of this Old Testament era, many prophets and wise men were pointing toward this next progressive step in God's salvation plans—the coming of a promised Messiah (e.g. Micah 5:2, Isaiah 11:1-5, 53:1-12).

The River of God wasn't finished. In fact, in many ways, it was just beginning. Israel had reached thousands of people through the old covenant. But the loving God longed for billions more to come into relationship with him.

A cascading waterfall would soon appear—from the very being of God himself in heaven. The revelation needed completion—totality. Whereas the devil appeared as a serpent to drag man down into the dirt of unbelief, God planned to do the opposite to elevate human beings to saving faith. God must become man to reveal his true heart—face-to-face.

Scene Four—God with Us

In the year 6/5 B.C., a young virgin named Mary and her carpenter husband, Joseph, wearily trudged down the dusty roads of Palestine from their village of Nazareth to Joseph's hometown of Bethlehem—as required by a new Roman census. They arrived after dark and were forced to stay in a humble stable. Four hundred years had passed since the collapse of the Jewish nation. That night Mary would give birth to her first son, while unbeknownst to her, shepherds would shake with fear as angels sang from heaven and certain Magi (Eastern astrologers known as "wise men") launched a search for the most important birth in the history of man.

Mary's son—later known as Jesus Christ (Salvation—Anointed One or Messiah)—remains the most significant person in history. The message of the Bible's New Testament (New Covenant) boldly proclaims that God loves people so passionately that He left the splendor of Heaven and came to earth in human form (Galatians 4: 4,5).

His great love story—from Adam and Eve, through Abraham, Moses, and the nation of Israel—required a permanent solution. Animal sacrifice was temporary. The moral laws of love only described proper God-man and person-to-person relationships. But human beings had failed in their covenant assignments, and Israel had not taken God's forgiveness to the nations.

Enter Jesus of Nazareth—God-in-the-flesh (John 1:14)—the second member of the trinity. He would complete the progressive revelation of the river of God's love.

There is no one in history like Jesus. As God's "holiness" means that he is "different" or "unique" from human beings, Jesus from Nazareth remains the most holy or *unique* figure the world has ever seen. David Marshall states, "The world that Jesus brings us to is the culmination of the sights of sages and mythmakers . . . Jesus was not denying glimmers and sparks of truth with each tradition. But he was claiming some unique relationship to the ultimate source of light."[182]

As a part of examining Jesus' amazing expansion of God's river of love, we must first understand the incredible uniqueness of the person of Jesus Christ. How is Jesus of Nazareth unique in every way to history and the world of religion?

1. Jesus is unique in *historical verification.*
    When we read the history books, we often assume that ancient historical figures such as Alexander the Great, or Plato or Julius Caesar, can be easily verified by historical records. That is not true.

Very few ancient manuscripts exist that confirm the reality of *any* ancient history-maker—especially books or parchments that go back over one thousand years.

But Jesus is different. First, there are twenty-seven different New Testament sources that describe his life and ministry. [183] Second, his life is mentioned by numerous non-biblical authors such as Cornelius Tacitus (born A.D. 52-54), the great Jewish historian Flavius Josephus (born A.D. 37), Seutonius (Roman historian), Tertullian (African jurist-theologian), and even the Jewish Talmuds (written A.D. 100-500).[184]

The Encyclopedia Britannica once used 20,000 words to describe Jesus—more than Aristotle, Cicero, Alexander, Julius Caesar, Buddha, Confucius, Mohammed, or Napoleon Bonaparte combined. There is unprecedented proof that Jesus of Nazareth walked this earth some two thousand years ago.

2. Jesus is unique in the *prophecies* related to his life and work.
Jesus' life purpose was announced by numerous prophecies hundreds of years before his coming in 6/5 B.C. The Old Testament contains three hundred references to the Messiah that could have been fulfilled *only* in the person of Jesus.[185] These include him being a Jew (Numbers 24:17), from the tribe of Judah (Genesis 49:10), in family line of David (Jeremiah 23:5), and born in David's hometown of Bethlehem (Micah 5:2). He was preceded by a messenger (Isaiah 40:3), betrayed by a close friend (Psalm 41:9), sold for thirty pieces of silver (Zechariah 11:12), crucified with thieves (Psalm 22:16, Isaiah 53:12), and buried in a rich man's tomb (Isaiah 53:9).

Peter Stoner states in *Science Speaks* that the odds of Jesus fulfilling only eight of the major prophecies are one in 100,000,000,000,000,000 (10 to the 17th power).[186] He concludes, "The prophets had just one chance in 10 to the 17th power of having them come true in any man, but they all came true in Christ."[187]

Allow that scientific probability to sink deeply into your heart. Jesus' claim to be the Messiah has no parallel in history.

3. Jesus is unique in his *birth*.

    Jesus' unique and utterly miraculous birth is celebrated all over the world each Christmas. Two detailed accounts of the amazing circumstances are recorded in Matthew 1-2 and Luke 1-2. Besides the angel Gabriel announcing the birth (Luke 1:26-38), the extreme humility of being born in a cave or barn reserved for animals (Luke 2:6), or the choir of angels that sang for some startled shepherds, Jesus being conceived of the Holy Spirit and born to a woman who was a virgin is unparalleled in human experience. But this, too, was prophesied: "The Lord himself will choose the sign: Look! The virgin will conceived a child! She will give birth to a son and call him Immanuel—'God is with us'" (Isaiah 7:14).

    Do you know of any other "virgin" births?—or *any* child conceptions that produced a life anywhere near that of Jesus Christ? As the creeds finally delineated, Jesus was fully God and fully man. God himself had taken on human form. Can we imagine anything more wondrous than Incarnation? This act exemplified the *second* greatest act of humility of all time—God stooping to become a part of his fallen creation. The *greatest* act of humility is still to come.

4. Jesus is unique in his *supernatural powers*.

    If anything stands out in the four gospels (good news accounts) of the life of Jesus Christ, it is God's love expressed through miracles that freed and benefitted people. The first gospel, written by John Mark, contains fast-paced stories where Jesus heals peoples' diseases, casts out demons, multiplies food for thousands, and even raises people from the dead (e.g. Mark 2:1-12, 6:34-44, 9:14-29). John's gospel, written by the disciple whom Jesus' loved (John 20:2), builds its case on eight miracles that demonstrated the power and divinity of Jesus Christ.[188]

A careful study of the New Testament reveals at least thirty amazing signs and wonders that Jesus performed while on the earth.[189] No other person validated their ministry by supernatural means as did Jesus who "went around doing good and healing all who were oppressed by the Devil, for God was with him" (Acts 10:38).

5. Jesus is unique in his *perfectly holy life.*

Jesus Christ remains to this day the only person who backed up his claims by a sinless life. You don't find any youthful indiscretions such as plagued the early years of Saint Augustine of Hippo. His adult years revealed no adulteries or crusades of violence such are recorded about Muhammad, the founder of Islam. On the contrary, when questioned about his teachings or his unique moral authority, Jesus responded humbly and confidently to his accusers: "Which of you convicts me of sin?" (John 8:46). Deafening silence followed.

Jesus made it quite clear to all that followed him that the secret to his success was found in perfect obedience to his heavenly father. "I always do the things that are pleasing to him" (John 8:29). Did any other human being dare to make that claim? History and personal experience say *no.* Philip Schaff confirms, "It is his absolute perfection which raises [Jesus'] character high above of all other men and makes it an exception to a universal rule, a moral miracle in history."[190]

How did he do it? Jesus was not a mere man—he was God in human form. The great French general Napoleon Bonaparte acknowledged that fact when he said, "I know men and I will tell you that Jesus Christ is no mere man. Between him and every other person in the world there is no possible term of comparison. Alexander, Caesar, Charlemagne, and I have founded empires. But on what did we rest the creations of our genius? Upon force. Jesus Christ founded his empire upon love; and at this hour, millions of men would die for him"[191]

6. Jesus is unique in his *teachings*.

   Many of the world's most memorable sayings and teachings came from the lips of the God/man, Jesus Christ. Years ago, the first section of Scripture that I memorized was the incomparable "Sermon on the Mount" found in Matthew 5-7. It begins with the "Beatitudes" which describe the life that God honors, such as "Blessed are the poor in spirit for theirs is the kingdom of heaven" (Matthew 5:3). A few verses later, we find sentences still quoted two thousand years later by United States presidents: "You are the light of the world. A city set on a hill cannot be hidden" (Matthew 5:14).

   These remarkable chapters conclude with the famous warning: "But everyone who hears these sayings of mine, and does not do them, will be like a foolish man who built his house on the sand: and the rain descended, the floods came, and the winds blew and beat on that house; and it fell. And great was its fall. And so it was, when Jesus had ended these sayings, that the people were astonished at his teaching, for he taught them as one having authority, and not as the scribes" (Matthew 7:26-29).

   Jesus also told forty memorable parables. They include "The Lost Sheep" (Matthew 18:12-14), "The Rich Man and Lazarus" (Luke 16:19-31), "The Pearl of Great Price" (Matthew 13:45, 36), and "The Prodigal Son" (Luke 15:11-32). No wonder those who heard him said, "Never did a man speak the way this man speaks" (John 7: 46).

   The power and impact of Jesus' words, beloved by millions for two thousand years, hold a special place in history and human literature. Jesus himself could say with confidence: "Heaven and earth will pass away but my words will not pass away" (Luke 21:33). And Mary Hopkins could echo, "No revolution that has ever taken place in society can be compared to that which has been produced by the words of Jesus Christ."[192]

7. Jesus is unique in *claims to deity*.

Biblical faith makes a revolutionary assertion: the Creator God of the universe came to earth in the person of Jesus Christ and *lived among us*. According to both the Old and New Testaments, the coming of Jesus consists in nothing less than "God with us" (Isaiah 7:14, Matthew 1:23)—not simply a guru, a holy man, a religious founder, a wise man, or political leader. Jesus is the only figure in history to claim to be God and back it up by living proofs.

Josh McDowell points out in *Evidence That Demands a Verdict* that there are three areas of Jesus' life that point to his deity.[193] The first represent his *direct* claims. These include numerous references to himself where he stated unequivocally his equality with the Father (e.g. John 10:30-33, John 14:9). At his mock trial before the Sanhedrin, he answered the Jewish leaders question of his divinity by saying, "You say that I am" (Mark 14:62)—a Greek idiom for *yes*. When questioned about his age and authority in John 8:58, he famously declared, "Most assuredly I say to you, before Abraham was, I AM" *(eimi)*—equating himself directly with Jehovah, the eternally existent God (Exodus 3:14, Deuteronomy 32:39, Isaiah 43:10.)

The second area reveals Jesus' *indirect* claims to divinity. Norman Geisler lists seventeen references where Jesus used terms that equated him with Jehovah. They include being the Creator (John 1:3), Savior (John 4:42), Forgiver of sins (Mark 2:7, 10), First and the Last Revelation 1:17, 2:8), the Judge (Matthew 25:31), and the Redeemer (Revelation 5:9).[194]

Finally, the Bible reveals sixteen different *titles* that Jesus openly shared in unique relationship to the Father. Among them are: Jehovah (John 8:58), Lord (Matthew 13:14, 15), Son of God (John 5:19-27), Son of Man (Daniel 7:13, 14, Matthew 8:20), Abba—Father (John 5:18). Albert Wells sums up well the unique aspect of the deity of Christ: "Not one recognized religious leader, not Moses, Paul, Buddha, Mohammed, Confucius etc. have ever claimed to be God; that is, with the exception of Jesus Christ. Christ is the only religious leader who has ever claimed to be deity and the only individual ever who has convinced a great portion of the world that he is God."[195]

There remains one category in the uniqueness of Jesus. I will discuss it by returning to the story of the river of God's love. It exposes the very reason that Jesus came to earth.

Scene Five—The Greatest Love of All
Jesus walked the earth for a little over three decades. He healed the sick, taught and fed the masses, cast demons out of the oppressed and even raised people from the dead. His message stated that the fullness of God's Kingdom had arrived and that people "must turn from their sins and believe this Good News!" (Mark 1:15). In Jesus' own words, we learn his purpose:

> As Moses lifted up a bronze snake on a pole in the wilderness, so I, the Son of Man, must be lifted up on a pole, so that everyone who believes in me will not perish but have eternal life. For God so loved the world that He gave his only Son, so that everyone who believes in him will not perish but have eternal life. God did not send his Son into the world to condemn it, but to save it. (John 3:14-16).

Jesus Christ came to earth to be the Savior of the world. He was born to die for the sins of all people. Just before his death, Jesus told his disciples, "Greater love has no one than this; than to lay down his life for his friends" (John 15:13). He would fulfill the greatest act of love the world had ever seen—a holy God substituting his own agonizing sufferings on behalf of sinful people to reconcile them to Himself. He would save them by *dying* for them.

Through his death, they could experience *eternal life*—if they believed.

Jesus' mission was crystal clear. As I point out in my book, *If God Has A Plan for My Life, Then Why Can't I Find It?,* more than twenty-five times in the gospels he explained he'd been *sent* by the Father. Here are a few examples: "Anyone who does not honor the Son does not honor the Father who *sent* him . . . I try to please the One who *sent* me . . . Whoever hears what I say and believes in the One who *sent* me has eternal life . . . The things I do, which are the things God gave me to do, prove that the Father *sent* me (John 5:23, 30, 24, 36).[196]

Sent to do what? John 3:14-16 told us. He came to earth to reveal God's love for the entire world in a personal, intimate way; He was sent to die for our sins; and through his death, those who put their trust in him could be restored to right relationship with God.

Why do human beings need a sacrifice for sins? Gordon Olson reminds us that sacrificial offerings had been practiced since the days of Adam and Eve, including the Old Covenant sacrificial offering system during the days of the Jewish nation.[197] They served two vital purposes: 1) Propitiation— providing forgiveness of sin before a holy God, and 2) Transformation— showing the seriousness of sin, prompting hatred of it, engendering guilt and humility in the human heart, and providing a tangible object for faith while pointing to God's great love and rightful supremacy in our lives.[198] In other words, sacrifices revealed God's true nature (Romans 3:21-26) and brought necessary humility to human hearts. God and men can walk in fellowship through atonement and faith (Romans 5:6-11).

Eighty-nine chapters of the New Testament gospels share the incomparable life of Jesus. Nearly thirty percent of them (25 out of 89) focus on his last week alive—the period of his sacrificial death. They share his entrance into Jerusalem (Matthew 21:1-10), his trial before the Sanhedrin (John 18:13-23), being spit upon and mocked by Roman soldiers (Mark 15:16-20), his condemnation by Pontius Pilate (Luke 23:13-23), his cruel suffering via crucifixion (John 19:1-30), his last words (Matthew 27:45-51), and his heart-rending death (Mark 15:37-39).

The gospel writers focused their accounts like a laser. Yes, they'd previously recorded his miracles, wrote down his amazing teachings, and vividly described his three years of caring for people. But they also knew why he came: *He came to die for the sins of the world.* This was the Good News! In the greatest act of humility ever contemplated, the omnipotent Ruler of time and space substituted his own sufferings in the place of sinful men.

Today we call that amazing day "Good Friday." Good for whom? Not for God—not a day without excruciating pain, suffering and death. But EXCEEDINGLY GOOD for all of humankind whose sins could now be forgiven and whose lives could be restored by humble faith to a living relationship with their Creator.

Scene Six—The Greatest Proof
But the spellbinding narratives of the four Gospels don't end there. One more scene still needed to be played out. We will let the remarkable words speaks for themselves:

> Now after the Sabbath, as the first day of the week began to dawn, Mary Magdalene and the other Mary came to see the tomb. And behold, there was a great earthquake, for an angel of the Lord descended from heaven, and came and rolled back the stone from the door, and sat on it. His countenance was like lightning, and his clothing as white as snow. And the guards shook for fear of him, and became like dead men.
>
> But the angel answered and said to the women, "Do not be afraid, for I know that you seek Jesus who was crucified. He is not here; for he is risen as he said. Come see the place where the Lord lay. And go quickly and tell his disciples that he is risen from the dead, and indeed he is going before you into Galilee; there you will see Him. Behold I have told you."

So they went out quickly from the tomb with fear and great joy, and ran to bring his disciples word. And as they went to tell his disciples, behold Jesus met them saying, "Rejoice!" So they came and held him by the feet and worshipped Him. Then Jesus said to them, "Do not be afraid. God and tell My brethren to go to Galilee, and there they will see Me."

Then the eleven disciples went away into Galilee, to the mountain which Jesus had appointed for them. When they saw him, they worshipped Him; but some doubted.

And Jesus came and spoke to them, saying, "All authority has been given to me in heaven and on earth. Go therefore and makes disciples of all nations, baptizing them in the name of the Father and of the Son, and of the Holy Spirit, teaching them to observe all things that I have commanded you; and lo, I am with you always, even to the end of the age." (Matthew 28: 1-10, 16-20).

Jesus Christ, the wondrously unique God/man, died for the sins for the world and rose from the dead to prove beyond a shadow of a doubt he was more than a human being. Resurrection served as the final witness in his trial for credibility.

Josh McDowell devotes eighty-five pages of his classic work, *Evidence That Demands a Verdict,* to the historical, logical, and literary proofs for the resurrection of Jesus Christ. His risen life remains one of the most provable events of ancient times.[199] He points out that human beings living since the death and resurrection of Jesus are faced with only three choices relating to the Son of God. Either he was a lunatic who made crazy claims—a liar who has deceived billions—or the Lord of life that he claimed to be.[200]

G.B. Hardy exclaims: "Here is the record. Confucius' tomb—occupied. Buddha's tomb—occupied. Mohammed's tomb—occupied. Jesus' tomb — EMPTY. The decision is yours to make; the evidence speaks for itself. It says very clearly—Christ is risen indeed!"[201]

Scene Seven—Rivers of Living Water

We must conclude our love story of the history of biblical faith with the fruits of God's plan of salvation. Jesus said, "If anyone thirsts, let him come to me and drink. He who believes in me, as the Scripture has said, out of his heart will flow rivers of living water" (John 7:37, 38).

"Rivers of living water" sound quite familiar. Since the time of Jesus Christ, nearly two thousand years ago, the River has grown into a veritable *ocean* of love that is lapping up on the shores of the nations of the world. When Jesus left the earth, he possessed only hundreds of disciples. Today, biblical faith counts over two billion followers worldwide and the number is exploding.[202] Plus, the number is not complete though the goal of world evangelization is in sight. But that story is the subject of another book.[203]

So how does the biblical narrative of faith in a loving God answer the essential questions of life and the truth test? The answers may pleasantly surprise you.

QUESTIONS THAT BIBLICAL FAITH MUST ANSWER

* God—Who's in Charge?

  The God of the Bible is an awesomely great being who is both *transcendent* (beyond our natural order) and *immanent* (close and near). In transcendent power, God is the uncreated Creator of the universe (Genesis 1:1) existing in a triune Godhead made up of Father, Son, and Holy Spirit (Matthew 28:19). The persons of the Godhead are eternal (Psalm 90:2), all-powerful (Genesis 17:1), rule the universe (Revelation 19:6), possess all knowledge (Psalm 147:5), and are present everywhere (Jeremiah 23:24). "He rules over everything" (Psalm 103:19)—*God most High.*

  But this amazing trinity is also near to his creation (immanent). The Godhead are personalities—thinking (Isaiah 1:18), feeling Hosea 11:8), and acting (Psalm 145:4). God possesses wondrous moral characteristics including truthfulness (Psalm 108:4), grace and mercy (Ephesians 2:4-10), great patience (2 Peter 3:9), perfect justice (Deuteronomy 32:4), tender intimacy (Song of Solomon 5:2), and whose essential nature emanates love (1 John 4:8). He is the Lord "who exercises lovingkindess, justice and righteousness on earth, for I delight in these things" (Jeremiah 9:23, 24)—*God Most Nigh.*

The biblical God created the universe, controls its function and destiny, formed and implemented the plan of salvation, and gives meaning to true loving relationships.

• Source—Is the Guidebook Reliable?

As we discussed in Chapter Four, the Holy Bible continues to be the most widely read and trusted religious text ever written. It consists of a library of sixty-six books, written by over forty different authors in three different languages over sixteen hundred years. The Bible stands unique in its continuity of revelation, its breadth of circulation, its number of translations, and its fulfilled prophecies. Gutenberg made it the world's first published book; it was the first text taken into outer space (on micro-film); and it remains the world's number one bestseller.

Professor M. Montiero-Williams, a professor of Sanskrit, spent forty-two years studying Eastern religious texts, and said this in comparing them with the Bible: "Pile them if you will on the left side of the study table; but place your own Holy Bible on the right side—all by itself, all alone—and put a wide gap between them . . . There is a gulf between it and the so-called sacred books of the East—a veritable gulf which cannot be bridged over by any science of religious thought."[204] The Bible has no equal in the history of literature or religion. It claims to be the "inspired word of God" (2 Timothy 3:16).

• Origins—How Did We Get Here?

The book of Genesis gives a clear and precise account of the creation of the world and man's role upon the earth. In his book, *The Creator and the Cosmos*, Canadian astrophysicist Hugh Ross reveals that his study of Genesis 1 & 2—including the exact *order* of God's creation—led him to biblical faith because the creation sequence written down thousands of years ago matched the discoveries of science today.[205]

Winfried Corduan says that "according to special revelation, the history of humanity began with the creation of human beings who had a direct relationship with God, the Creator. After the human beings disobeyed the Creator, their relationship with him was broken, but certainly not their knowledge of him. There is a good reason to believe in the common descent of all human beings from the original pair, both on revelatory and scientific grounds."[206]

• Organization—What's the Structure?

The Bible reveals that the organization of the universe features three sets of moral beings that include the Godhead, angels (both good and evil), and human beings (see Chapter Four). In the case of mankind, God exercises his moral government over intelligent creatures by rewarding their good choices with good consequences and punishing their bad choices with bad consequences (Joshua 24:15, Deuteronomy 30:19). Right choices reap good consequences and poor choices bring bad consequences (Deuteronomy 28:1-68).

All aspects of human society—from family life to governmental laws—work according to these same principles of free moral agency (e.g. Romans 13:1-6). Jonathan Edwards, America's most famous theologian, explains: "When moral creatures are brought into existence there must be a moral government. This is the dictate of reason from the nature of things."[207]

On the other hand, God governs the physical world (animate and inanimate creation) through laws of instinct (Numbers 22:22, 23) and cause and effect (Exodus 14:21-29). God always get what he wants in these realms due to his absolute control. Scientific discoveries simply name and explain God's governance over inanimate creation.

In the moral world, God rarely gets what he wants due to the sinfulness of man (Genesis 6:5, 6). He occasionally suspends human free will providentially to direct human history and guide his plan of salvation (Exodus 11:9, 10).[208]

- Human Beings—What is Their Nature and Calling?
Biblical faith asserts that human beings possess both a material side to their nature (our bodies—e.g. 1 Corinthians 15:48) and a spiritual dimension created in God's image (Genesis 1:26-28). Our immaterial self includes the human spirit or mind (Ephesians 4:23), the soul or emotions (Psalm 42:4-6), and the human will (often referred to as "the heart"—e.g. 1 Samuel 16:7). People are encouraged in Mark 12:30 to love God with all elements of their physical and spiritual being: "with all your heart (will), all your soul (emotions), all your mind (spirit), and all your strength (body)."

Human beings were placed on the earth to care for it and improve it (Genesis 1:26, 9:1, 2). God personally forms every human being in the womb with a special destiny and purpose (Psalm 139:13-16). God created human beings as the highest level of creation on earth, just a little lower in power than the angels (Psalm 8:3-8). We were designed to exercise loving dominion over the earth.

- Morality—What's the Basis of Right and Wrong?
The Bible teaches a clear concept of morality that emanates from the character of God. I call it the "Law of Love." This universal

moral standard can be stated in three principles: 1) Good has intrinsic value—it ought to be willed for its own sake, 2) God's good is of supreme value to the universe—it ought to be chosen supremely, and 3) My good is equal to that of other human beings. It ought to be chosen equally.

To summarize our moral responsibilities: All moral beings ought to love God supremely and each other equally. This law of love has always been the standard of right and wrong, though it has been revealed progressively in history. It operated through intuition and conscience from the Garden of Eden to the rise of the nation of Israel; On Mount Sinai, God wrote it down in the form of ten commandments (Exodus 20:1-17); Jesus then summed it up in two commands (Matthew 22:37-40); Through the Apostle Paul, the universal law moral law was condensed into one word—love (Romans 13:8-10).

Jonathan Edwards called it the "theory of virtue." He taught that since God is the being who has the 'most of being,' he is the supreme object of choice; and men, since they are in general of the same importance, will have equal chances in the choices of virtuous beings. Hence this theory of virtue is summarized in the biblical rule that we are to love God with all our heart and our neighbor as ourselves.[209]

It is right to love God supremely and right to love other human beings equally. This truth could be understood in kindergarten. The failure to practice it remains our greatest challenge.

• Sin—Why is the World a Mess?
The biblical answer is very simple: *sin*. Human beings have refused to live up to their moral responsibilities, both to God and their fellow humans. Man is fallen—not basically good.

The Old Testament uses eleven different Hebrew words to describe man's rebellion against the law of love. They include: To miss the mark, to act perversely, to break away from authority, to refuse to obey, to refuse to serve God, to act treacherously, to be rebellious, to be stubbornly disobedient, to be wicked or impious, to live worthlessly, and to be evil (literally to "dash to pieces" your moral humanity). The New Testament uses eight Greek words that carry similar meanings.[210]

All problems in human relationships, including national wars and conflicts, are ultimately caused by selfish desires and actions. These choices come from a willful attitude (Jeremiah 12:3), selfishness (Jude 12), lawless behavior (1 John 3:4), disobedience to truth (James 4:17), wrong motivations (1 Corinthians 4:5), and constitute moral insanity (Ecclesiastes 9:3).

Because God is just, and human beings are immortal (in spirit and soul), the penalty for sin is eternal separation from God.

•   Salvation—How Can the World Be Made Right?
We discuss salvation at length in Chapter Six. During ancient times, God provided atonement (a "covering" for sin) through animal sacrifices to reveal his justice and holiness, and transform guilty hearts into humble repentance and submissive faith in God's provision for sin.

Then God took the ultimate step of love: "When the right time came, God sent his Son, born of a woman, subject to the law. God sent him to buy freedom for us who were slaves to the law, so that he might adopt us as his very own children" (Galatians 4:4). Jesus' death on the cross served as God's greatest and final atonement for sin (Hebrews 10:12-18).

Man's part is to repent and believe (Mark 1:15). God initiated the reconciliation—human beings are invited to respond. I suggest a timeless, universal definition of salvation: *Trusting in both God's provision for sin and empowering for right living.* Millard Erickson confirms, "This faith was an utter abandonment of reliance on one's own strength, righteousness, effort, or that of anyone other than God himself. It was also a belief in the gracious, merciful provision of that holy, loving God." [211] Terance Tiessen agrees: "People experience the salvation that God has accomplished in Christ when they respond to God in a way that satisfies him, which the Bible calls 'faith.'" [212]

When people humble themselves before God, turn away from a self-centered life, and put their faith in Christ (God's atonement for sin), another amazing thing happens: God comes to live inside of them through the power of the Holy Spirit. (Romans 8:1-11, 2 Peter 1:2-11). God not only forgives—he transforms us from the inside out through his Spirit (John 14-16).

Salvation is *faith working through love*, by God's grace and power.

- Earth—How Should Human Beings Treat the Earth?
The dominion mandate given first to Adam (Genesis 1:26-28) and then to Noah and his descendants after the Flood (Genesis 9:1-3) describes mankind's superiority over and responsibility toward the plant and animal worlds. Human beings are not brute beasts—they are rational animals—finite, miniature copies of the infinite God.

This innate superiority doesn't give us license to rape and pillage the animate and inanimate creation, but rather to wisely develop it for human civilization to the glory of God. People shouldn't treat sub-human animals the same way they act toward humans (e.g. killing an animal is not a crime), but all levels of God's creation should be respected, not abused (Proverbs 12:10). When God gave instructions about righteous warfare in Old Testament times, he specifically told the Israelites "you shall not destroy its trees by wielding an axe against them" (Deuteronomy 2:19, 20)—in other words, don't abuse the natural world as if it has no value. We must acts like good stewards—not careless barbarians.

God loved human beings enough to die for them. He desires *us* to exercise dominion over nature with grateful respect and good stewardship over all that he has made.[213]

- Heaven—Is There a Future and a Hope?

Biblical revelation begins with the story of God's astounding creation of the cosmos *ex nihilo* (Genesis 1-2), and ends in the book of Revelation with his creation of "a new heaven and a new earth, for the first heaven and the first earth passed away" (Revelation 21:1). All human beings will either spend eternity with God in heaven because of their faith or be separated from him forever due to unbelief (Revelation 20:11-15).

Living with God in heaven—experiencing eternal life—not only will be stunningly beautiful and fulfilling (see the amazing description in Revelation 21 and 22), but "[God] will dwell with them, and they shall be his people, and God himself will be with them, and be their God. And God will wipe away every tear from their eyes; there shall be no more death, nor sorrow, nor crying; and there shall be no more pain, for the former things have passed away" (Revelation 21:3, 4).

Prior to this glorious future for the people of faith, the Church's job (those "called out" from the world) consists in sharing the Good News of salvation with everyone in the world. When all have received a chance to be saved from their sins (Matthew 24:14), then Jesus will return to establish God's kingdom in its fullness (1 Thessalonians 4: 13-18).

As numerous books have recently chronicled, heaven is for real—an eternal existence of life and blessedness, all made possible by the God of pursuing love.[214]

THE TRUTH TEST AND BIBLICAL FAITH

We have walked the road of biblical faith from the Garden of Eden to Heaven's shores. I've shared its straightforward answers to life's most important questions. Finally, we must assess whether biblical faith meets the "truth test" that we presented in Chapter Three.

Is biblical faith clear and simple? Its concepts of God, man, freedom, sin, salvation, hope, and many other subjects not only make sense, but also build upon one another as if a part of a well organized system of understanding. Faith itself is *childlike*—as Jesus said it should be (Matthew 18:3). Perhaps the most complex idea in the Bible remains the concept of a triune, not singular God—three in one. Yet, trinity love provides the answer for our longing for loving relationships. We were created for love by a Godhead who is the source of that love.

Is biblical faith reasonable? God invites us to reason with him (Isaiah 1:18), and the Bible's explanations about life, morality, humanity, love and relationships appear reasonable and valid. It is worth noting that modern science—based on human reason—arose out of the biblical worldview, and that many of the early scientists believed that a reasonable God created a world that man could explore and seek to understand.[215] Vishal Mangalwadi explains: "The West's intellectual openness (reason), which set it apart from Islam and Plato, is the result of biblical theology,"[216] Biblical faith invites people to freely use their minds for the glory of God and the improvement of life on earth.[217]

Is biblical faith based on evidence? It contains the greatest array of evidence of any religious tradition. From its voluminous manuscript evidence, to its eyewitness accounts, to its fool-proof logic (Jesus is a liar, a lunatic, or the Lord), to its life-transforming power experienced by billions of people—biblical faith stands strong as a worldview based on facts. Faith is not intellectually blind. It is an *act of trust* based on solid evidence. If biblical faith went on trial, its substantial claims would persuade many open-minded jurors to vote for approval.

Does conscience testify to the truth of biblical faith? The moral law of God—loving God supremely and loving others equally—lines up squarely with man's universal sense of obligation and duty. Even those who disbelieve in God recognize the validity of the Golden Rule and its importance in human behavior. When it comes to right and wrong, the human conscience (if cultivated and nurtured properly) lines up solidly with biblical revelation (Romans 2:15).

Is biblical faith lasting and eternal? It reveals an eternal God who created immortal human beings whose choices determine their destiny in this life and beyond. Man's dichotomous nature (immaterial and material) requires eternal answers to the great questions of existence. Biblical faith supplies those answers and looks to persuade people to turn away from eternal judgment to the joys of eternal relationship with God (Acts 24:14-16, 26: 28, 29).

Is biblical faith universal? It spans from Adam and Eve, Abel and Enoch, through Abraham and the nation of Israel, and Jesus and the birth of the Church, to having over two billion followers today. [218] It is the only truly global religion with 33 nations in Africa, 5 nations in Asia, 43 nations in Europe, 53 nations in the Americas, 25 nations in the Pacific, and a total of 159 of 199 nations in the world having a majority of biblical believers.[219] Both in time and global scope, biblical faith is unique among the religions of man.

FORMS OF FAITH

I conclude our survey of biblical faith with a listing of its major branches or forms. Catholic and Orthodox followers of faith are a declining percentage of the world population, but make up 19 percent of the faith-based total. Evangelicals (Protestants and Independents) are gaining in influence and outreach (11 percent of the people of faith), with Pentecostal believers leading a global revival of biblical faith (from nearly zero in 1900 to 177 million today).[220] In recent years, Messianic Jews have surged in number worldwide.

Only God knows those who truly *trust in his provision for sin and empowering for right living* through the death and resurrection of Jesus Christ. They are the people of biblical faith.

111

Distorting Faith

There are a number of groups that fit the faith tradition but may have deviated from its central tenets. These include organizations and denominations such as The Church of Jesus Christ of Latter Day Saints (Mormons) and Jehovah's Witnesses who profess faith but also add extra-biblical teachings and personal revelations that dilute the biblical message. Some mainline denominations commit this same error—they are biblical in name, but not in heart and practice. Terance Tiessen laments that this type of distortion "is bound to occur in that process of transmission and tradition, but some truth may also remain."[221] This was my own personal experience during my early years. Biblical faith is not a mental assent to certain ideas. It consists in repentance from sin and faith in God that works through love (Galatians 5:6).

CONCLUSION

I believe that biblical faith is unique among religious worldviews as our response to the most complete self-revelation of God who lived among us as one of us.[222] I also agree with the once-agnostic-turned-Christian C.S. Lewis that "I believe in Christianity as I believe that the sun has risen: not only because I see it, but because by it I see everything else."[223]

The River of God flows throughout history, beckoning people into right relationship with their Creator, but that pristine stream has been diverted by four false distributaries. The first one developed early in human history. It contained a very clever twist—by someone very experienced at lying to others.

The liar was angry as he paced about his lair. Even his demon sentries with swords brandished appeared nervous as they awaited his orders. The liar snarled and wheezed while dark, sulfurous breaths wafted into the air. He was thinking.

So far his plan had gone devilishly well. Humankind—rotted vermin in his eyes—had been cast out of the Garden as desired. Their once friendly relationship with the Creator had been broken—and he grinned at the genius of it all. The liar had convinced them to "build a tower up to heaven"—and God had scattered them across the earth. But the humans continued to sacrifice and remember his creative powers ("did they really think He would forgive them?"). What should he do next?

Just then, Zeus, the spirit power of Mesopotamia, strode into the room. He was dark as soot, and sculpted with bulging muscles. "My Baal," he whispered to the Demon Prince. "I have an idea." "What is it?" bellowed the liar. "The human scum have fatally lowered their vision. They no longer see the Enemy as He is. In fact they don't want to see! Let me take my legions—we will convince them that the sun that warms them is their god—the rivers that provide water are their benefactors! We will fill the world with new objects of love and affection that dissolves their memory of Him!"

"Will that be enough?" growled the Prince of Darkness. "Sometimes, the thoughts of his creation draw them back to the beginning." Just then another hideously voluptuous demon entered the lair. "My lord," began Ishtar. "There is another step to be taken. I will kill them with lust for all that defiles them. In the end, they will even sacrifice the lives of their children to deal with their guilt."

Chapter Six

Many Gods

"To an image carved from a piece of wood they say, 'You are my father!' To an idol chiseled out of stone they say, 'You are my mother.' . . . For you have as many gods as there are cities and towns." (Jeremiah 2:27-28)

I remember visiting the *Jefferson National Memorial Museum of Westward Expansion* in St. Louis some years ago. It tells the story of the Lewis & Clark Expedition of the early nineteenth century. Thomas Jefferson had famously commissioned Meriwether Lewis and William Clark to explore the lands of the Louisiana Purchase from Missouri to the Pacific. The museum contains entries from their actual diaries written during the historic trek in 1803-04.

One thing really stood out as I read their journals—how *different* the American frontier appeared in the early nineteenth century with its lush vegetation, vast herds of buffalo and other animals, and the sheer abundance and grandeur of the fields, forests, and waterways that flowed westward. Their accounts praised the wonders of nature—the immense size of fish, trees, and animal life that they encountered. I felt like I was glimpsing life on another planet—one that no longer existed in our modern, sterile world.

It is an even greater stretch of imagination to go back thousands of years and picture the beauty, enchantment, and teeming spiritual and material abundance of the ancient world. By all accounts it was a magical world where the memory of the Creator God still existed and everyone had heard his voice.[224] Angels and demons interacted with human beings— starting with Satan himself in the Garden of Eden (Genesis 3). The Bible even suggests that angels had sexual relations with early peoples: " In those days, and even afterwards, giants lived on earth, for whenever the sons of God had intercourse with human women, they gave birth to children who became heroes mentioned in legends of old" (Genesis 6:1-4)—an angelic/human coupling of sorts. The ancient world enjoyed a nearly enchanted mixture of spiritual and physical vitality.

THE FIRST FALSE FORK IN THE RIVER—POLYTHEISM

Into this vibrant and magical world came the first distortion of human views about God. As early human beings got further from the Garden of Eden and one another, they forgot their common heritage, and over thousands of years began to associate the Creator God (High God) with aspects of his created world, both physical and spiritual. Romans 1:20-23 shares what happened:

> For since the creation of the world, His invisible attributes are clearly seen, being understood by the things that are made, even his eternal power and Godhead, so that they are without excuse, because although they knew God, they did not glorify Him as God, nor were they thankful, but became futile in their thoughts, and their foolish hearts were darkened. Professing to be wise, they became fools, and changed the glory of the incorruptible God into an image made like corruptible man—and birds, and four-footed

beasts, and creeping things . . . who exchanged the truth
of God for a lie, and worshipped and served the creature
rather than the Creator who is blessed forever" (New King
James Version).

This change in religious allegiance took time—and is not difficult to understand. The Old Testament is replete with examples of Israel following
God for a time—then forgetting him—and turning to false gods. One generation after God revealed himself at Mt. Sinai (around 1406-05 B.C.),
Moses warned the Hebrew nation: "Take heed lest you lift up your eyes to
heaven, and when you see the sun, the moon, and the stars, all the host of
heaven, and you feel driven to worship them and serve them" (Deuteronomy 4:19).

Apparently God knows the human tendency to "lower our sights" and
diminish him. In ancient times, over thousands of years, I propose that
many people and civilizations lost their view of the loving Creator God
and began to attribute deity-like qualities to angels and demons, the forces
of nature, and even powerful, yet fallen, human beings. The result produced
an explosion of polytheism—the worship of *many gods.*

In their book *The Religious Traditions of the World*, James Lewis and
William Travis explain: "Polytheism literally means 'many gods.' Most ancient peoples and many modern ones have constructed a spirit world with
multiple good and evil beings, often as personifications of the forces of nature. But polytheism is more than nature religion; it is also an attempt to
explain human experience, the longings of the human soul, and encounters
with the divine."

Why did ancient peoples turn from worshiping the Creator (High
God) to idolizing nature, angels, or even fellow human beings (even if
they were giants)?

First of all, human beings are prone to confuse "causes" with "effects"—especially objects that "amaze" them. I'm sure that even some
moderns have viewed beautiful works of art, admiring their intricate design

and style—then given more conscious appreciation to the painting instead of the artist who created it. That error is easier to commit when viewing the splendor of creation where the magnificent sun, romantic moon, powerful winds, and mighty rivers provoke near worship and awe. The "painting" can easily become confused with the artist.

Second, man's daily dependence on and fear of nature may have also contributed to the switch from the High God to lesser ones millenniums ago. The sun provided warmth. The rivers ran with life-giving water. The soil produced food. Out of fertile wombs, babies entered the world. Over time, ancient peoples began to *personify* God's protection and provision via these elements they could see, taste, and touch, or feared.

Rodney Stark agrees that polytheistic naturism has its origins in the personification of natural forces and 'myths' that arise from these personifications." [225] He believes the evidence shows that early religions seemed to have 'devolved' from a focus on High Gods into lush polytheism.[226] He states: "Early peoples worshipped the usual collection of nature and functional Gods (sky, moon, rain, war, fertility, wisdom, etc.) and devoted their time to performing rites."[227]

The final perversion of the concept of a loving Creator God showed itself in ascribing god-like qualities to other human beings who were necessary for provision and protection—such as the war-like "leader" of a city state. In the twentieth century, the Japanese emperor and the "Supreme Leader" of North Korea enjoyed similar human worship and adulation. Stark explains: "The Gods of Sumer, Egypt, Greece, and of the Aztec, and Mayan Empires were conceived of as ordinary humans, aside from some supernatural powers and (usually) being immortal. That is, most of the Gods looked like human beings and had all the human desires and defects: they thirsted, hungered, bathed, lied, stole, murdered, envied, hated loved and lusted."[228]

People seemed more comfortable with gods that were less awe-inspiring, less demanding, and more permissive—gods who were easily propitiated with sacrifices. There also seemed to be some preference for specialized

Gods so that a person could seek fertility from one, rain from another, and victory from another."[229]

A "lush polytheism" had diverted people from the River to a false and polluted tributary of fear, ritual, lewdness, and even human sacrifice.

Ancient Forms of Polytheism

Polytheism remains today a global phenomenon—one of the five major views about God. Before we look at its modern forms, we need to examine its ancient roots. Many gods flourished in the river deltas of the ancient world. We will follow the path of those waterways to understand the ancient phenomenon of polytheism.

The Tigris & Euphrates

The Gods of Sumer

Archaeologist Samuel Noah Kramer famously stated that "History begins at Sumer."[230] In fact, due to significant archeological finds, we know far more about the religion of the Sumerians (and later Akkadians) than about the religions of later civilizations as Egypt, Greece, or even Rome. Sumer, located in the southeast corner of the Fertile Crescent (what is now southern Iraq), was the world's first *recorded* civilization. Bruce Feiler sets the stage for us:

> By 3000 B.C. a flourishing civilization existed in southern Iraq that called itself 'the place of civilized lord' and its population 'the black-headed people.' Sumer, as this land was later named, comprised as area of around ten thousand square miles, stretching from Baghdad to the gulf, and made up of city-states separated from open steppe. Sumer rose and fell numerous times but reached a peak with the reign of Ur-Nammu, lasting for around a century, from 2112 to 2004 B.C. This was the period of the ziggurat and around the time the Bible suggests Abraham was born. Flush with technology, elite Sumerians invented the

potter's wheel, the arch, the dome, and other amenities of civilized life . . . Sumer's reputation as the provenance of Western civilization rests primarily on two innovations: its breakthrough use of the written word and its vision of a god-centered world.[231]

Why do the Sumerians claim to be the world's first great civilization? First, because they developed closest to man's beginnings in the Garden of Eden—having been possibly founded by Nimrod after the global dispersion of humanity after Babel (Genesis 10:9).[232] They developed between the original rivers (Tigris and Euphrates) from which man's origins began.

Yet, the main reason "history begins at Sumer" is that they were the first group of people to develop a written language so we could hear their tale. Around 3300 B.C. they began drawing pictures and symbols in what we now call "pictographs." By 2800 B.C., the picture-symbols had turned to signs which represented syllables—600 in all. A scribe would write by pressing a pencil-like writing stick called a *stylus* into a soft, clay tablet. The different symbols appeared wedge-shaped, and this is the reason their writing is called cuneiform.[233]

Fortunately, substantial archaeological treasures of the Sumerian civilization were discovered in the past few centuries, including clay fragments, now housed at the Sumerian library at Nippur. Under Ur-Nammu, the Sumerians also developed first law code in history which was expanded by Sargon, the leader of Akkadian civilization (Accad in Genesis 10:10). Both ancient cultures developed flourishing polytheistic societies.[234]

Hundreds of Sumerian deities littered the landscape. Six gained great prominence as the gods of a large city-state. An (Anu) ruled as the sky god; Enlil (Bel), a great warrior, controlled the lands under the sky; Nanna (Sin) was the moon god, and Utu (Shamash), the sun god. Enki (Ea) was worshipped as the water god, but also as the god of wisdom (an interesting concept of rivers being associated with revelation). Finally, Ninhursag, served as the mother goddess. But she was unmarried! The rest had consorts and enjoyed numerous sexual escapades.[235]

Most venerated among the ancient Sumerian gods was *Ishtar*, goddess of fertility (her counterparts are the Phoenician—Astarte; Greek—Aphrodite; and Roman—Venus). Lewis and Travis explain: "Ishtar gave conception to women and life to the ground. She was also the queen of heaven, and a warrior goddess to some. Worship of Ishtar continued beyond the life of Sumer . . . moving to Palestine and Egypt. God statutes, wood plated with gold, were in temples. The gods could "see" and "eat" and twice a day meals were served to them.[236]

John B. Noss in *Man's Religions* summarizes the evolution of the Sumerian pantheon of gods: "The gods of the fields and streams and those of the sky overhead took to the towns, organized themselves into a super state, with governing power lodged in a council of the gods, fought, made love, and merged into a vast pantheon with names almost beyond counting."[237]

What do we learn from the early Sumerian deities? That ancient peoples gravitated to personified naturalistic and mythical gods to protect and provide for them—and that these gods were "made in man's image," sometimes, like Ishtar, with an obsession for sexual proclivity.

The Gods of Babylon

The next great civilization to rise between the Tigris and Euphrates Rivers was the Babylonians (1790–559 B.C.), of whom Hammurabi, the great lawgiver, and Nebuchadnezzar of biblical fame (Daniel 1-4) are among its hundreds of warrior-leaders. Polytheism continued to flourish during this era. The Babylonians possessed fertile imaginations and loved to tell stories about their gods.[238] Interestingly, during these centuries, the Babylonians crafted a number of mythical stories that lent credibility to the events recorded in the Bible,

The Story of Creation. The "Epic of Creation" (*Enuma elish*—"when on high") describes a watery realm ruled by Apsu and Tiamat, god and goddess of the deep. This primeval realm was disrupted by Apsu who wished to kill them, but he was murdered by the water god Enki, and this aroused Tiamat to create angry monsters, snakes, and demons. She gave some "tablets of destiny" to her second husband, Kingu, and started war on the gods. Only Marduk, the supreme god of the Babylonians, was able to subdue Tiamat. Here's the description of the battle that created the world and all human beings:

> "Tiamat, and the champion of the gods, Marduk, engaged, were entangled in a single combat, joined in battle. The lord spread out his net encompassing her; the tempest, following after, he loosed in her face. Tiamat opened her mouth as far as she could; he drove in the tempest lest she close her lips. The fierce winds filled her belly, Her insides congested and she opened wide her mouth; je let fly an arrow, it split her belly, cut through her inward parts, and gashed the heart. He held her fast, extinguishing her life."
>
> Marduk then cut her in two, and used her carcass to create the universe—on half the sky and other half earth. From her eyes flowed the Tigris and Euphrates rivers. Turning next to Kingu, Marduk took from him the tablets of destiny and mixed clay with the blood from Kingu's cut veins to create humanity." [239]

This obviously embellished tale gives a hint of how ancient peoples retained a vague memory of earth's true creation, but used their supernaturally laden world and vivid imaginations to expand the narrative with the involvement of "many gods."

The Story of the Flood. "The Epic of Gilgamesh" remains one of the most famous tales of the Babylonian period, and gives an amazing parallel account of the global flood (Genesis 7, 8). In the story, Gilgamesh meets one of his ancestors, Utnapishtim, who recalls the story of the global deluge.[240] Warning that the gods were going to destroy the earth, Utnapishtim built a large boat and took refuge in it with his wife and two each of all animals. After the floodwaters subsided, Utnapishtim recounts what happened:

> All mankind was turned to clay . . . I opened the window and the light fell upon my face. I bowed, I sat down, I wept, and over my face ran my tears. I looked upon the world—all was sea . . . I sent forth a dove and let her go. The dove flew to and fro, but there was no resting place and she returned. I sent forth a shallow and let he go. The swallow flew to and fro, but there was no resting place and she returned. I sent forth a raven and let her go. The raven flew away. She saw the abasement of the waters. She drew near; she waded, she croaked, and came not back. Then I sent everything forth to the four quarters of the heaven. I offered a sacrifice. I made a libation upon the mountains peak."[241]

As a result of their obedience, Utnapishtim and his wife are rewarded with "the gift of immortality," which they explain to Gilgamesh can be obtained by eating a plant that grows in the sea. Gilgamesh finds the plant, but before he eats it, a snake steals it away and gains immortality. A humbled Gilgamesh returns to his city of Uruk (Erech in Genesis 10:10) and is painfully aware that he does not possess immortality. The story ends unresolved.[242]

I share portions of these narratives to demonstrate the "memory" of real events that ancient peoples passed down in a confusing culture of raucous polytheism. As a result, the stories were embellished and twisted over time. It is similar to the game of speaking in someone's ear, and then passing it on to twenty successive people. Usually the words heard by the last participant are quite different from the original message.

Imagine that same process among ancient peoples, over thousands of years, where myriads of gods, belief in magic, animal and human sacrifice, sexual inhibition, and even astrology impacted the transmission of the truth.[243]

The Gods of Persia

The Persian Empire succeeded the Babylonian era from 550–330 B.C. The "many gods" of the Fertile Crescent continued to "fight, protect, provide, have sex, require sacrifice, and give guidance to the people."[244] A notable exception was the emergence of Zoroaster (of whom the biblical King Darius—522–486 B.C.—was a convert). As the founder of Zoroastrianism, Zoroaster (618–541 B.C.) brought a ray of light into the muddled world of the gods by denying there was a pantheon of deities in continual conflict and stressing the struggle between the one true God and an evil adversary. Stark reminds us that Zoroaster emerged during the sixth century B.C. as one of a number of religious innovators.[245]

Zoroaster's message was simple—and very biblical. Ahura Mazda (Wise Lord) is locked in an age long struggle with Ahriman, (Fiendish Spirit)—the spirit of evil. Human beings should use their free wills to join the side of Ahura Mazda who will triumph ultimately through the works of Saoshyant—a messiah-like figure. Each person must take responsibility to choose between the Wise Lord and Ahriman, the liar. Human beings determine their own fate.

Through good works, the righteous receives an everlasting reward, the through choosing the lie, the unrighteous face eternal misery.[246] Rodney Stark comments: "To fully appreciate Zoroaster, we must acknowledge him as the first to put forward the dualistic solution to the problem of evil and monotheism, and recognize what a great achievement it was"[247] Zoroaster, for a time, pointed the Persian Empire backed to original truths about God.

But now we must visit another civilization in ancient history that also flourished beside a very important river—the Nile. They, too, rose to world prominence——-eight hundred miles to the west of the Fertile Crescent—during this period of lush polytheism. We know them as the Egyptians. Their leaders were known as *gods*.

The Nile Valley

The Gods of Egypt—(3100–30 B.C.)

The flooding of the Nile River (the world's longest at 4,037 miles) each September or October leaves a rich deposit of silt along its banks which is known by the name Kemet or "black lands." In ancient times, three crops could be harvested from the rich soil. From this prosperous river delta came a powerful civilization (3100 to 30 B.C.)—led by great Pharaohs who were considered "divine rulers."[248] They, too, embraced a belief in multiple gods.

Over thousands of years, the Egyptians grew to worship 104 significant deities and possibly up to 450.[249] The people shared four different "creation myths," each connected with a different city. For example, in Heliopolis, the story went that Atum, the high God, created the universe. Bi-sexual in nature, he produced a male companion, Shu (the god of the air), and a female one, Tefnut (goddess of moisture). Somehow separated from the two companions, Atum was later reunited with them, and from his tears, human beings were formed. Shu and Tefnut then produced Geb (god of earth) and Nut (sky-goddess), who in turn produced Osiris (god of fertility and the underworld) and Isis (enchantress with greatest power). The latter's son, Horus (god of the sky—protector), was the symbol of the pharaohs. Ra ruled as the sun god.[250]

Lewis and Travis explain: "[The god myths] supported the Egyptian political and social order, particularly the crucial role played by the pharaohs. The accounts also relate the universe to the local Egyptian way of life, thereby sanctioning both the people and their place in the cosmos." [251] The Egyptians were fascinated with death and afterlife, which was "an underworld" parallel to the Nile Valley. Once there, each person's heart was judged on the balance scales by Anubis (god of death). If the heart on the one balance did not outweigh the *feather* on the other, the person was announced 'justified.' Guilty spirits were torn to pieces by a fierce monster."[252]

The nation of Israel lived among the vast polytheism of Egypt for four hundred years. Only when Yahweh proved his power over the gods of

Egypt (Exodus 4-15), did the Israelites' "exodus" Egypt for the worship of the true God.

Two other ancient civilizations built upon the "many gods" cultures of the Tigris-Euphrates and Nile Valleys. They rimmed another body of water that plays a large role in the development of mankind. We wrap up our tour of early polytheism with a visit to ancient Greece and Rome.

The Waters of the Mediterranean
The Gods of Greece & Rome

The Greek and Roman Empires ruled the known world from the ninth century B.C. to the fifth century A.D. Rome was founded as a city by Romulus and Remus in 753 B.C., but it was Greek culture and their gods that dominated until after the coming of Jesus Christ. The great Greek historian Herodotus (c.484–425 B.C.) claimed that the Gods of the Greeks had been adopted from Egypt, and many modern scholars agree.[253] Classical scholar C. Kerenyi lists 370 Greek gods that might have gone by 646 names.[254]

It was the blind poet Homer, writer of the famous *Iliad* and *The Odyssey*, who spoke of Okeanos (Oceanus) as the "origin of the gods" and the "origin of everything." Okeanos was a river-god, and like other river gods, he possessed inexhaustible powers of begetting. But Okeanos was no ordinary river god. He continued to flow to the outermost edge of the earth, "flowing back upon himself in a circle." The rivers, springs, fountains—indeed the whole sea—issued continually from his broad mighty stream.[255]

This ancient tale contains a very interesting parallel to the River we discussed in Chapters Five. (I wonder if Homer is reading from a "similar script?) However, the similarities soon end as we learn of Okeanos' wife, Tethys, and his begetting many other gods, while warring, sleeping around, and distributing his water throughout the earth.[256]

Greek mythology begins with "Twelve Titans"—"celestial gods who were defeated by Zeus (Jupiter). Zeus stands out in most Greek literature as the king of the gods, the ruler of Mount Olympus and the god of the sky, weather, thunder, lightning, law, order, and fate. His dominion came through multiple marriages[257] and defeating the Titans who are vanquished to Tartarus— a hell-like abode that sits "as deep below the earth as the earth is below the sky."[258]

In ancient Greek prose, we also find the "diffusion" of the Sumerian goddess Ishtar in the form of Aphrodite (Venus for Romans). She purports to be the daughter of Zeus, and according to Homer, "the beautiful shy goddess who arose from the water, and young grass sprouted at her feet. Eros (Cupid) and Himeros (Desire) accompanied her as she was born and became a goddess." She makes love everywhere, even betraying her husband, Hephaistos (the crippled god of fire).[259]

During their zenith, the Roman Empire basically accepted and expanded the Greek pantheon. [260] This led the Apostle Paul, sharing the Good News of Jesus in Roman-occupied Athens around 60 A.D., to remark: "I notice that you are very religious" (Acts 17:22).

That was an understatement. From Sumer to Rome, ancient peoples filled their lives, temples, and city-states with multitudes of gods and goddesses who, while carrying some faint vestiges of true divinity, were more likely to war, gluttonize, sodomize, murder, and keep their gullible subjects in fear—just like the fallen demons and human beings around them intended.

Maybe that was a cue. The high and holy God has been replaced with rapacious monsters. And those forms were just as vile in other parts of the "unknown world."

Gods of the Americas and the Far East

While polytheism was born and proliferated out of the Middle East, it also found willing adherents in ancient American civilization such as the Mayas and Aztecs as reported by Father Bernardino de Sanhagun in the *Florentine Codex* and unveiled after the decoding of the Mayan script a generation ago.[261] They, too, worshipped the forces of nature and supernatural and human counterparts. What stunned the Spaniards upon their arrival in the

New World were the immense ritual slaughters that were taking place—human sacrifice—at regular festivals averaging 2,000 victims a day, and on special occasions, exceeding 20,000.[262] Stark comments that "even primitive peoples understood that blood was the stuff of life"[263]—but instead of practicing loving, substituted atonement, a death orgy of humans was being offered to the gods.

In Asia, ancient forms of polytheism took hold along the Indus River Valley soon after the Mesopotamian diffusion, and spread in various strains of Hinduism (India), Buddhism (northeast Asia), and religious Taoism (China) and Shintoism (Japan).

Whereas most of Middle Eastern polytheism died over a thousand years ago, some major Asian forms remain today. Let's turn our attention now to polytheistic beliefs in the modern world. We begin with the largest and most universal form of polytheism. As you will remember, Edward Burnett Tyler named it Animism.

Animism (Folk Religion)

Many people might be surprised to learn that animistic polytheism makes up the world's largest religious practice with 17 percent of peoples practicing a pure form, and another 33 percent a mixed blend of animistic beliefs within another religion.[264] So just what is animism?

Dean C. Halverson gives us a clear definition: "The term 'animism' comes from the Latin word *anima* which means "soul" or "breath." As such, it refers to that which empowers or gives life to something. It follows, then, that animism is the religion that sees the physical world as interpenetrated by spiritual forces."[265] Animism, tribal, or folk religion is a belief in *spiritual powers* behind all aspects of the material world.

Here's how it operates. Human beings need to "interact" with these spiritual forces (both good and bad), often using "intermediate connectors" (personal or impersonal), to gain what they desire. These "connectors" can be mediums, shamans, priests, (i.e. religious specialists) for the purpose of obtaining something they want such as power, prosperity, protection, health, crops, children and so forth. The human agenda in this transaction is to obtain *blessing*. If the spiritual beings are "good," then the agendas match. But if the "connectors" are "bad," then their agenda might be quite different (such as false dependence, deception, and destruction).

In folk religion, contact with spirits often comes through a human specialist who knows how to use the following special forms: *the right words, the right object, in the right place, at the right time, with the right ritual.* By this mechanical means, a person will automatically receive the desired results from interaction with spirits or spiritual forces.

On every continent of the world, animistic polytheism is being practiced today—from offering food to the gods of eastern temples, to performing tribal dances for rain in West Africa, to voodoo ceremonies in Haiti, to reading the zodiac in a New York newspaper. In the movie *Chariots of Fire*, Harold Abrahams' track coach gives the Jewish athlete a "good luck charm" to wear around his neck during his Olympic race. This is a classic example of "mixed animism"—where a Jew combines animistic practices with his monotheistic faith.

Animism is not really worship—it is *superstition*. Animists believe the world is both physical and material, that there are spiritual forces that govern that world, and that human beings need special help to exist and prosper. We must interact with those spiritual forces through religious specialists using prayers, potions, holy days, rites, relics, or special places (temples, altars, trees).

Folk—tribal—animistic religion is more of a *formula* than a relationship to God. It reveals its strength in recognizing that there *are* powerful forces in this world. But in not seeing the loving Creator God above those powers, it resorts to legalistic methods and means to achieve its objectives. Animism was the first religious distortion in history when Satan, in the form of a serpent, tempted Adam and Eve to "gain something" (being God-like, knowledge, power) by means of an object (special fruit).

Possibly 50 percent of people the world dabble in the waters of animistic superstition.[266]

Polytheistic Hinduism

We will discuss Hinduism in depth in Chapter Eight because its primary focus is pantheistic (the Godness of everything)—not polytheistic in nature. However, "folk Hinduism," as a mixed form of animism, lives up to its reputation as one of the world's largest polytheistic expressions. After all, folk Hinduism involves possibly 330 million gods! (That's nearly one for every three people in India.) [267] John Noss explains how it normally works:

> The ordinary villager, who in his everyday life takes no thought for the morrow of a subsequent existence, is content to worship the village gods to whom he looks for rain, bountiful harvests, and escape from plague . . . There are, as it were, two religions: a work-a-day religion to meet the requirements of everyday existence and a higher religion . . . which the ordinary man does not attempt to understand."[268]

Polytheistic Buddhism

We will likewise restrain our discussion of the religious worldview of Buddhism until Chapter Ten due to the fact that the Buddha and his central teachings—found in Theravada Buddhism—is not polytheistic or pantheistic, but actually *atheistic* in nature.[269]

However, there is one form of Buddhism—Mayahana Buddhism—that falls in the polytheistic category. Mahayana adherents (which means "greater vehicle") developed a later form of Buddhism to attempt to draw more people—not just monks—into the practices of the religion. Over time, they came to recognize other Buddhas ("enlightened ones") such as Avalokiteśvara, Amitabha, and Bhaisajy-aguru, but also developed a special category of beings called *bodhisattvas* (bode-e-SOT-vas), who demonstrated wisdom in their enlightenment (Nirvana) and felt compassion to help others to obtain it.[270]

Mahayana Buddhists believe that at least eighteen *bodhisattvas,* including Maitreya, Avalokitesvara, Ksitigarbha, and Samanthadabra, exist in a heavenly realm but intervene in the human sphere. Buddhists pray to them for help rather than worshipping them (although certainly in folk-Buddhism the distinction blurs). In Tibetan Buddhism the idea was extended to the Lama concept—where a *bodhisattva* is repeatedly reborn as a human to teach Buddhism anew.[271] Thus, Mahayana Buddhism produces an eastern version of polytheism.

Both religious Taoism (China) and Shintoism (Japan) qualify as polytheistic forms of their various religions. We will discuss them later on in the context of their major worldviews.

We now conclude our tour of ancient and modern polytheism—the first false fork of the River of God—by looking at its answers life's questions and fitness regarding truth.

QUESTION POLYTHEISM MUST ANSWER

- God—Who's in Charge?

  As we've seen, polytheists sometimes believe in supreme gods, but they are usually crafted in mythical human from with all our subsequent failures and shortcomings. In polytheism, "many gods" are in charge—and in conflict with one another. In animism, it is the *spirits* who control things—and it is imperative for human beings to get on their right side. In Mahayana Buddhism, there are *Buddhas* and *bodhisattvas*—and technically no gods.[272]

- Source—Is the Guidebook Reliable?

  Most polytheistic religions contain no holy books—just poetic *myths*. Mahayana Buddhism has its *Tripitika* ("three baskets" or sections)—one of which deals with rules for monks and nuns, the second shares conversations with the Buddha, and the third contains doctrine.[273] It is seventy times larger than the Bible [274] (and very diverse).

- Origins—How Did We Get Here?

  There are creator Gods in most polytheistic traditions, but many creation stories appear unrealistic. Animists believe in spirit beings, but no one knows how they got here.

- Organization—What's the Structure?

Many gods fight and rule—sort of a polytheistic "survival of the fittest." The gods' consorts and many children make the structure of the universe look "family centered"—but most of them are dysfunctional families who sleep around and are at war with each other.

- Human Beings—What is Their Nature and Calling?

Man's nature is not clear in polytheism, though there is a belief in mans' material/immaterial components (body and soul). In Mahayana Buddhism, every person's true nature is a Buddha-nature, an "impermanent collection of aggregates,"[275] but most people are ignorant of this fact.

- Morality—What's the Basis of Right and Wrong?

Whatever the gods or Buddhas or bodhisattvas decide—which is why many polytheistic societies have trouble with morality, or even sacrifice (murder) thousands of their people. Mahayana Buddhism shares the "Eight-fold Path" with its Theravada cousin—but Buddhism, overall, is a "do-it-yourself" religion where almost all forms of morality are tolerated.[276]

- Sin—Why is the World a Mess?

In animism, it is because of complex relations with the spirit world. In Mahayana Buddhism, sin is centered in *desire* which must be terminated.[277] In ancient polytheism, the petulant gods were the problem! They were dysfunctional—and created problems on earth.

- Salvation—How Can the World Be Made Right?

In Mahayana Buddhism, liberation from *samsara* (cycle of death and rebirth) is the ultimate goal.[278] Rituals are critical as well as help from other Buddhas and bodhisattvas. Depending on the sect, entry into paradise is attained by faith, visualization, or invoking the Buddha's name.[279] In other forms of polytheism, salvation comes by *appeasing the gods.*

- Earth—How Should Human Beings Look at the Earth?

Polytheistic peoples have little concern for earth. Life is survival, and for some, attaining Nirvana. The reason is their perspective—looking *back* and not forward into a more prosperous future. Huston Smith explains: "Primal religions give the appearance of looking toward the past. Primal time is not linear . . . it is a temporal; an eternal now . . . For primal peoples "past" means preeminently closer to the originating Source of things."[280] Most polytheists live for today.

- Heaven—Is There a Future and a Hope?
  In Mahayana Buddhism, there is re-incarnation and various heavens and hells before hopefully reaching Nirvana, a state of ecstasy which is beyond description.[281] Other polytheistic peoples believe in an afterlife—heaven and hell—but neither is certain.

THE TRUTH TEST AND POLYTHEISM

Is polytheism clear and simple? Its global differences create incredible complexity, and its array of gods and goddesses are really quite astounding—especially in folk-Hinduism where there are 330 million of them!

Is polytheism reasonable? It is sensible to believe in spirits (angels and demons), but not in multitudes of gods. Most of its gods are also unreasonable beings that lie, kill, rape, and pillage to get their way. These are not "reasonable" ways for gods to act.

Is polytheism based on evidence? The evidence comes up short—with few books, and less historical verification. The stories that exist are mostly *myths*—and that tells you something. Mahayana Buddhism has its texts, but these are quite varied—not a uniform source of truth.

Does conscience testify to the truth of polytheism? The presence of spirit beings seems to align with reality, but the acts of the gods, and the things they require of people (like human sacrifice), go against the teachings of conscience. Polytheism generally lacks a moral compass.

Is polytheism lasting and eternal? Animism focuses on the "now" with vague concepts of heaven. The demise of ancient polytheism reveals a lack of lasting character. Mahayana Buddhism points to an eternal paradise, but few make it, and re-incarnations can be endless.

Is polytheism universal? As we have shared, animism is a global phenomenon that lends credence to the idea of *spiritual forces* existing in the universe. The question remains: which ones are angels, or demons, and how should we interact with them? Mahayana Buddhism is limited in both time and geography. It is an Asian religion that lacks appeal on a global scale.

Conclusion

Polytheism developed as a powerful force in the ancient world. C.S. Lewis saw the worship of many gods as the "real, but unfocussed gleams of divine truth falling upon human imagination."[282] It deviated from the original revelation of a loving Creator God and spiraled down into fear, appeasement, immorality and even sacrificial death to its practitioners.

It still holds sway over hundreds of millions of people today via folk religion which is a distant memory of its original Fertile Crescent forms. Polytheism sees the spiritual world, but fails to properly analyze and organize it.

While polytheism was growing in the Middle East, another very different form of religion was being born in the fertile Indus River Valley of India. A new distributary off the River was being created.

Whereas the inhabitants of the Fertile Crescent saw God as a personal being, the Hindus would re-define him into an *impersonal force.*

The liar was thrilled with the news. All over the earth, the narrow-sighted humans were forgetting their original relationship to the Enemy and were ascribing his attributes to the things he made. Zeus and his minions had them worshipping every conceivable aspect of creation—and over time, they even built temples dedicated to the sun, moon, even frogs and gnats! "The stupid vermin," the liar grinned in his heart. "They should take dominion over nature, but instead they're bowing down! We've even convinced them to WORSHIP pieces of wood and stone!" His devilish heart roared at the prospect.

He was most proud of Ishtar—the sensuous one. She had drawn many of the peoples of the earth into sexual lust with a roll of her eyes, the draw of human nakedness, and her promises of fertility. The liar had never experienced sex—it seemed a quaint form of "pleasure" to him. "But the foolish humans crave it," he mused in his heart. Then to deal with their guilt, Ishtar had them kill their own children! "Marvelous," thought the master of evil. They were killing thousands every solstice! "At least they're keeping Hades busy," he boasted to himself.

Just then a hideous, yellow-skinned creature entered the demonic lair. "My Baal" drooled Brahman, the Archangel of the East. "The descendants of Shem and Ham have agreed to our scheme to 'create' different classes of humans. But now in their servitude, (which is our sheer delight!) they are looking for the Enemy."

"Can you keep their eyes off of Him?" The liar growled.

"Yes, my Baal," continued Brahman. We will dull their pain by getting them to think lofty thoughts. We will convince them to worship the cosmos! I will use my own name."

The liar fiendishly laughed. "And they will think they're on the way to paradise."

Chapter Seven

All is God

"Verily, this whole world is Brahman. Tranquil, let one worship." (Upanishad Chand 3.1) [283]

I'll never forget my first visits to Asia—seeing the teeming masses of humanity in India and China, countries that contain nearly one-third of all people on earth. One summer we visited a massive Buddhist temple that straddled a lush, green, semi-tropical hillside. It housed thousands of statues and shrines, with special foods being offered to idols, devoted monks scurrying to their places of meditation, and incense wafting lazily heavenward from the altars.

Near the top of one endless maze of shrines lay a four hundred foot "Dead Buddha" statute. At the time, I didn't realize that that India's history held the key to understanding the religions of the East. Their amazing story developed—as we've seen in other parts of the world— along the shores of a river, the Indus River, which flows through Pakistan and India. It is beside the waters of the Indus that India, Hinduism, and pantheism all emerged.

THE SECOND FALSE FORK IN THE RIVER—PANTHEISM

The history of pantheism is the story of the *Hindu* people—a Persian word which means– "people who lived east of the Indus River"—a spacious land where 850 million people today claim to be Hindu (80 percent of the population, but it is decreasing).[284] Hindus also boast sizable populations in Bangladesh (11 percent), Bhutan (25 percent), Fiji (41 percent), Mauritius (50 percent), Nepal (89 percent), Sri Lanka (15 percent), Surinam (27 percent), and Trinidad (25 percent). All told, Hindus currently make up 15 percent of the world's population.[285] It all began in and around the fertile Indus River valley which begins in the Himalayas and is considered the celestial home of the gods.[286]

Distinguished Indian historian Sudhakar Chattopadhyaya once said, "Hinduism is perhaps the only major religion in the world that has not been started by a prophet. It's a religion that originated with the people, it really has no beginning."[287] This "peoples' story" stands inextricably entwined with the history of the Indian nation, and remains one of the most fascinating, complex, contradictory, and mystical narratives in the history of mankind—bursting with incredible poetry, poverty, optimism and despair. Chattopadhyaya tries to explain:

> The Indian faiths comprehended under the term *Hinduism* have an almost unlimited diversity. No possibility exists of bringing them under one rubric or saying that they are in agreement about what should be said and done in the world. They are really not one religion, but rather a family of religions. The word *Hinduism*, in fact, should not at all imply that Hindus put their faith in a completed system of doctrines . . . Hinduism is instead fluid and changing. It comprehends the living faiths of the people of India who call themselves Hindus.[288]

Hinduism *is* exceedingly complex. Why? Many "poets" create many interpretations. These divergent voices produced a unique Hindu pluralism that means that Hinduism can be all things to all human beings. According to Indian professor Arvind Sharma, there is not one thing that one Hindu says that is not denied by another."[289]

The religious journey traveled by the Hindu people is noted in John B. Noss' seminal book, *World Religions*. His chapter explaining early Hinduism, "The Passage from Ritual Sacrifice to Mystical Union," sums up the Asian movement from polytheism to pantheism.[290]

Noss notes that Hindus consider themselves pantheists, polytheists, monotheists, agnostics, atheists, pluralists, and monists! They can follow moral standards or ascribe to a sublime mysticism. They can be active or contemplative, have rituals or none, go to a temple or not. He says their "only general obligation, whatever their divergences, is to abide by the rituals and rules of their caste and trust that by doing so, their next birth will be happier." [291]

Instead of special revelation to guide them, Hindus formulated a vast mosaic of poems, myths, instructions, and philosophical treatises, all quilted together into a worldview that went from optimistic in ancient days to resigned and pessimistic. In the end, they dealt with their depression by inventing a way to be released (extinguished) into a Greater Reality.

Hundreds of years before Christ, eastern polytheism created something new. They reduced divinity to a subjective state—'all the gods are within me,' said one sacred text. Another taught: "The highest *Brahman*, in all forms, is the supreme reality of the universe, which is the most subtle of the subtle and which is eternal, is *nothing but yourself.* "[292]

The High God had shrunk to "gods"— then, an inner oneness with the *All.*

The History of Pantheism

The Indus River Valley

The story begins millenniums ago when an ancient people migrated two thousand miles south from the Fertile Crescent, navigated through the three thousand foot Khyber Pass (in later years, the gateway to the "Silk Road") and discovered a tantalizing and hidden world—the Indus River Valley. Along this beautiful waterway—the twenty-first largest river system in the world—they *worshipped*—and established what would become one of the world's largest civilizations.

Most scholars divide the development of ancient India and the birth of Hindu pantheism into four periods: The Pre-Vedic, Vedic, Upanisadic, and Post-Upanisadic eras.[293] We will begin our journey there—then fast forward to the present.

Pre-Vedic (3000-1500 B.C.)—From High God to Spirits
Some historians believe the Hindu people are a combination of the original post-Babel races that migrated into the Indus Valley and an Aryan race (eastern European) people who swept down and conquered them around 1800 B.C. Other scholars dispute the Aryan invasion theory based on more recent archaeological findings.[294] At any rate, by 1500 B.C., the Indus River Valley region was thriving—and much more densely populated than either the Nile or Tigris-Euphrates valleys.[295] That remains true to this day.

Some amazing finds have been unearthed. The most notable sites are Mohenjo-daro and Harappa, which were discovered in 1856 when some workmen on the first railroad line through the river valley region stumbled onto the ruins in a dense jungle area.[296] They were startled to find one- and two-story homes in a gridiron fashion (right angle streets!) that sported such luxuries as swimming pools, sewers, forced-air heating, and even hot showers. [297]

The ancient Indians shunned war (their word for warfare meant "a desire for cows"), produced beautiful linens, developed the world's first alphabet with 250 characters, and recited an eerily-similar-to-the-Bible flood story where Satyauata and his wife and three sons (Iyapeti, Sharma, and Charma) survived the deluge.[298] When the ancient Hindus engaged in public worship, they did it under the open sky, like the ancient Iranians—and used three main holy sites for their animistic celebrations.[299] They were a vibrant and optimistic people.

The Vedic Period (1500-700 B.C.)—*From Spirits to Many Gods*

But changes were coming. Around 1500 B.C., the early Hindus developed a new written language called Sanskrit, and great literature flowed from the pens of numerous Sanskrit writers which became known as the *Vedas* (Knowledge)—composed along the shores of the Indus River. The Vedas contained both poetic and practical writings on religion, life, death, philosophy and music. The *Rig Veda* (Knowledge of Sacred Formulas), which numbers ten volumes of prose in 1028 lyrics, is five time larger than the Psalms and contains many penetrating insights on the meaning of life. Salvation in the *Rig Veda* comes through prayer.

Many of the Vedas were hymns to the nature gods—of which there were at least thirty-three.[300] They expressed "cosmic prayers" such as the following: "Thou hast made prayers the means of thine exalting, therefore we wait on thee with hymns, O Indra . . . Mark well our sacrificial cake, delighted; Indra, drink Soma and the milk commingled. Here on the sacrificer's grass be seated." [301] Indra was a chief god of the early people—thought to be in charge of war, storms, and rainfall, but who sometimes got into mischief. The Vedic theory of the sacrifice, its hymns, prayers and its results as an exchange of gifts between gods and men, is the fundamental focus of the whole Vedic religion.[302]

Ancient worship took place in families or clans, but eventually "professional" priests (*brahmins*) appeared who took over the responsibilities for the rites and sacrifices. To guide them in their tasks, the *Brahmanas* (priestly texts) were written, giving detailed instructions for performing the more complicated rituals. Over two thousand years, the Hindu writers gathered a broad, interwoven collection of writings into *Four Vedas*—Samhitas (Collections), Brahmanas (separate prose attached to Samhitas), Aranyakas (Forest Texts—meditating on sacrifice as an inner experience), and Upanishads (dialogues between a guru, i.e. teacher, and truth-seeking disciples).[303] Thirteen "important" Upanishads stand paramount. There is little consistency of ideas among the varied writings.

However, one concept that haunts the Indian people today—*the caste system*—appeared during the Vedic period and would guide their religious destiny. During this era, four castes (social classes) came to prominence: 1) Brahmins, the priestly elite, 2) Kshatriyas, the warrior leaders such as kings and princes, 3) Vaishya—middle-class farmers and merchants, and 4) Sudra — laborers/servants who owned no land.[304] Much later "untouchables" (*dalits)* joined the program—and the caste system, eventually expanded to over 3000 sub-categories.

A Vedic writing explains the origins of the caste system: "One fourth of the Supreme Being constitutes all beings, while three fourths of him are immortal and stand above. With the one fourth below, he extended on all sides into the animate and inanimate . . . His face became the Brahman. His arms were made into the Ksatriya, his thighs became the Vaisya; from his feet the Sudra was born" (Rigveda X, 90).[305]

Notice the emerging concept of deity. The Hindus were moving toward the idea of God as a mystical, ultimate force of some kind. The priests had begun asking the question: "Could the ultimate reality of the world be called Brahman?"[306]

Here's what was happening. Due to the rigidity of the caste system (you could not change classes throughout your lifetime), a once optimistic people were becoming pessimistic—totally disillusioned with life stuck in caste concrete.[307] (Some older historians who share the "Aryan invasion" theory argue that leaving a nomadic lifestyle and the intense heat of the region also affected the Hindu psyche.) Earlier peoples had faced life positively and confidently, giving promise of great things to come.[308] But over the centuries, as the Vedic writers explored the need to escape the fatalistic cycle created by the caste system, they devised a way to be delivered (*moksha*) from this life and find true existence and freedom.

Thus, *Brahman and Nirvana* were born.[309] Here's how.

Toward end of the Vedic period, there emerged a deep yearning for assurance of unity in the totality of things. The 129th hymn of the tenth Veda addressed to a great cosmic reality referred to as *That One Thing*—a neutral principle or activity said to have existed before the universe began.[310] "That

One Thing" became known as *Brahman,* although major confusion existed about him or it. Here's a Vedic example: "Whether the world was made or was self-made, He knows with full assurance, he alone. Who in the highest heaven guards and watches; He knows indeed, but then, perhaps, he knows not!"[311] It is hard to have confidence in a God which is a "Thing" and may or may not know the answers to life.

The Upanisadic Period (700 to 200 B.C.)—From Many Gods to All is God
Over a three-to-four hundred year time period, another collection of writings developed and gave permanence to the idea of Brahman—the new pantheistic faith. The *Upanisads* (literally "sittings near a teacher" i.e. discussions on ultimate wisdom) contained two hundred writings that tried to explain the new Brahman religion.[312] By this time, Hindu civilization had expanded to the Ganges River basin—and here the Upanisads—somewhat like the New Testament to the Old Testament—became the successor to the Vedas.

Whereas the ancient Vedas had primarily explored external religious sacrifices to the gods, the Upanisads encouraged *asceticism*—giving up the world (in response to the dreary caste system) and seeking inner emancipation from its illusion and pain. The trend shifted away from ritualism and embraced the "inner sacrifice" of soul or self (*atman*).[313]

John B. Noss explains the new worldview: "Ultimately, all things are bound together in *being.* Man comes to see not his separateness from the gods and his fellows, but his and their identity with an eternal, all-inclusive Being or Reality, and begins to seek his deliverance (*moksha*) from separateness by mystical union with it. This all-inclusive being or reality is most commonly called Brahman."[314]

The central feature of the New Hinduism was an intense focus on the "self" (*atman*) and how it was linked to Brahman, the unifying spiritual force that underlies all existence and gives meaning to all ritual practices.[315] Major ideas included:

- *Brahman*—an impersonal reality, unknowable except by an experience best described as direct perception, unmediated knowledge, or intuition.[316]

- *Atman* (soul)—The essence of the universe (Brahman) and the essence of the individual self (*atman*) are identical. "That thou art" (*tat tvam asi*).[317] Atman-Brahman is often used to describe the final reality of the universe.

- *Samsara*—Life is suffering and wandering—an endless round or cycle of births and deaths. This is the theory of the transmigration of the soul—more popularly known as reincarnation. It is referred to as "The Wheel"—life has endless cycles of rebirth.[318]

- *Karma*—(deed or work). This denotes the fatalistic law of good or bad consequences. Listen to an early Upanishad statement on karma: "They who were of pleasant conduct here . . . they will enter into a pleasant womb, either womb of a Brahmin or the womb of a Kshatriya, or the womb of a Vaisya. But those who are of stinking conduct here—the prospect is indeed, that they will either enter the womb of a dog, or the womb of a swine, or the womb of an outcast." Karma provided a "satisfactory explanation of the mystery of suffering." [319]

- *Nirvana*—The pantheistic "Paradise" where one finds "release" (*moksha)*—an escape from the cycle of birth, death, and rebirth into an ultimate state of unconscious everlasting bliss."[320]

- *Ahimsa*—People should refrain from harming any creature (non-violence)—which follows the idea that human beings can be reincarnated as insects, animals, etc. Causing as little pain and suffering to others as possible is the highest moral virtue.[321]

The start of the sixth century B.C. saw new religious innovators emerge who paralleled what historians refer to as the "second urbanization" that took place in the Ganges River valley (as opposed to the earlier Indus civilizations). In many ways, their rise happened as a reaction to the now established pantheistic religion—

which spoke of endless, despair-producing reincarnations. We will briefly mention two religious movements here, and detail one later.

- *Jainism*—founded, by Mahavira, an Indian holy man. Mahavira was a charismatic guru (spiritual teacher) who railed against the dominance of the priests and the Vedas. [322] He lived an ascetic life, walked around naked, renounced all sexual pleasures, and taught that the aim of human existence is to escape the successions of re-births through self-mortification. Jainism grew rapidly in India and occupies eleven pages in *Man's Religions*.[323] Jainism remains a rel-atively godless religious sub-sect.

- *Buddhism*—especially the Theravada (pure) version. Siddhartha Gautama—more commonly known by his title—The Buddha (En-lightened or Awakened One)—was born at the same time as Ma-havira and just one hundred miles to the west. He also disliked the fixed castes, paid priests, bribable deities, and questioned the Vedas.[324] He practiced meditation for enlightenment, and birthed a movement that flourished in India, then spread to other parts of Asia. Many people do not realize that Buddhism is really an eastern version of *atheism*—so we will cover it in subsequent chapters.

The Post-Upanisadic Period (200 B.C. to 200 A.D.)—From All is God to Di-vine Trinity

During this period, the Vedic Scriptures re-surfaced in popularity and swung Hinduism's "All is God" mantra back toward the personification of Brahman. It even included emphasis on a Hindu Divine Trinity. The chal-lenge of godless Jainism and Buddhism were ascending during this time, and Brahman needed to be brought closer to the people.[325]

The "Divine Trinity"—a re-packaged Brahman—consisted firstly of Brahma, a personification of the unfathomable ground of reality. Next was Vishnu, the sustainer and preserver of the world in its present form. Vishnu is believed to pervade existence and hold everything together (an interesting parallel to Jesus Christ, the second Person of the Godhead, mentioned in

Colossians 1:17)[326] Vishnu is believed to take on an additional ten distinct Godly forms or *avatars* (beings that "descended" to lower or animal-like forms.) [327] Shiva makes up the final member of the Hindu trinity—a being who is capable of both uniting and destroying the universe. [328] He is the Lord of Sleep, who governs the end of all existence and who takes pleasure in destruction (while wearing a snake around his neck).[329] The Divine Trinity in Hinduism resembles the Father, Jesus Christ, and Lucifer—not the biblical Godhead of Father, Son, and Holy Spirit.

The Divine Trinity in evolving Hindu theology represented the three primary realities of life: creation, preservation, and destruction. Most Hindu teachers do not regard them as separate Gods, but as three aspects of Brahman—-what Ninian Smart called "a three-fold symbol of the one Being." (This explanation contains an interesting parallel to the biblical Godhead.) However, the Hindus also accept numerous other gods, so this new twist amounts to a pantheistic form of polytheism.[330] Another difference with biblical faith: Most, if not all of the gods in Hinduism, including the Divine Trinity, have consorts!

One of the more popular writings of Hinduism—*The Bhavagad Vita* (Song of the Lord)—containing seven hundred verses of prose, was produced during this era and is considered by many to be the "Fifth Veda." The Bhavagad Vita is a dramatic poem that reveals Krishna as the supreme lord god, and has been popularized in modern times by the Hare Krishna sect (God's Divine Energy) and through the Beatles song, "My Sweet Lord" by George Harrison, who embraced the Hare Krishna tradition. Harrison's ashes were "immersed" in the Ganges River in December, 2001, following his death.

Hinduism in the Common Era (200 A.D. to the present)—Brahman, Allah, Yoga
By A.D. 300, the religious tide had turned back to Brahmanism (All is God). Then Islamic traders entered the south in the seventh century, and through invasions in the eleventh century which produced Muslim rule from A.D. 1000–1858. During the Middle Ages, Muslims limited the

practice of Hinduism for five hundred years. Restrictions loosened under Muslim sultan Jalaluddin Akbar (1542–1605). For a period, a movement to try and unite Hindu and Islamic beliefs emerged (in reaction to the spread of Sikhism), but a revival of Islam in the eighteenth century and colonization of India by Great Britain in nineteenth century stopped that syncretism.[331]

The British brought civilization to India in the 1800s, and a backward and virtually uneducated people took avidly to Western learning. In an interesting twist, the early Christian missionaries used their printing presses to mass produce the Vedic and Upanisadic writings for the first time in India's history. Prior to the nineteenth century, the Hindu texts had been memorized and orally communicated as the sole domain of the brahmins (Hindu priests). Thus "the Britisher was the middle man and Christianity the mid-wife . . . in transforming Hinduism from a religion of the medieval world into a religion of the modern world." [332]

Modern Practices of Hinduism

Hindu professor Arvind Sharma reminds us that in the modern world, the acceptance of Vedic authority is perhaps the sole formal test of orthodoxy in Hinduism.[333] In other words, you can pick whatever part of the Hindu texts that you like—and practice them—and that makes you a Hindu pantheist. He says: "A Hindu may be identified as one who does not deny being one." [334] How's that for easy entrance?

In practical terms, especially in the Western world, modern day "All is God and God is All" philosophy displays itself primarily in "yoga" which means "to join" (yoking). Yoga connects the human with the divine, and carries with it five different forms: 1) Body—Hatha Yoga, 2) Mind—Raja Yoga, 3) Knowing—Jnana Yoga, 4) Feeling—Bhakti Yoga, and 5) Willing—Karma Yoga).[335] Transcendental meditation often accompanies yoga training and has been mainstreamed in the West by various gurus for many years.

Other Forms of Pantheism

Sikhism is a branch within Hinduism founded by Guru Nanak Dev (1469-1538) who preached a unifying message that "There is no Hindu, there is no Muslim." Sikh devotees number 20 million worldwide, of whom 80 percent live in India (many having moved from Pakistan when the two nations were divided in 1947). Some authorities claim Sikhism is monotheistic, but others place it in the pantheistic camp.[336] Some Sikhs (Learners or Disciples) desire to create an independent Sikh nation between Pakistan and India to be named Khalistan (Land of the Pure).[337]

Western groups that promote pantheistic include Theosophy, the Divine Light Mission, Self-Realization Fellowship, Ananda Marga, Hare Krishna, and the more generalized New Age movement. The worship of Gaia (Mother Earth) is a relative to Hindu pantheism—seeing God as the sum total of the universe. John Toland first used the word *pantheism* in 1705. James Lovelock popularized the concept in his book *A New Look at Life on* Earth published in 1979.

To sum up, over thousands of years, the heavy weight of a dehumanizing caste system drew a creative and optimistic people into the depths of despair. Their longing for freedom blurred the image of God into an impersonal Ultimate Force through whom they sought deliverance. This clouded vision produced the world's first "do-it-yourself religion" where each individual is tasked to find his or her own golden thread in the tangled skein of Hinduism's mass of beliefs and practices.[338]

QUESTIONS PANTHEISM MUST ANSWER

We now turn to the questions that Hindu pantheism must answer to be a credible worldview or pathway to the truth.

- God—Who's in Charge?
  Early Hinduism proposed Atman-Brahman (Universal Spirit/Power of God)—the one reality and ground of the entire cosmos.[339] Brahman is understood as the absolute, infinite, eternal, omnipresent, impersonal,

indescribable, neuter Being into which the individual human spirit must merge.[340] Later Hinduism personalized Brahman as Brahma, Vishnu, and Siva. [341] But there are 330 million other gods that many Hindus worship.

So, who's really in charge? In philosophical Hinduism, the answer is *you*.

• Source—Is the Guidebook Reliable?

Hinduism contains a large collection of writings. The ancient *Vedas* were shared orally for 3000 years. Amazingly, when they were written down for the first time in the nineteenth century, though drawn from many sources, they contained "hardly an error."[342] Besides the ancient Vedas (mainly prayers), there are numerous other sacred texts. The *Brahmanas* emphasize the duties of priests and focus on sacrifice.[343] The Upanisads became the third important set of writings, adding youth and women to the formerly male-dominated discussions of religion. They focus on speculation about the pantheistic Brahman. Around 250 B.C., the *Law-Book of Manu* included the four stages (*asramas*) of a devout life:1) Youth—student, 2) Young adult—marriage and family, 3) Middle age—meditation, and 4) Old age—spiritual hermit.[344] Later on, the *Bhavagad Vita* rose to become the most beloved devotional poem of Hindu literature. And finally, *The Epics* (two) and *Puranas* (eighteen) helped to popularize Hindu thought both within and outside the confines of India.

The Hindu writings are an elaborate collection of stories, rituals, discussions, and prescriptions for life. The greatest drawback is their vast contradictions.

• Origins—How Did We Get Here?

Hindus hold to a bewildering variety of speculations and theories on the origins of the universe. They include the *Hymn of Creation* attributed to Sankara (788–820 A.D.?)—"Whence all creation had its origin, he, whether he fashioned it or whether he did not, he, who surveys it all from highest heaven, he knows—or maybe even he does not know." [345] On the other hand: "Brahman is the cause from which the world proceeds. Yet the world is not created since this would imply purposeful acts by an intelligent being which Brahman is not."[346]

So which is it? Created or not created? It depends on which Hindu you ask.

- Organization—What's the Structure?

If the ultimate reality is Atman-Brahman, then no structure exists in the universe—just *being*. However, in practical Hinduism, there are many structures. The most destructive is the caste system which has kept people in poverty and bondage for thousands of years.[347] On the spiritual side, Arvind Sharma says that three religious orientations form the "spiritual superstructure" of Hinduism: *jnana* (knowledge), *bhakti* (devotion), and *karma* (action).[348] He explains that Hinduism is not a thing; it is a process. It is a method of discovering spiritual truth, of engaging the ultimate.[349]

- Human Beings—What is Their Nature and Calling?

Robert E. Hume states: "In Hinduism, the human individual is an emanation or temporary manifestation of the impersonal Supreme, is not inherently or permanently worthful, is not responsible before God, and is not permitted to be brotherly with all fellow human beings" (outside his caste).[350] In other words, pantheism gives little dignity or worth to people.

As to man's nature, we are divided vertically into a dichotomy of body/soul or matter/mind. Horizontally, the human personality is divided into knowing, feeling, and willing.[351] Every human being possesses an imperishable soul (atman) that continues to exist through the entire cycle of death and rebirth. However, this "individual" *atman* is actually an aspect of the Atman-Brahman, sharing all of Atman-Brahman's qualities, including infinity and eternity.[352]

As to man's calling on earth, the focus is simple: Be One with Brahman and "follow the vocation of the family into which one is born.[353]

- Morality—What's the Basis of Right and Wrong?
  Hindu morality varies greatly because, "One is pretty much free to do as one chooses in the realm of one's spiritual life."[354] This is true because morality constitutes a means through which salvation may be won, but only one of the stepping stones on the way to its achievement.[355] Many pantheists demonstrate their beliefs through *yoga* which contains a "synthesis of beliefs and practices and is a natural correlate of pluralism."[356]

  Designing your own morality allows people a free hand in choosing the kind of god they want to worship and how they want to worship it.[357] Christianity and Islam have a *core*; Hinduism is a circumference seeking a center.

  So, what should a good Hindu do? Arvind Sharma suggests there are four Hindu goals of life (*purusarthas*) 1) Acting righteously (*dharma*), 2) Earning money and helping others (*artha*), 3) Satisfying human desires by enjoying music, food, and relationships in a restrained manner (*kama*), and 4) Liberation—(*moksha*)—from the cycle of death and rebirth.

- Sin—Why is the World a Mess?
  There is no concept of sin in pantheism because no God exists to whom we are accountable. John Noss explains: "By and large, philosophical Hinduism is based on the conviction that the chief error of man lies in his thinking; his miseries are due to fallacies in the conception of things, rather than to sin in his living."[358] To the philosophical Hindu, sin—as well as the whole of human life—is an illusion (*maya*).

- Salvation—How Can the World Be Made Right?
  Salvation comes through Oneness with Brahman. There are a number of different ways to get there including breaking away from the natural world through asceticism and meditation, which amounts to 'abandoning the body' and 'freeing the soul.'"[359] According to the *Upanisads*, salvation is primarily attained through one's own philosophic speculation upon a pantheistic Supreme Being.[360] Essentially, Hinduism is an

array of techniques for establishing linkages between the human world and the transcendental world beyond it.[361]

- Earth—How Should Human Beings Look at the Earth?
The material world is either illusion (*maya*) or is temporal and unimportant. This faulty worldview remains a primary reason why India has a long history of poverty.[362]

- Heaven—Is There a Future and a Hope?
Two possibilities remain. Those who attain union with Brahman experience Nirvana—a state of unending bliss. Those who fail experience endless reincarnations. For millenniums, the teaching of reincarnation has depressed and disillusioned millions of Hindus.

THE TRUTH TEST AND PANTHEISM

Is pantheism clear and simple? Hindu pantheism portrays the least simplicity and greatest complexity of the five religious worldviews. When thousands of people over millenniums of years knit their ideas into a patchwork quilt of opinions, then religious chaos is bound to result. Indian thinker Bibhuti S. Yadav laments: "Hinduism is a rolling conference of conceptual spaces . . . a living contradiction. Hinduism is a moving form of life whose predicament is to be incomplete to its own logics; it is a history of contradictions in flesh, fortunately demanding that their resolution be constantly postponed."[363]

Is pantheism reasonable? As Indian thinker Vishal Mangawadi points out in his book *Truth and Transformation,* the Hindu concept on meditation involves *emptying* the mind, not engaging in rational thought. He says that Hindu monks were "trying hard *not* to think—and they succeeded." This is why they did not develop technology, universities, and science.[364]

Pantheism isn't reasonable because it suppresses reason. God makes no sense, the world is illusory, and history and theology are twisted. Arvind Sharma explains: "Hindus do not always attach the same theological value to historical events as they do in the West. The Hindus pull a switch here: They derive theological value from converting history into myth."[365] When reality becomes myth, no matter how great the poetry, the result is deception.

Is pantheism based on evidence? Hinduism's vast collection of writings speaks to its historical reality—but not to its truthfulness. In fact, the vast contradictions in its writings act as a judge and jury against its claims. Sharma points out: "This is of course the great danger; that in wanting to be all things to all human beings, Hinduism might be found wanting by all, precisely because it wants to be all things to all."[366] Being all things to all people might be helpful in human relationships, but it is suicidal to a world-view that makes claims leading to paradise.

Does conscience testify to the truth of pantheism? The moral relativism of Hindu pantheism leaves conscience without a compass. Thus cows can be revered more than people, caste systems create animosity between human beings, and "every person does what is right in their own eyes." Do-it-yourself religion is suicidal to the healthy functioning of conscience.

Is pantheism eternal? It speaks of the eternal, but few arrive at the destination. In practical terms, endless reincarnations are the greatest reality for the majority of people.

Is pantheism universal? Pantheism came from one nation—India—and spread to a few others over time. However, Hinduism is inextricably intertwined with being Indian. It remains the least universal religion among the five views of God.

Conclusion

The Indus River valley produced the second major fork off the original River of God's revelation of. In reality, this new religious waterway was a fork off the second stream of polytheism. Human worship had moved from the true God of love, to the many gods of nature and spirits, to the Brahman (All is God) of ancient India.

Two more detours from the River of God would be crafted by *the liar*. One of them contained two troubling, but very clever opposites—one blossoming in the East and the other forming in the West. One would negate reason; the other, exalt it. Both produce the same effect: where there is no God, *man becomes his own deity.*

The demonic trinity had been holed up in the vast earthly dungeon for days. The bulging Zeus paced about like a caged lion. Brahman slithered from wall-to-wall relishing his power in this unseen Triad of Evil. They shouted, they ranted, and they flailed at one another as chugs of sulfurous breath filled the cavern with smoke.

The liar was irate: "The Enemy's Chosen One is coming soon!" he bellowed. The thought of it made his stomach churn. He knew the Coming was centuries away, but time seemed to move more quickly in their dimension than on the human side of the Curtain. "We must act to confuse and destroy the human rats!" the liar bellowed and wheezed.

Brahman spoke first. "I have a crafty demon prince who might help our cause in the East," he spoke mockingly at the Lord of the demons. "Bring him in," said the liar, who seemed to spill out the words like vomit. A grotesquely large demon entered the darkness. "My name is Gautama," he spoke softly to the gathered demon princes as he bowed before them. As three sets of piercing red eyes focused their hollow gaze upon him, he continued: "The vermin sons of Shem and Ham in the Middle Kingdom are learning that desire is a dead end. We must take the next step. I will convince them that desire is the problem and that it must be snuffed out."

Gautama continued. "But as you know, my baals, the sons of Japheth are of a different mind. Whereas we've crushed the inhabitants of the East, the inhabitants of the West are haughty. Inflate their desire to be gods themselves. That will cause their ruin. In the East, we will empty them of all desire. Then there will be nothing left to kill."

The demon masters nodded in agreement. The liar spoke, "Let the new deception begin."

Chapter Eight

No God

"We have killed God. The most sacred and powerful force the world has hitherto possessed now bleeds beneath our knife . . . The grandeur of this act is too great for us. Is it not necessary that, as a result of this act, we become gods ourselves?"—Friedrich Nietzsche[367]

On Saturday, March 24, 2012, some 20,000 atheists demonstrated in Washington, D.C., for a "Reason Rally" protesting religion. British scientist and leading proponent of atheism Richard Dawkins was the headliner. He didn't appear until five hours into the event, but when he strode to the podium, the crowd cheered wildly. He announced: "We're never antagonistic toward religious believers; we're antagonistic toward religious belief. There is no good, honest reason to believe in a god or gods of any kind, or indeed in anything supernatural. The only reason to believe something is that you have evidence for it."[368]

The crowd whistled and cheered for his familiar lines such as: "I don't despise religious people. I despise what they stand for." And, "Evolution is not just true, it's beautiful." Then Dawkins called on the crowd not only to challenge religious people but to "ridicule and show contempt" for their doctrines and sacraments, including the Eucharist. Outrage was the parlance of the day. Television host Adam Savage told the masses: "There really *is* someone who loves and protects me and watches over my actions—it's *me!*"

Man-centered atheism/secularism comprises one of the five worldviews that go back to ancient times. Yet, there has been a substantial surge in global atheism in the past four decades.[369] What is atheism? An "atheist" says there is sufficient evidence to show that God does not exist. An "agnostic" says there is insufficient evidence to know whether God exists or not. A "practical atheist" is a person who lives as if God does exist.

I will use the word "secularist" (worldly; supreme attention to the things of this life)[370] as synonymous with "atheist." The term *secularism* was first coined by in 1846 by George Jacob Holyoake (1817-1906). If you combine the numbers for both "atheists" and the "non-religious," the total number of secularists is about 20 percent of the world's population.[371]

Atheism developed as the fourth false distributary of the River of God. Human beings were becoming more civilized (less dependent on God's protection), educated (philosophical about life), industrial (more prosperous), technological (more creative), and scientific (understanding how the world works). This growth in human development brought a mystical humanism to the East and rational secularism to the West. Both exalted man. Some replaced God with the State.

EASTERN FORMS OF ATHEISM

Our look at atheism takes us to different parts of the globe. We will begin our tour in the Far East, where, as we saw earlier, a caste-bound people in India developed a despairing worldview that blurred God into the cosmos. In the sixth century B.C., one of their princes spiritually catapulted them another direction—into the darkened waters of disbelief.

History knows him as the Buddha. His contemporaries called him Siddhartha.

Buddhism as Mystical Atheism: Emptying the Individual

Siddhartha Gautama (563–483 B.C.) was born into the warrior caste of the Shakya tribe in Kapilavastu, in northeastern India (now a part of Nepal).[372] His first thirty years were spent in luxury as a prince, living in a palace where his kingly father desired to shelter him from suffering. He married Gopa at sixteen and they produced a child named Rahula.[373] One day, Siddhartha left the palace and encountered a crippled old man, a sick man, a decaying corpse, and a wandering guru.[374] The experience caused him to become disillusioned with his wealth and he became deeply concerned about the causes of suffering in the world.

For the next six years, Siddhartha abandoned his family and became an ascetic. After years of poverty and seeking, he realized that extreme asceticism did not bring enlightenment or answer his questions. He then sat under a *Bodhi* tree in the city of Bodh Gaya and vowed he wouldn't arise until he gained enlightenment. According to different sources, he meditated there between one and forty-nine days—after which he became the "Buddha" (The Enlightened One).

Soon thereafter, Buddha traveled to Benares and preached his first sermon in which he introduced what would come to be known as the Fourth Noble Truths of the Middle Way. The "Middle Way" taught people to avoid the extremes of wealth on one hand and asceticism on the other. Over the years he won thousands of followers who formed communities called *sanghas* (early monastic orders). After forty-five years of preaching meditation as the means to enlightenment, Buddha died, probably as a result of food poisoning. His last words declared: "Decay is inherent in all component things! Work out your salvation with diligence."[375]

Today, some 350–400 million people call themselves Buddhists— roughly 6 percent of the world's population. Some forms of Buddhism inculcate polytheistic folk religion or espouse pantheism. But the original followers of the Buddha—now designated Theravada Buddhists— believed in a "morality without god and atheism without Nature."[376] German scholar

Hermann Oldenberg (1854-1920) concluded succinctly that Buddhism, at its core, is "a religion without god."[377]

Buddha built his "godless religion" on Four Noble Truths which state: 1) Life consists of suffering (*dukkha*), 2) The cause of suffering is *desire* for impermanent things (*samudaya*), 3) Suffering can cease through *eliminating* that desire (*nirodha*), and 4) The way of liberation (*marga*) is the Eightfold Path. This path helps one move toward enlightenment through 1) *wisdom*—right understanding, right thought, 2) *ethical conduct* - right speech, right action, right livelihood, and 3) *mental discipline*—right effort, right awareness, and right concentration.[378]

Buddha believed the problem in the world was "self"—not a bad conclusion. However, his answer didn't involve submitting "self" to God or improving "self" in any meaningful way. Enlightenment came through *eliminating* "self" as a reality—a concept called *sunyata* or "emptiness." Though various Buddhist scholars try to romanticize the concept of "emptiness"—it comes down to killing all aspects of individual identity.[379] You are free from desire when *you* no longer exist. This liberation comes primarily through *zen*—the discipline of *meditation*.

Theravada Buddhism is an eastern, mystical form of atheism. There is no God, and selfish desires are the problem. You must get rid of self and commit "spiritual suicide" through the "Triple Gem" which includes belief in Buddha, the teachings of Buddhism (*Dharma*), and refuge in a community of monks (*Sangha*). Buddhists also believe in numerous re-incarnations—like Hindus—on the road to enlightenment. What's the final destination? Buddhist professor Masao Abe, Purdue University, sums it up: "If the doctrine of early Buddhism were to be summarized in one word, it would be Nirvana."[380] And Nirvana is nothing less than "the blowing out of all cravings, a state of nothingness."[381]

We must also mention two other forms of eastern atheism. Neither of these religions spans the globe—but both made a huge impact in China, the most populous nation on earth.

Confucianism as Socio-political Atheism: Changing the Individual and Society
The Yellow River in China originates in western China and flows through
nine different provinces to the Bohai Sea. It is the sixth largest river in the
world (3,395 miles long) and is considered "the cradle of Chinese civilization"—the most prosperous region of early Chinese history. As we've seen
with other rivers of the world, the Yellow River basin birthed two religions
that dominate its history. We begin with Confucianism, which means *a family of scholars* signifying a genealogy, a school, or a tradition of learning.[382]
Its most famous scholar is Kung Fu-tzu, whose Latinized name is Confucius (551–479 B.C.).

Though facts about Confucius are scant, he lived during a time of political instability and disunity among the various tribes who populated
the vast river plains. Confucius was a well-educated intellectual who
served as a minister of justice of the State of Lu, and spent twelve years
(ages 56–68) traveling extensively throughout China trying to promote a
peaceful and secure cultural and political order. His crusade failed—and
he spent the last five years of his life writing and a teaching a small group
of followers who wrote his ideas down in what became known as the
Analects (Selections).[383]

His disciples eventually formed eight distinct schools that championed
the Confucian work ethic which involves strong families, moral virtues,
and a stable political society. Harvard University professor Tu Wei Ming
says Confucius characterized himself as, "a fellow human being with a
Heaven-ordained mission to transmit the Way as an inexhaustible student
and tireless teacher."[384] Confucius' "Heaven" was like Plato's "Good." He
made no reference to a personal God.

To sum up, Confucius set out "to devise a set of moral and political
beliefs which, if widely and consistently acted on in human society, would
produce the greatest good of which he could conceive, namely a stable social and political order in which human beings could flourish."[385] Confucius' famous edict stated, "Conquer yourself."[386] He was China's most
influential humanist.

Confucius believed that man was basically good (*jen*) but needed to grow his moral virtues through strenuous discipline.[387] This included self-reflection, cultivating one's moral and mental faculties, and acting responsibly according to one's true (good) nature.[388] Confucian humanism was the moral re-armament of its day and formed many branches. It eventually became the official ideology of the Han Chinese, China's dominant people group. Many people credit the Confucian work ethic with the rapid economic growth experienced in China and East Asia today. It is a godless socio-political ethic with anywhere from 6 to 350 million adherents.[389]

Taoism as Natural Atheism: Going with the Flow of Nature
Next to Confucianism, the most important and influential ancient Chinese philosophy was Taoism (pronounced DOW-ism—meaning "the Way"). Whereas Confucius spoke of the "Way of Heaven," The Taoists developed a total rejection of the socio-political order, which they believed to be the source of spiritual pollution.[390]

Most scholars believe that Lao Tzu (LAO-tzee—The Old Master), a senior contemporary of both Confucius and the Buddha, made the greatest contribution to the metaphysical concept of the Tao through his writings which became known as *Tao Te Ching*. In most translations, they begin with the following two lines: *The Tao (Way) that can be told is not the eternal Tao; The name that can be named is not the eternal name.*[391]

To Lao Tzu, the Tao was a mysterious thing. He regarded it as the general impersonal source of the universe. Princeton Taoist professor Liu Xiaogan explains: "Tao determines all things, or everything depends on it. Tao is the prime source, the One primordial being or the Chaos." [392] The Tao is the force of existence from which the world flows, but it is also the "Way" or "Pattern" within that world.[393] This natural "flow" of life is the underlying principle of the Tao. By aligning ourselves with nature, we can experience harmony, health and peace.

Confucius had stressed that the way to harmony in life came through strenuous moral discipline i.e. *force*, from the outside, enacted through family and society. Lao Tzu countered that "the way" occurred when we "go with the flow"—natural, spontaneous *inactivity*, from the within, where individuals return to natural patterns and rhythms.

Confucius was the activist; Lao Tzu, the pacifist.

Three main principles comprised the teachings of Lao Tzu and others that followed him. 1) The *Te* (The Pattern)—we should be true to who we are in our unique nature and work in harmony with the natural flow of the universe. 2) *Wu-Wei* (Inactivity)—take no unnatural action, but let nature or the Tao take its course, 3) *Yin Yang*—the most popularized Taoist teaching that says we must balance the interacting forces within nature.[394] To Lao Tzu, there were about seventy concepts of things in "pairs," summed up by activity versus passivity, toughness versus softness, and competition versus forbearance. To accomplish anything, a person needed to think backwards—to start with the opposite of what is being sought.[395] In practical terms, this meant "going with the flow" emphasizing the value of restraint.[396]

Tao philosophy creates three inner virtues (The Three Jewels) that stand paramount: humility, compassion, and moderation. Contemporary Taoists tend to be hygiene-conscious, environmentally aware, and concerned to promote sexual health and longevity. There are as many as 55 million Taoists in the world today with 31 million living outside of China.[397]

Buddhism, Confucianism and Taoism remain the dominant religions of China and other Asian nations. All three philosophies are man-centered i.e. *humanistic*. They contain numerous religious forms that worship thousands of gods or focus on ritual. But the heart of these influential worldviews centers on *man*—not God. One says to empty self; another to improve self; and the third, to flow with self. But self is paramount.

WESTERN FORMS OF ATHEISM

Now let's turn to the other side of the globe. Present-day expressions of atheism in the Western world also show themselves in different forms. We will call them philosophical, practical, and militant atheism (secularism.)[398] Ignace Lepp gives us an overview:

Contemporary atheism, at least in the developed countries
of Christian civilization is distinguished from the atheism
of other times and other civilizations above all by its extension. It is no longer a phenomenon of a few individuals
protesting the taboos of society, nor the privilege of a mi-
nority who consider themselves especially "enlightened"
in the manner of the eighteenth century rationalists. It is
the common lot of at least a considerable portion, if not of
the majority, of our contemporaries and is well on its way
to becoming the common norm of society. The intellectu-
als were the first to break with traditional faith; the bour-
geois followed them; then came the masses, and, finally
the peasants.[399]

The Ancient Greeks—Early Science and Reason
As we learned in Chapter Three, many early Greek philosophers moved
away from a High God or gods and elevated man's reason as the ultimate
authority in life. Thomas Oden adds another key: "Science had originally
been invented by the Greeks, not because they were the first to observe and
study nature but because they sought the intelligible, unchanging and permanent 'something' behind all the flux of observation, and tried to formu-
late it into abstract theory."[400] During the coming centuries, the re-discovery
of classical literature would "marry" man's reason and science into a burgeoning movement of man-centered ideals.

Let's re-trace the history and discover the key players in the rise of the
Western form of atheism.

The Renaissance (ca. A.D. 1400–1600)—*The Birth of Empirical Science*
An explosion in knowledge had burst across Europe during the close of
the Middle Ages. Johan Gutenberg's invention of the printing press, with
movable type, made both ancient and modern writings available to the
masses for the first time. That produced two streams: one created an

awareness of God's Word that led to the Protestant Reformation. The other pursued humanistic themes, passed down from Greek and Roman thinkers. It led to a "re-birth" of humanity's sense of independence and individualism, i.e. atheism.[401]

Toward the end of the Renaissance period, the modern methods of empirical science emerged through people like Nicholaus Copernicus (1473–1543), Johannes Kepler (1571–1630), and Galileo Galilei (1564–1642). The vast majority of the early scientists believed in a loving Creator who desired them to discover his natural laws. Galileo said God wrote two "books"—the Bible and nature.[402] Rodney Stark devotes a chapter in his book, *For the Glory of God,* to debunking the myth that the Renaissance scientists were all atheists. On the contrary, fully two-thirds of them were deeply committed Christians.[403]

Both Dean Halverson and Rodney Stark point out that the conflict between the Medieval Church and science has been greatly exaggerated in modern times in an attempt to elevate atheism and discredit biblical faith.[404] It's true that a gulf developed during this era between science and the Church—but it's equally true that biblical faith in a rational Creator *gave birth* to modern science.[405]

The Enlightenment (ca.1600–1800)—*The Growth of Philosophical Atheism*
French philosopher Rene' Descartes (1596–1650) carries the title of the "Father of Modern Philosophy." His famous statement *cogito ergo sum* ("I think, therefore I am") indicated that a doubter could only be certain of one fact—*his own existence.* Descartes promoted skepticism, but he did so by proposing that the surest way to find truth was to doubt everything until one found something "indubitable" (unable to undermine conviction). On that foundation, he himself built and encouraged others to build. This new line of reasoning shook the Christian world to its core and shifted the foundation for certainty about life from God to man.[406]

The scientific revolution of the 1600s also presented something new—a change in the way men saw the world and their role in it. It was a shift that placed emphasis on experiment and mathematics. According to Thomas F. O'Dea, science began to "geometrize" abstract thought.[407]

Next, philosopher David Hume (1711-1776) questioned why we should trust the mind to be our model for looking at the world. Isn't it all just matter? He theorized that: "Matter may contain the source, or spring of order originally, within itself, as well as the mind does." [408] By such reasoning, Hume questioned the philosophical necessity for believing in God, and although he was "irreligious," he supported "general theism" in some forms.[409] Hume also stressed the importance of experience (not just the mind) teaching us about causal relationships. His contribution to the development of humanistic thinking has been termed "unmitigated skepticism."[410]

Immanuel Kant (1704-1824) then picked up the question of epistemology. How do we know that we know? Kant was a complex, religious man who probably became atheistic toward the end of his life. He was ambivalent about the transcendent reality of God. No thinker placed greater emphasis on reason's boundaries than Kant, yet no one was ever been bolder in asserting its unqualified role to rule our lives.[411] Kant declared: "The proposition, 'There is a God,' says nothing more than . . . there is in the human mind . . . self-determining Reason which determines itself."[412]

Kant held two truths in tension. First, by perceiving and knowing *we* invent our own world. Second, through matter, this world has a reality of its own. Though Kant wrote extensively about various arguments for the existence of God, "moral faith," and the concept of God and our consciousness as moral agents,[413] he also sowed the seeds of modern skepticism which stated that the problems of philosophy were unanswerable—so, we must depend on the realm of science. If the *noumena* (objects of the mind) were unknowable, it would follow that the intelligent person should concentrate upon *phenomena* (objects of the senses).[414]

Thus science became more authoritative in an increasingly secularized world.

Modern Atheism (1800–Present)—Going Global

A.N. Wilson, in *God's Funeral*, lists thirty-seven theologians, philosophers, poets, artists, scientists and revolutionaries who figure as prominent proponents of atheism in the past two centuries.[415] H. Wayne House mentions thirteen different leaders, from Bertrand Russell to Richard Dawkins, who've led the growing atheist expansion of the past forty years.[416] All have advanced the "God is Dead" movement in various ways. The title from Wilson's book is taken from Thomas Hardy's poem, "God's Funeral" which describes the death of God in the West. Two of the stanzas tell the story:

> *"And tricked by our own earthly dream and seek of solace, we grew self-deceived. Our making soon our maker did we deem, and what we had imagined we believed."*
>
> *"Till, in Time's stayless stealthy swing, uncompromising rude reality mangled the Monarch of our fashioning, who quavered, sank; and now has ceased to be.[417]*

God had been killed by the philosophers. But how could we be sure?

Evolution—Scientific Atheism

Enter reason's "consort"—the realm of science. Charles Darwin's *The Origin of the Species* was not meant to actively promote materialism or even propose a theory of evolution—many of scientists and philosophers had already done that. Rather, he created a concept called "natural selection" which removed the necessity for a special creation by God. [418] Darwin had finally made it possible to be an intellectually fulfilled atheist.[419]

Interestingly, Darwin had his own doubts. In his book he remarked: "If it could be demonstrated that any complex organ existed which could not possibly have been formed by numerous successive slight modifications, my theory would absolutely break down."[420] Today, advanced molecular biology has revealed the irreducible complexity of parts of the human cell. Michael Behe and others have demonstrated that the various "chemical machines" of the human cell "could not have possibly been formed by numerous successive slight modifications."[421] If Darwin were alive today, he might reject his own theory. But atheism has not.

Secular Humanism—Philosophical Atheism

Humanism had blossomed in Europe as an opening up of ideas, sciences, arts, and exposure to new countries and peoples generally within Christian culture. For example, Desiderius Erasmus (1466–1536) was a noted humanist as well as a Christian scholar. But the Enlightenment caused humanism to take a decidedly atheistic direction in ensuing centuries.[422]

German philosopher Friedrich Nietzsche, whose uncle and two grandfathers were Lutheran pastors, thrust atheism into center of the modern world with his open denial of God and need for him. Nietzsche boasted:

> God is dead. God remains dead. And we have killed him. How shall we comfort ourselves, the murderers of all murderers? What was holiest and mightiest of all that the world has yet owned has bled to death under our knives: who will wipe this blood off us? What water is there for us to clean ourselves? What festivals of atonement, what sacred games shall we have to invent? Is not the greatness of this deed too great for us? Must we ourselves not become gods simply to appear worthy of it? [423]

Nietzsche made a profound intellectual impact during the nineteenth century which carried over in to the twentieth. His concept of the "Will to Power" inspired Adolph Hitler in the development of the Third Reich, which led to the slaughter of millions of Jews and Christians.[424]

Others brought the philosophy of humanism into different dimensions of Western life. Sigmund Freud attributed an atheistic assumption into his understanding of human nature.[425] John Dewey left no room for the supernatural by formulating a thoroughly secularist philosophy of education.

Though Romantic poet Percy Bysshe Shelley's *Necessity of Atheism* (1811) was probably the first English treatise on atheism, Dewey helped articulate the core beliefs of secular humanism in the more widely distributed Humanist Manifesto I written in 1933.

Three major Humanist Manifestos, I (1933), II (1972) and III (2003), established atheism in the twentieth century and twenty-first centuries as the new darling of religion. In the first manifesto, Dewey and others described their new creation as "a vital, fearless, and frank *religion.*" NOTE: not just ideas, but a religion. The first manifesto contains fifteen affirmations of belief (or non-unbelief), beginning with the following:

> FIRST: Religious humanists regard the universe as self-existing and not created.

> SECOND: Humanism believes that man is a part of nature and that he has emerged as a result of a continuous process.

> THIRD: Holding an organic view of life, humanists find that the traditional dualism of mind and body must be rejected.[426]

The most public expression of the religious nature of atheism remains the widely cited phrase "secular humanism" found in the 1961 U. S. Supreme Court *Torcaso vs. Watkins* where Justice Hugo Black used the term in a footnote to the text of the judicial decision.

Whereas humanism originally focused on man and his capacity for goodness while emphasizing his role as a creator of culture and an agent of his own self-realization,[427] over the centuries, it evolved to being an enemy of God and faith. Hanns Lilje warns us: "For the socialist thinker, the requirement of decisive atheism is unavoidable because every form of religion destroys the dignity of man . . . Religion everywhere has sanctioned the oppression of the working man . . . Peaceful co-existence with religion is unbearable; it is absolutely incompatible with socialistic humanism."[428]

In recent years, global atheism has increased its clout through a slate of books including Richard Dawkins' *The God Illusion,* Christopher Hitchens' *God Is Not Great,* Sam Harris' *The End of Faith*, and Daniel Dennett's *Breaking the Spell: Religion As a Natural Phenomenon.* Atheism has come out of closet—with brazen contempt for those who believe in God.

That brings us to the final form of modern day atheism—the militant version—which has been lethal to more people than any other ideology in the history of the world.

Communism—Militant Atheism

Karl Marx (1818–1883) and Friedrich Engels 1820–1895), founders of modern communism, built their idea of dialectic materialism on Georg W. F. Hegel's (1770–1831) concept of dialectical idealism. Hegel believed that everything in history develops through a process of change—the dialectic—moving from thesis (conflict) to antithesis, causing synthesis to be formed. Reality is not static or fixed, but is in a constant historical process of change and development. [429]

Marx and Engels applied Hegel's theory to social movements, especially those that denied the hand of God in history. Engels, who was Marx's financial benefactor, boasted: "All the possibilities of religion are exhausted."[430] Karl Marx's God-denying central idea was that human societies are the products of economic forces. Freedom is an illusion. We are products of our times and the times are products of economics.

Marx was expelled from the Rhineland (Germany) in 1849 for his radical views and settled in England. Three of his children died young because of poverty. He was one of literature's great phrasemakers—a self-hating anti-Semite who believed that money was the real god of the Jews. He wrote at age twenty-six: "Religion is the opium of the people."[431]

His atheistic masterpiece was *Das Kapital* which played upon the economic injustices of the nineteenth century and encouraged the masses to cast off the chains of capitalism. In a visionary sense, Marxism was the greatest alternative to Christianity which has ever been formulated."[432] His theories caught fire in Europe, as people became convinced that *they* deserved to be the supreme drivers of history. [433]

The political expression that atheism/Marxism birthed we know as *communism.* It produced Lenin and Stalin in the Soviet Union, Mao Zedong and others in China, Fidel Castro in Cuba, and many other twentieth and twenty-first century "statist" dictators. It is estimated that over 100 million people lost their lives due to the ideology of communism in the twentieth century. [434] If those figures include the secular humanist promotion of abortion on demand, the number of murdered human beings could rise to over *two billion.*[435]

Militant atheism is, by far, the bloodiest religion ever practiced on earth.

QUESTIONS ATHEISM MUST ANSWER

We now turn our attention to the questions that humanism/atheism/secularism must answer to be a credible worldview. We will look at the answers through the lens of their two largest expressions: the European social democracies and Communist China. Both Europe and China, in their governmental expressions, manifest a strong secular outlook on life. Many other examples could be used including the ancient Greek democracies, and more recently Nazi Germany, or the former Soviet Union.

*   God—Who's in Charge?
    Matter in one form or another, is all that has existed from eternity and all that will ever exist.[436] Human reason must shape the material world for its purposes. In practical terms, this means that human beings rule their lives autonomously and human reason is paramount. Each person becomes god, and the strongest man becomes the leader of a statist, god-like government. In atheism, men and governments become God.
*   Source—Is the Guidebook Reliable?
    There are no sourcebooks, just the writings of the philosophers and scientists. However, in the past fifty years, different "statements" have

emerged that include the following: Humanist Manifestos I-III, A Secular Humanist Declaration (1980), A Declaration of Interdependence (1988), Humanism: Why, What and What For? (1996), the Humanist Manifesto 2000: A Call for a New Plantetary Humanism, The Affirmations of Humanism: A Statement of Principles (2001), The Amsterdam Declaration (2002), and the Humanist Manifesto III: Humanism and Its Aspirations (2003).[437]

- Origins—How Did We Get Here?

The material universe is either eternally existent or the Big Bang brought it into existence without a supernatural cause.[438] Macro-evolution over billions of years is the only acceptable scientific explanation of our origins. Young Hegelian Arnold Ruge stated, "This communism, as a perfect naturalism, is equivalent to humanism; and as a perfect humanism it is equivalent to naturalism. It is the true resolution of the conflict between man and nature."[439]

- Organization—What's the Structure?

There is no structure but natural selection and survival of the fittest. This is also true of autocratic governments that arise from the atheistic worldview.

- Human Beings—What is Their Nature and Calling?

In secularism/atheism, man is basically good—just unenlightened or uneducated. Humanity is monistic because people consist only of matter. Humanity represents the highest point of the gradual and random processes of evolution.[440] Philosopher Jean Paul Sartre explains: "Every man must create his own essence—each man must do it himself. Each man must take the responsibility to make himself. In all this, God has no part.[441]

- Morality—What's the Basis of Right and Wrong?

H. Wayne House tells us that in atheism: "Ethics is seen as an autonomous field of inquiry wherein moral judgments can be made without recourse to revealed religion, and human beings are capable of cultivating moral wisdom and living virtuous lives independent of their belief in or reliance on God or gods."[442] In practical terms, with no God except individual autonomy, there are no moral absolutes—just "tolerance of everything" but absolutes.

Sin—Why is the World a Mess?

- Because of ignorance and superstition fostered by religion. Mankind must reject the escapist promises of religion and face problems squarely believing that humankind has the potential to create a world in which peace and justice will prevail.[443] Sin is relative. Do what you want as long as "you do no harm." Without a moral standard, atheists tend to be progressive or liberal on such social issues as abortion and homosexuality.[444]

- Salvation—How Can the World Be Made Right?

Salvation comes through education, human striving, government and science. According to Dean Halverson it entails: "Extending the scientific method of rational inquiry into all aspects of life, while at the same time maintaining a sense of compassion for the individual (do no harm)."[445]

- Earth—How Should Human Beings Look at the Earth?

"Man is the master and possessor of nature," boasted Rene' Descartes.[446] Humanists either regard the environment as something to be relentlessly exploited (as in communist nations), or they deify it and place the interests of birds and plants on a level with those of human beings (as in some Western social democracies).

- Heaven—Is There a Future and a Hope?

Atheism offers no heaven. There is no survival of the person's consciousness after death. The future is a world utopian society ably described by Mark Levin: "Utopianism is the ideological and doctrinal foundation for statism . . . it strips the individual of his uniqueness . . . but assigns him a group identity based on race, ethnicity, age, gender, income, etc . . . It is equality in misery."[447] Atheism's present-and-near future means big governments, tyrannical leaders, submissive masses, and possibly a global society. In the faraway future, its vision becomes "Star Wars"—an inter-galactic version of its goals on earth.

THE TRUTH TEST AND ATHEISM

Is atheism clear and simple? Atheism/secularism contains a clear and simple premise: man is the most highly evolved being in a purposeless material world.

Is atheism reasonable? The focus on reason recognizes humanity's superiority over creation, but fails to answer how we got here (macro-evolution contradicts the laws of science at several points). It lacks a credible rational for morality and human rights, and presents little optimism for the future.

Is atheism based on evidence? Some scientific evidence points toward an old earth and cosmos, but there are many questions and contradictions. The universality of God-consciousness and human morality makes little sense in secularized thought. Neither does evidence for the supernatural world and the afterlife.[448] The evils of tyrannical governments that atheism almost always produces speak volumes against its validity as a worldview.

Does conscience testify to the truths of atheism? Since atheism essentially teaches that "every man does what's right in his own eyes," then conscience can be molded into believing almost anything—even the killing of millions of innocent people for "the common good."[449]

Is atheism eternal? The only eternal aspect of atheism is the endless evolution of the material world. Karl Gustav Jung has stated: "Man positively needs general ideas and convictions that will give a meaning to his life and enable him to find a place for himself in the universe."[450] Atheism supplies none.

Is atheism universal? Its modern-day prophets say *yes.* Georg W. F. Hegel taught that: "The truth (of atheism) is inherently universal, essential, and substantial . . . But that spiritual principle which we call God is . . . individual and subjective truth."[451] Atheism was not widespread for thousands of years, but developed as a more recent phenomenon of history. Atheism/secularism is a worldview found primarily in the secular democracies of the West, in Communist China, and through Thervada Buddhists in Asia.

Conclusion

Atheism sprouted ancient roots in both the East and the West many millenniums ago, but its strongest growth is occurring today. In Asia, the *liar* successfully convinced people to "kill the self" in their pursuit of divinity or distract it with social or natural concerns. In the West, the strategy was to "kill God" by exalting human reason through science and civilization.

But another deception was coming to further pollute the pure and life-giving streams of the River. One more false fork would be placed strategically at the "center of the world"—today's Middle East. The new religion would not kill self or God.

It would kill *people*—in the name of God.

The liar was discouraged. The Chosen One had come to earth and outmaneuvered him. He thought he could tempt him to join the rebellion, but the King had refused, been killed on cross, and had risen! Now the liar knew the Enemy's plan: provide a sacrifice that would melt every vermin heart, then, fill it with his own Spirit!

The thought of it made him sick. He winced to himself: "The Enemy loving and living inside the vermin." How could he have been so stupid? Why couldn't he have stopped the Plan? And now the Chosen One's bride—what he called "The Church"—was taking the Roman world by storm. He hated the term church because it meant "the called out ones." "Called out of our brilliant deceptions," he fumed. It pained him to know that almost half the Roman Empire had left their selfishness and idolatry to follow the Enemy's Prince. And he had heard the Chosen One announce his goal: "Go into all the world and make disciples of all nations." The thought almost made him vomit.

But lately, the Church's growth had slowed down in the center of the earth. The Chosen One's followers were drifting back to things the liar had hoped for—legalism, apathy, and self-seeking. The liar knew he must act quickly. He must light one more fire of deception. He barked to his doting sentries, "Bring in Khalid!" A swarthy demon lord, entered the satanic stronghold. "Yes, my Baal," rasped the archangel of Mesopotamia. "Here are your orders!" bellowed the liar. "Time is short. Convince your people there is one god and no son of God. Give them our vision for taking over the world. Desecrate the holy land. March throughout the earth. Hold nothing back. Those who convert, reward them. Those who don't, simply kill."

Hussein grinned fiendishly. He could already taste the blood on his lips.

Chapter Nine

Warring God

"Make war on them (infidels) until idolatry shall cease and
God's religion shall reign supreme."

Sura 2:193—The Koran

My first visit to a Muslim nation took place decades ago when I landed in
Istanbul, Turkey, with a European tour group. The imposing presence of
mosques and minarets, the piercing yet melancholic "call to prayer" five
times a day, the women scurrying about in head-to-toe Muslim garb, and the
backwardness of the nation compared to others (the cars were twenty years
older than those in Europe)—told me I'd landed in a vastly different world.

Life also seemed chaotic in Istanbul—former Constantinople of the
Byzantine Empire. People acted fearful and distrusting. We needed to "body-
guard" our female members in public because Muslim men cast nodding,
lustful stares and attempted to grope them on public buses or in elevators.
After arriving at our first hotel, we failed to guard our luggage after getting
off the bus—and instantly some bags disappeared into the evening shadows.

This large Muslim nation—once the center of Islamic civilization—
struck me as corrupt, lustful, fearful, thieving nation that was locked in the

backwardness of the past. Yet, Turkey was the freest and most modern of the Muslim nations! If this was freedom, what would bondage look like? In later years I found out when visiting more radical Islamic states.

Islam was the final world religion to emerge in history—very near to where it all began. It views itself as the final link in a chain of prophecy that goes back to Adam. [452] Islam is one of the fastest growing religions in the world—though primarily through birthrate. There are 1.3 billion Muslims (people that possess *islam*). They make up 23 percent of the world's population.

Eighteen percent of Muslims (234 million) reside in Arab nations, and 20 percent (260 million) live in sub-Saharan Africa. There are 55 majority-Muslim nations in the world with Indonesia being the largest (100 million). At least two million Muslims reside in the United States, and significant populations live in Europe, the former USSR, and South America.[453]

Nominal or corrupted biblical faith in the Arabian Peninsula set the stage for the birth of this unique, monotheistic twisting of biblical truth. The collapse of the Roman Empire had left an emptiness and insecurity that nearly invited a new religious power to emerge.

Along came a "prophet" named Muhammad, who declared that "Submission" (*Islam*) formed the essence of true religion. Christian missiologist Don Richardson explains the meaning: "Islam means *submission* . . . submission to God, submission to Muhammad as the ultimate prophet of God, submission to the Koran as the ultimate revelation of God, submission of women to men and submission of everyone to the caliph, sultan, shah, or whichever kind of Muslim ruler is in power."[454] Godly submission *does* create blessing when it is voluntary and motivated by love. This brand, however, would be motivated by a very different spirit.

Islam gained converts, territory, and power through the means of violent military force. There are at least 109 identifiable *war verses* in the Koran, which is Islam's holy book—one out of every fifty-five.[455] George Washington University Professor Seyyed Hossein Nasr says that Islam is the terminal religion of humanity.[456]

He may be right. From the very beginning, the Muslim God was a warring god.

The History of Islam

The story begins with Muhammad (or Mohammed) who was born in Mecca, on the Arabian Peninsula in A.D. 570. Mecca ruled as the city that guarded the *Ka'aba*—a religious shrine sheltering 360 idols that represented the gods the Arabs worshipped. Muhammad was orphaned as a child and raised by an uncle. He never became literate. At an early age, Muhammad became a religious man who was surrounded by idolatry and weak biblical faith.

He married a rich widow named Khadija at the age of twenty-five after working for her caravan business. She was fifteen years his elder. She bore him four daughters, and after he became "the Prophet," Khadija became one of his first converts.[457]

Around 610, Muhammad reportedly had a visitation from an angel named Gabriel who told him to "recite" words he would receive from Allah.[458] Khadija persuaded him that Allah was calling him to be a prophet. He began to assail the idolatry in Mecca, but his strong message of monotheism brought a violent reaction, and he was forced to flee about 280 miles north to the city of Yathrib. This migration, called *Hijra* began in A.D. 622. It is the beginning of the Muslim calendar today.

In Yathrib (the name later changed to Medina—"city of the Prophet"), Muhammad served as an arbiter of disputes. To supplement his income and build his religious following, Muhammad and his followers began plundering traveling caravans (the major form of commerce at that time). In the words of author Ibn Warraq, Mu:

Muhammad was, "no more than the head of a robber community, unwilling to earn an honest living."[459] He drew Arab men into his army by the almost irresistible lure of sex with captured -slave women.[460]

After six years of consolidating power in Medina, Muhammad made a treaty in 628 with the leaders of Mecca, allowing his forces to visit and make pilgrimage. Two years later he broke the treaty by attacking Mecca with an army of ten thousand, who took control of the city, destroyed all the images and idols in the *Ka'aba*, and executed some of the people. Muhammad was now the undisputed political and religious leader of Arabia.[461]

In 632, the tenth year of *Hijra*, Muhammad died. The Koran or Qur'an (The Reading), which had been given to Muhammad over a twenty-two year period, was transcribed forty years after his death. Former Shiite Muslim Reza Safa summarizes the growth of Islam from that point:

> Upon receiving a modified revelation, from "let there be no compulsion in religion" (Sura [Chapter] 2:256) to "kill those who join other gods" (Sura 9:5), many tribes in Arabia could no longer resist Muhammad, but were forced to surrender, convert, and submit to Islam and to Muhammad as its prophet. It was conversion to Islam or death. Islam developed form a small sect into a major Arabian power. One generation later it had become a vast Arab empire, and in another two to three generations, Islam had turned into a cosmopolitan civilization stretching across three continents, absorbing the heritage of many different cultures.[462]

After Muhammad's death, a power struggle ensued among his followers leading to division and warfare among various groups. Different branches or sects arose including the Shia (Shiites) and the Sunni (Sunnites). Abu Bakr, was one of Muhammad's first converts, became the first *caliph* (Muslim leader) and brought all the tribes on the Arabian Peninsula under the rule of Islam. Under Omar, the second caliph, the Muslim armies defeated the Persian and Byzantine armies and launched a bloody expansion that lasted one hundred years.

The Muslim hordes swept through present-day Iraq and Iran and into Central Asia and the Punjab (northwest corner of Pakistan and India). They conquered all the Asian territories of the decaying Roman Empire except modern-day Turkey. Northward they occupied Syria and made Damascus the capital of the Umayyad Dynasty (A.D. 661–750). Then they invaded Egypt and moved across North Africa and into Europe. This "First Jihad"— which Don Richardson calls "the Islamic holocaust"— was stopped when Charles Martel (Charlemagne) defeated the Muslims in the battle of Tours, France, in 732.

The Abbasid caliphate (A.D. 750–1258) thrust Islam into a higher dimension of political power and wealth as the "Dark Ages" descended upon European civilization. Baghdad became the major political and economic center during this period and the Islamic community experienced its only major renaissance in art, education, science, and commerce and law.[463] In 1258, Baghdad fell to the Mongols, though they eventually converted their Mongol and Tatar conquerors and recovered their power by the fifteenth century.

During the fifteenth–eighteenth centuries A.D., Islam expanded into three new empires—the Mughal in India, the Safavieh in Iran, and the Ottoman in Anatolia (Turkey). The Ottoman Empire emerged as the most aggressive of the three, and launched the "Second Jihad," bringing about the fall of Constantinople in 1453—bringing Turkey into its orbit. On September 12, 1683, the Turkish Muslim armies failed once again to capture Vienna. Europe was saved, but the empire lasted until World War I.

The current fifty-five Muslim majority nations were conquered during these centuries of Islamic expansion. Reza Safa states: "Islam has left a fingerprint of blood through every page of its history."[464] The latest version—the "Third Jihad"— began in 1979 with the revival of Wahhabism in Saudi Arabia, the rise of Ayatollah Khomeini in Iran and the new Ali Pasha (Field Marshall) of Islam, Osama bin Laden. The Muslim terrorists who hijacked and flew commercial planes into the World Trade Center and Pentagon on September 11, 2001—killing 3,000 innocent people—followed in the bloody footprints of Muhammad and his followers.

Islam contains three major branches. The Shiites are authority-driven, adhering to the teachings of *imams* and enforcing *al-Shariah* (Divine Law) in personal and social life. Shiites await the return of the Twelfth Imam

(Muslim Messiah-figure) who will bring peace and justice to the world and bring human history to a close.[465] Shiites make up 12 to 13 percent of the Muslim religion and trace their roots to Muhammad's cousin and son-in-law, Ali.

The Sunnis, who make up 87 to 88 percent of all Muslims, emphasize the "consensus" of the written traditions which includes the Koran, Hadith, and the *Sunna* (Customs) from which they derive their name. They also believe in the division of religious and political power. *Sufism* survives as the third mystical wing of Islam—denouncing worldliness, seeing God in all things, and the assimilating of self into the Vast Being of God (a pantheistic version of Islam).[466]

Modern-day jihadists continue Muhammad's struggle to bring about global "submission" to Allah and his prophet.

THE DARKS SIDE OF MOHAMMED'S ISLAM

There is a tendency in the modern world to view all religions in a positive light—to put a "spin" on history that glosses over historical realities. This is especially true of the historical roots and teachings of the Prophet Muhammad. Muslim clerics and apologists often leave out the facts about his life, some of the Koran's controversial teachings, and the means Muslims have used to "convert" the world to Islam. We will highlight some of those glaring omissions here.

We now turn to the secretive, dark side of Mohammed's Islam. Many contemporary Muslims may reject these methods or activities, but since they remain at the core of the Koran's teachings, we must take them seriously until the teachings and/or the Koran itself are repudiated. They continue to impact millions of lives.

Thievery and Kidnapping

During his time in Medina, Muhammad took part in no less than thirty-eight raids on traveling caravans through the area, killing people, seizing plunder, and giving the women as slaves to his men.[467] Muhammad built his empire on thievery, goods, riches, and people. Islam's *Hadith* (Statements) mention a young man who took part in nineteen raids under Muhammad's direct leadership. Other sources claim Muhammad personally led 27 out of 65 military campaigns that he authorized against Jews, Christians, and other Arabs who refused to acknowledge him as a prophet.[468] Muhammad often functioned more as a terrorist than a religious figure/teacher.

Centuries later, the rulers of the Ottoman Empire kidnapped thousands of Christian children to be trained as the Sultan's special guards (*janissaries*).[469] In the twenty-first century, thousands of people are being assassinated and killed by suicide missions in numerous nations. They point back to Muhammad's grandson, Hussein (Lord of the Martyrs), who was murdered in A.D. 680 along with seventy-two people including women and children. From the time of *Hijra,* when Muhammad and his men emigrated from Mecca to Medina—up to this present hour—fear, terror and bloodshed have been the primary strategy of Islam.[470]

Sexual Exploitation

Muhammad and his men appear to have been sex-crazed. The historical record clearly reveals that Muhammad's tactics in recruiting Arab men to his cause involved promises of military prowess, plunder, and sex (women slaves).[471] Historian Maxime Rodison states in her biography of the Prophet: "Muhammad distributed women and girls he captured on raids to be sex slaves for his male followers. He kept some for himself, of course."[472]

But that wasn't all. Five passages in the Koran promise heavenly virgins (*houris*) for the pleasure of Muslim men in Heaven—for all eternity. Unlimited sex on earth and also in heaven! That will draw recruits. A story is told about one of Muhammad's men named Umar Ibn al-Humam, who heard Muhammad promise that martyrs they would have virgins in heaven. Al-Humam shouted, "Fine! Fine! Have I only to get myself killed by these men to enter into paradise? Grasping his sword [he] plunged into the thick of battle and was soon killed."[473]

While Muhammad apparently lived in a monogamous relationship with his first wife, Khadija for twenty-five years, she died three years before he fled to Medina. After that, his sexual appetite grew. He married a child named Aisha at six, and had sex with her at nine. This left him open to charges of pedophilia. He kept adding more wives to his harem, even getting a "special dispensation from Allah:" "O Prophet! Surely to you we had made lawful your wives . . . especially for you (not for the rest of believers . . . You may take to your bed any of them you please" (Sura 33:50, 51).[474] In the end he "bedded" at least twelve wives and two concubines.[475] The pursuit of sex was paramount in Muhammad's personal life and army.

Violence and Murder

Sexual slaves were procured through warfare. While out to rob a caravan near Medina, Muhammad's men encountered 300 fighters from Mecca. His smaller force defeated them, and killed 49 men. One of his fighters threw a severed head at the feet of Muhammad who responded: "It [the severed head] is more acceptable to me than the choicest camel in Arabia."[476] From that time forward, murdering those who refused to convert became Islam's rationalization for terrorism—slaughter a few; reap the conversion of many.[477]

In another confrontation to control the Jewish Banu Qurayza tribe, the people were told to lay down their weapons. Muhammad then ordered that every Jewish man be beheaded. Multiple sources describe Muhammad himself presiding over the beheading of at least 500-900 Jewish men—five at a time. Their bodies were buried in a ditch.[478] Muhammad then seized Rayhana, widow of a Jew he had killed, and forced her to become his concubine. When Muhammad ordered the murder of a dissident poet named Kab ibn al-Ashraf, he told his men: "Kill any Jew you are able to kill."[479] The seeds of anti-Semitism were sown in blood in Medina.

Some Muslims maintain that Islam and Christianity have the same historical record of crusades and the use of violence. There is a huge difference:

Islam was and remains violent because its founding Scriptures *authorize* violence. The Christian crusaders tragically used retaliatory violence and cruelty to reclaim lands lost to the Muslims during the Middles Ages. But to do so, the practitioners had to *violate* their Scriptures. The Koran contains 109 war verses that encourage violence. The New Testament contains none. Let that comparison sink in for a moment.

Abusing Women

From the early days of Islam, women were viewed as "property" to be used and abused by men (including their husbands). Even today, in many Muslim nations, women are forced to stay at home, not go out in public alone, aren't allowed to attend school or pursue careers, and must cover their bodies from head to toe. Muslim women may possess the least human rights of any population segment of the world.[480]

Sometimes Muslim authorities cruelly humiliate women. In July of 2009, 164 Muslim women were sentenced to a public flogging for "crimes" such as wearing pants in public or having sex outside of marriage. Lubna Hussein, a Sudanese journalist was among thirteen women arrested by police at a Sudanese café and charged with violating the country's "decency laws" by wearing pants. She was sentenced to be flogged with forty lashes.

In Sudan, women are lashed for adultery three times more than men. Why? Muslim males escape punishment for extramarital sex by denying the charges. Women who become pregnant after sex find their babies used as evidence against them. In 2006, the Islamic government of the Maldives sentenced 184 people to flogging— 146 were women.[481]

One more example of female abuse will suffice. Jean Sasson, author of *Daughters of Arabia* reports: "Islam's widespread practice of amputating the clitoris and sometimes part or even all of the vulva from the genitalia of Muslim women, affirmed in the *Hadith* by Muhammad himself, most likely traces back to the founder's deliberate abuse of sex to lure pagan males into his cult."[482] This was done to suppress the female sex drive so men could more easily use and abuse them without their arousal. This prolonged the men's orgiastic ecstasies."

Abuse of women remains a major problem in nearly all Muslim societies.

Expanding Slavery

Muslims are also the world's greatest practitioners of slavery—both past and present. The word "slave" derives from *Slav*—when the ancient Romans captured Eastern Europeans and sold them throughout the Roman Empire. Rodney Stark points out in *For the Glory of God* that the explosive growth of Christianity during the first three centuries of the Church not only brought fifty percent of the Roman Empire to faith in Christ, but it also practically eliminated the power and presence of slavery for hundreds of years.[483]

It was the Muslim traders who "brought slavery back" by force-marching perhaps a million African slaves 1200 miles through the Sahara Desert to sell in North African slave bazaars from the eighth century A.D. onward. Their example, and its economic benefits, "revived" the practice of slavery in Europe in the 1600s as European civilization imitated the Muslim traders to keep up financially.

During this time, and up to the present, the Koran stood on the side of the slave owners because Muhammad himself owned slaves. Others followed suit. For every African slave brought to the United States (prior to the Civil War and Emancipation), many more were abducted to Muslim North Africa, Arabia, and the Middle East. Islam is the only major religion to condone and sanction slavery today.

Here's an interesting mystery. Thirty million descendants of black slaves reside in America. Where are the possible 300 million descendants of African slaves that should be living in North Africa and the Middle East? The dirty secret is that Muslim slavers usually *castrated* black males so stop them from having sex with Muslim and black women whom the traders wanted for their own pleasures. The Koran sanctions the practice (Suras 23:5 and 70:30). There are few blacks in North Africa today, but there are tens of millions of *brown-skinned Haratin* people who are descendants of Arab fathers and black mothers. Mauritania alone is reported to have one million Haratin.[484]

Islam stands out in history as the world's greatest human trafficker. It is the *only* religion—in countries like Sudan—that allows the practice today

Promoting Jihad—the War Verses in the Koran

The most evil aspect of Islam remains the teachings of *jihad* (exertion in the way of God). There are 109 verses in the Koran, from *suras* (chapters) 2 to 73, which condone the killing of others (infidels) for the cause.[485] A few verses mention war in self-defense, but the majority involves what Muslims view as the two "camps" of the world: "The House of Islam" and the "House of War." If you reject Islam, then you are *attacking* Islam and that makes you an enemy of Muhammad, Islam, and even God—so war against you is justified.

Here are three examples from the Koran: "Seize them and put them to death wherever you find them" (Sura 4:89). "Believers, make war on the infidels who dwell around you" (Sura 9:123). "When you meet unbelievers in the battlefield, strike off their heads and, when you have laid them low, bind your captives firmly" (Sura 47:4).

Historian Bat Ye'or describes the horrors of early Islam: "The Arab conquest was accompanied by tremendous destruction . . . entire towns, innumerable villages given over to pillage, and fire, to massacres, slavery and deportation of populations."[486] Over time, Ye'or explains that a "method" of jihad was formulated:

> The general basic principles according to the Koran are as follows: the pre-eminence of Islam over all other religions (Koran 9:33); Islam is the true religion of Allah (3:17) and it should reign over all mankind (34:27); the *umma* [Muslim community] forms the party of Allah and is perfect (3:106), having been chosen above all peoples on earth, it

187

alone is qualified to rule, and thus elected by Allah to guide the world (35:37). The purpose of jihad, until this goal will be achieved, is an obligation (8:40) . . . [Other] peoples have the choice between war or submission to the *umma*, whereas idolaters are forced to convert to Islam or be killed . . . Either the individual or the tribe would convert to Islam . . . or conversion was replaced by the payment of a tribute."[487]

Despite their propensity for destruction, over time, the Muslim conquerors levied a severe tribute or poll tax (*jizya*) on conquered peoples instead of just killing them. Why? Dead people don't pay taxes—so murder gave way to financial gain. The "newly submissive converts" became known as *dhimmis* (non-Muslims).

The killing continued for centuries. It became the rationale for slaughtering one million Armenian Christians in the early 1900s. Sura 8:12-13 commands, "Strike off their heads. Strike off their fingertips! because they defied God and his Apostle."

Osama bin Laden used a similar rationale when he sent suicide bombers in hijacked airplanes on September 11, 2001, and killed 3,000 innocent Americans. They perished because they were a part of the "House of War." Yet, Muslim terrorists say they simply use the same tactics of the Christian crusaders in their killing sprees. Regretfully, the crusaders performed some horrible acts of violence during the Middle Ages. However, the analogy falls flat. Crusader atrocities *contradicted* the teachings of Jesus. Muslim atrocities *followed* the commands of Muhammad.

THE TRUTH MUST BE SHARED

I've focused on Islam's "dark areas" because Muslim scholars attempt to cover up the history. For example, while researching the Islam, I read George Washington University professor Seyyed Hossein Nasr's respected summary of "Islam" in *World Religions: The Seven World Religions Intro-*

duced By Preeminent Scholars from Each Tradition. Dr. Nasr is an author of a number of books and served as a professor at Tehran University in Iran and Temple University in the United States. His contribution in *World Religions* runs 105 pages.

Yet, in his presentation, he glowingly describes the prophet Muhammad as "the perfect man par excellence" who represents "perfect submission to Allah"— "the ideal model of human behavior."[488] He makes *no mention* of Muhammad being a robber baron in Medina, rewarding his band of thieves with sex slaves and concubines, marrying a six-year-old and having sex with her when she was nine, the vicious slaughter of the Banu Qurayza Jews, the betrayal of Mecca, or his leading numerous murdering, plundering raids. If Muhammad is the "ideal model of human behavior," then we all should become lust-driven terrorists! Wouldn't that make a wonderful, moral, and peaceful world?

Dr. Nasr also *rewrites history* when he states that "contrary to popular Western conceptions, [Islam] was not forced upon the people by the sword . . . Islam spread peacefully among the Turks of central Asia" and "spread peacefully" elsewhere.[489] That's a lie—or gross ignorance. Islam gained the majority of its territories by *terror*—either bloodshed or forced tribute. He also makes no mention of slavery, the subjection of women, or Islam's goal of global conquest. If Islam is to be considered as a viable worldview, the truth must be told.

Now we turn to the central beliefs of those who follow the God of war.

Islam's Five Pillars of Action

Five practices are required for faithful Muslims. They include:

1. The Confession (*shahadah*): To believe in one's heart that there is no God but Allah and to acknowledge that Muhammad is his Messenger. Making this confession of faith is all that is required to become a Muslim.[490]

2. Prayers (*salah*): Muslims should pray seventeen cycles of prayer a day, spread out over five time periods, ideally facing Mecca.

189

They can pray either individually or corporately. Friday at the mosque is the only required corporate meeting.[491]

3. Fasting during Ramadan (*sawm*): Ramadan is a month-long period of fasting and devotional activities during the daylight hours only in commemoration of Muhammad's receiving the Koran during the ninth lunar month of Ramadhan. During the fast, Muslims must abstain from eating, drinking, smoking and sex.[492]

4. Giving to the Poor (*zakat*): Muslims are commanded to give one-for-tieth of their income (2.5 percent) primarily to the poor and needy.[493]

5. Pilgrimage to Mecca (*hajj*): Every Muslim must make a trip to Mecca at least once during their lifetime, provided they are able with respect to health and finances. Each pilgrim must wear a white garment called *ihram*. The *hajj* normally takes a week.[494]

Many scholars believe that *jihad* (striving), more often called "holy war," comprises the sixth pillar of Islam. Don Richardson believes that radical Islam has only one genuine pillar—*jihad*. He warns, "The so-called five pillars of Islam, by comparison with radical Islam's jihad, are merely five little candles flickering atop Islam's primary pillar—the political one. The five little candles add a nicely distracting religious décor, but little more."[495]

In historical truth and context, Islam is a religion of deception, violence, and indignity to women. It supports fanatical behavior, operates by theocratic legalism and encourages poor stewardship of the earth. Islam condones slavery, and contains little freedom and hope for over one billion people.

Now let's look at the questions Islam must answer to be taken seriously as a worldview.

QUESTIONS ISLAM MUST ANSWER
• God—Who's in Charge?
  Strict monotheism—one God— is the main tenet of Islam. Allah is the Absolute, the Infinite, the Perfect Good, Pure Being, the Beyond Being, and the Supreme Reality of the Muslim faith. He is not personally

knowable by human beings.[496] Muslims make a special point to state that Allah is by himself, has no son, and no Trinity exists. To say that God is a trinity or has partners is the gravest sin. Allah is known by many names which include Rabb (Lord), Rahnam (Beneficent), Rahim (Merciful), and Malik (Master).[497]

- Source—Is the Guidebook Reliable?

Muslims recognize four Holy Books including the Jewish Torah (*Tawrat*), the Old Testament Psalms (Zabur), the Gospel of Jesus (*Injil*), and the Koran (*Qur'an*). Only the Koran remains uncorrupted. The Koran or Qur'an (The Reading) contains 114 suras (chapters) and 6,151 verses. Don Richardson warns, "We must ask ourselves: Are we talking about a book of peace or Muhammad's *Mein Kampf?*"[498] Edward Gibbon, author of the *Decline and Fall of the Roman Empire*, remarked:

> [The Koran is an] incoherent rhapsody of fable and precept and declamation which seldom excites a sentiment or idea . . . The use of fraud and perfidy (treachery), of cruelty and injustice, were often subservient to the propagation of the faith . . . Mohammed commanded or approved the assassination of Jews . . . abused the claims of a prophet . . . The female sex, without reserve, was abandoned to his desires.[499]

The Koran is supposed to be read in Arabic only, but Arabs make up only about 20 percent of the Arab world—so this leaves millions of Muslims without clear knowledge of its teachings.[500] Sunni Muslims also accept the *Hadith* which purport to be holy traditions, sayings, and actions of Mohammed and his followers.

- Origins—How Did We Get Here?

Allah created the universe out of nothing. He is before creation, and does not need anything in creation—though he has made his existence evident within creation. Humans only create secondarily from what Allah has created (Sura 45:3-5, 21:33).[501] Muslims reject the theory of evolution, believing that men and women did not ascend from lower forms of life but have descended from on high from a divine proto-type.[502]

- Organization—What's the Structure?

  Allah is the supreme arbitrary ruler. There are good angels and fallen ones—demons (*jinn*)—who are even capable of having sex with the *houris* (Sura 55:74). According to former Shiite Muslim, Reza Safa, the goal of Islam is to produce a theocracy with Allah as the ruler of society with no separation between church and state. This society would have no democracy, no free will, and no freedom of expres-sion.[503] According to the Koran, Allah has sent a prophet to every nation to preach there is one God. 124,000 prophets were sent, according to tradition.[504]

- Human Beings—What is Their Nature and Calling?

  Human beings are good by nature,[505] have dignity, but are *not* made in God's image since God's nature and man's nature are completely dif-ferent. Allah made the first human beings from the dust of the earth (Sura 15:26) and breathed life into them. Humans are God's vicegerents on earth[506] and were created to live in unconditional sur-render to the will of Allah.[507]

- Morality—What's the Basis of Right and Wrong?

  Right and wrong is determined by the edicts of Allah as revealed in the Koran. Each person has two angels assigned to him, one to record the person's good deeds, and the other to record the bad deeds.[508] Muslims view their task on earth as repaying their debt to God which involves the whole of their lives. Their bodies and lives belong to God and are not their own.[509] The *Shariah* or Divine Law of Islam (The Road) shows Muslims what Allah wants them to do in this life to gain happi-ness and in paradise to come.[510]

- Sin—Why is the World a Mess?

Muslims do not believe in Original Sin and say that the concept of human beings in rebellion against heaven is a Western conception.[511] Humans do not have sinful natures. People are sinless until they rebel against Allah. People should not behave according to their lower (animal) nature. Instead, they should use their wills to act in total submission to Allah.[512]

- Salvation—How Can the World Be Made Right?

A person may be saved if their good deeds outweigh the bad deeds. Salvation is based on human effort. [513] "Islam . . . has no redeemer, no mediator, and no forgiveness guarantor. Under Islam, every human defendant in God's court must face the ultimate judge without the help of an advocate. Hence, under Islam, there can be no assurance regarding one's eternal destiny."[514]

Individuals *may* be saved (especially men) through practicing the five pillars. The world as a whole can only be made right through submission to Allah and world conquest. Islam follows Nazism, fascism, and communism as the world's latest religion of force.

According to missiologist Don Richardson, Islam, by design, is the only religion in the world that contains *no* redemptive analogies.

- Earth—How Should Human Beings Look at the Earth?

Muslims view creation care as secondary to submission to Allah. The Koran says very little—outside of the war verses—about man's role on earth in developing planet earth. This is major reason why many Muslim nations are poor, backward, or undeveloped. Islam carries little vision for man's stewardship of creation.[515]

- Heaven—Is There a Future and a Hope?

The Angel of Death comes to take possession of a person's soul at death and takes them to a place where two angels interrogate the person about their life and the doctrines of Islam. Much later, at the time of Judgment, every departed soul will be given a resurrection body before Allah announces his verdict upon them—either everlasting torment or paradise.[516]

Paradise/Heaven amounts to an enormous God-owned bordello in the sky where, especially martyrs, will find a host of virgins called *houris* who forever satisfy their sexual cravings (Koran 38:51, 44:54, 55:55074, and 56:22, 34-36).[517] On the other hand, the Koran has an obsession with the threat of hell—one in every 7.9 verses (as opposed to one in every 120 verses in the New Testament.[518]

The Shiite Muslims await the return of the twelfth *Imam* (spiritual leader) called the *Mohammed al Mahdi* who will appear along with Jesus Christ.[519]

THE TRUTH TEST AND ISLAM

Is Islam clear and simple? Renowned German scholar Gerd R. Puin states that "The Koran claims for itself that it is *mubeen"* or "clear." But if you look at it [in the original Arabic] you will notice that every fifth sentence or so simply doesn't make sense . . . The fact is that a fifth of the Koranic text is *just incomprehensible.* This is what caused the tradition anxiety regarding translation."[520]

Islam's central message of "one God" rang clear during a time of diverse Arabian polytheism and nominal biblical faith. The five pillars are simple and straight-forward, though difficult to meet, and do not necessarily apply to women.

Is Islam reasonable? Islam makes sense if you believe in force, not freedom. In terms of a reasonable understanding of Islam's origins, Reza Safa states: "The spirit that raised Baal worship in Phoenicia and Canaan, and later in Babylon, is the same spirit that raised Islam in Arabia."[521] Allah appears very similar to Baal in his demand to be "master of all" by force. Islam's connection to immorality is also eerily similar to Baal worship. Baal was often linked with the goddess Astoreth or Ishtar (Judges 2:13) which plunged many societies into sexual obsession and perversion.

Is Islam based on evidence? The historical evidence for Mohammed, and the birth and expansion of Islam, is well chronicled in history. Hundreds of writings, from the Koran to the Hadith, tell the story of the Muslim faith, its tenets and its practices. However, that evidence also reveals a religion of violence and force that emanates from a God of war.

Does conscience testify to the truth of Islam? Not in areas of freedom, liberty, grace, love, and morality. In sexual matters, Mohammed's sexual appetite, pursued through twelve wives and concubines, created a problem with "common conscience," even among the sexually promiscuous early Muslim culture. Accordingly, the standard had to be lowered by direct edicts from Allah that gave coverings to his escapades. Don Richardson states: "Moderate Muslims can be commended for living on a much higher ethical plane than the so-called prophet."[522]

Does Islam speak of eternity? Islam teaches the immortality of the soul, and the *Koran* contains numerous statements about heaven (paradise) and, especially, the reality of hell for all infidels (unbelievers). The main difference between the Muslim and biblical heaven is the Islamic focus on sex liaisons with *houris* as opposed to an eternal love relationship with God.

Is Islam universal? Muslim professor Seyyed Hossein Nasr states: [The] primordial character of the Islamic message is reflected not only in its essentiality, universality, and simplicity but also in its inclusive attitude toward the religions and forms of wisdom that preceded it."[523] As the latest of the major religions, Islam suggests that former monotheists could be saved by Allah, but the incorruptible "final" teaching of the Koran—teaching submission to Allah and his prophet, Muhammad—remains the true way of salvation. Islam is a global religion, but remains small in the 144 non-Muslim-majority nations of the world.

Conclusion

The religion of Islam is a major force in our world today. At the heart of the Islamic faith lies the belief—actually the *duty*—of every Muslim to use force if necessary to advance the cause of Allah. Koran 2:193 and 8:40 state clearly: "Make war on them (infidels) until idolatry shall cease and God's religion shall reign supreme."

One of the greatest indicators that Islam is built on force and control is this fact: not *one* true democracy exists among the fifty-five Muslim-majority nations of the world. They operate largely as controlled societies where force is the means and global conquest the goal of the warring God.

Section Three

THE RIVER IS RISING

Chapter Ten

Comparisons

"It is serious folly to assume that all religions are leading people toward God by their own paths . . . The religions are one instrument that Satan, the "father of lies," uses to keep people from the only Savior."[5]

We have carefully examined the history and beliefs of the world's five religious worldviews. I have proposed that each of the thousands of religious expressions that exist in the world falls under one of the five major concepts of God. Let's review the five worldviews and the type of "religion" they generate:

1. Loving God—producing a religion of grace.
2. Many Gods—producing a religion of fear.
3. All is God—producing a religion of despair.
4. No God—producing a religion of men.
5. Warring God—producing a religion of force.

The following chart compares the main elements of the five religious worldviews:

AREAS	Loving God	Many Gods	All is God	No God	Warring God
God	Loving God Personal/ Infinite Triune	Many gods Personal/ Finite	All is God (Brahman) Impersonal/ Infinite	No God Men become God	Warring Go Personal/ Infinite
Source	Bible Conscience	Myths Legends	The Vedas Upanishads	Reason Human laws	Koran Hadith
Origins	Creator	creators	evolution	evolution	Creator
Human Beings	Made in God's image Material/ Immaterial. Created good but fallen	Made in image of gods	Part of creation	Animal Matter only	Created good- Material/ Immaterial
Sin	Fallen	Mixed	No such thing	Relative	Exists
Salvation	Faith in Christ (God) "Only God can save us"	Works "Appeasing gods may save us"	Oneness "Evolving consciousness may save us"	Self- improvement "Progress will save us"	Works "Good works may save us"
Earth	Steward/ Develop	At mercy of earth's elements	Part of cosmos including earth	Consume Radical environmen- talism	Unimportant
Future	Heaven/Hell	Unknown	Continuum	World Super-state Star Trek	Paradise/ Hell Unsure
Distortion	————————	Nature Angels & demons	Creation	Denial of God	God-Trinity- Faith - Jesus
Forms	(Yahwehism) (Judaism) Catholic Protestant Orthodox	Sumerians Mesopotamia Hinduism Zoroastrianism Jainism Buddhism	Hinduism Taoism Shinto Sikhism Bahai Gaia/New Age	Confucianis Secular Humanism Fascism Communism	Shia Sunni Sufi

COMPARING THE FIVE WORLDVIEWS OR CONCEPTS OF GOD

Now let's summarize each religion from the chart above and analyze its strengths and weaknesses. Our analysis will include "The Questions Each Worldview Must Answer" and how each one fares on the "Truth Test" (discussed in Chapter Three).

Let's begin with the strengths and weaknesses of faith in a *loving God*.

LOVING GOD — THE RELIGION OF GRACE

Strengths of Belief in a Loving God

Biblical faith teaches there is a triune God whose essence is love. God (Father, Son, and Holy Spirit) is personal, holy, pure, filled with every kind of goodness in an infinite degree, and is the source and example of all loving relationships. We learn about the loving God from the Bible, view his character and power through nature, and his moral characteristics resonate in the human conscience. The Godhead created the universe and all that exists.

God made man in his image with the ability of mind, emotions, and will. Man's spiritual dimension (spirit and soul) dwells in man's body and separates from it at death. Human beings have sinned and fallen short of God's standards. No amount of works or good deeds can bridge the gap between God's holiness and man's sin. Man can only be restored to relationship with God by *faith*—trusting in God's atonement for sin through the sacrificial death of Jesus Christ.

While on earth, believers in the loving God should use their gifts and talents to develop and improve the earth. Upon physical death, those who have trusted God to save them will enjoy an eternity of loving relationships with God and his people in heaven. Those who reject God's offer of grace will spend eternity in hell—away from his presence and grace. Saved (restored) human beings are privileged to take God's message of forgiveness to all people in the world.

Robert E. Hume served as professor of the History of Religions at Union Theological Seminary in New York. In his book, *The World's Living Religions*, he lists nine different strengths of biblical faith: 1) The concept of God as a loving, holy Father, 2) The character, teachings, and sacrifice of God's Son, Jesus Christ, 3) The presence of the Holy Spirit, providing for progress, 4) Teaching concerning God's kingdom, 5) The concept that death doesn't stop the development of human life, 6) A distinctive Scripture (The Bible), 7) A practical response to suffering, 8) A civilizing influence and 9) great missionary activity.[524]

Biblical faith gave rise to the birth of universities of higher learning in Europe, gave impetus to the development of science in the West, created the foundation for republican and democratic governments, and helped define unalienable human rights. The biblical worldview served as the engine of the Reformation, the Industrial Revolution, the development of capitalism and the creation of the middle class in many nations.

Followers of Jesus started the first hospitals, gave birth to the nursing profession, championed civil and women's rights, and continue to lead in mercy efforts and humanitarian aid around the world. Global missions have made significant contributions to political and economic development in Africa, Latin America, and Asia over the past two hundred years.

For over two thousand years, the religion of love has been the single greatest contributor to progress and prosperity among the nations of the world.

Questions and the Truth Test for a Loving God
Belief in a loving God provides clear responses to the "Questions That Every Worldview Must Answer."

- *God* - A triune loving God is in charge of the universe. The human desire to love and be loved makes sense and originates in a God who demonstrates that love.
- *Sourcebook* - The Bible is the world's most reputable religious sourcebook. Its histories are accurate, its poetry unsurpassed, its fulfilled prophecies have no equal, and its literary quality is superb. The stunning beauty and accuracy of the Bible remains one of the greatest testimonies to the truth of biblical faith.

- *Origins* - God created the world *ex nihilo* (out of nothing). The only other viable option is evolution—and the evidence for its validity remains unverified.
- *Structure* - God's multi-faceted kingdom over animate and inanimate creation involving both sovereignty and free will, gives clarity to how the cosmos operates. The presence of angels and demons answers many questions related to the presence of the supernatural. Both God's sovereignty and human free will make history and human action understandable.
- *Man* - Man's two-part being accounts for near-death experiences. The dignity of man as made in God's image has fueled education, science, business and technology, civil governments, and human rights for centuries. The biblical worldview stands as the primary fountain of progress in history.
- *Morality* - God's moral character and laws give clear understanding of right and wrong. His law of love resonates with the human conscience and forms the basis of most human laws in the world's most just, free, and safe societies.
- *Sin* - Man's fallen state—unique to the five worldviews—gives great insight into the problem of sin and evil. Sin *is* the reason the world is a mess.
- *Salvation* - Salvation comes from God through his sacrificial atonement. Human beings respond in humble faith. People cannot save themselves. A loving God can.
- *Earth* - Biblical faith produces a respect for the earth—and desire to steward and improve it. The greatest advances in human technological development and conservation of the earth have come from nations operating out of a biblical worldview.
- *Heaven* - Since human beings are immortal, those who are reconciled to God will share eternal love and relationship together with him in heaven. Those who don't will be separated from the glories of heaven—in an eternal abode known as hell.

Faith in a loving God also gets a high grade on the "Truth Test." Its message is clear and simple. It is reasonable because God's existence and ways make sense. Biblical faith is based on vast historical and rational evidence. There is a clear witness of conscience, both to God's existence and moral laws. It describes relationships and realities that meet the eternal time test. And biblical faith in a loving God has expressions in all eras of time and every part of the world.

Weaknesses of Belief in a Loving God

Hume lists five weaknesses of biblical faith, but they all relate to human failures: relapsing, forgetting, failing to practice, abusing, or perverting God's revelations.[524] Those failures are due to sin and human imperfections—which is actually a strong point in the worldview. Many atheists fault biblical faith for lack of supernatural evidence.[525] But God *has* revealed himself personally in history on numerous occasions (think the nation of Israel and the coming of Jesus), or through angels—and those experiences did not necessarily elevate faith. God is a humble being who possesses no personal need of egotistical manifestation (as earthly leaders do), and has designed his kingdom for the humble who are willing to seek and find him (Acts 17:27).

Some believe the doctrine of the trinity poses a weakness in biblical faith. How can God be one but yet three? On the other hand, the reality of a triune God gives real meaning to the concept of love. A singular God would have nothing to love or even a reason to love. The Triune God *demonstrates* love (1 John 4:8) in the way the Father, Son, and Holy Spirit relate to each other, and created other moral beings to enter into their fellowship. The trinity remains a *mystery*—but one that answers the question of love.

Now we must analyze the strengths and weaknesses of belief in *many gods*.

MANY GODS — THE RELIGION OF FEAR

Strengths of Belief in Polytheism

Polytheism—the belief in many gods—has taken many forms over thousands of years, with animism (folk religions) being its largest expression today. The many gods of polytheism are usually personal, but finite. We find writings about them mostly in the myths and legends of ancient cultures—not books that claim revelation.

The gods of polytheism are very similar to human beings—both in good and evil—leading to the conclusion that "man is made in the image of the gods." The concept of sin is vague or mixed, with the gods often sinning as much as people. Salvation comes through "appeasing" the gods, primarily by sacrifices and acts of devotion. Since many polytheistic gods are associated with nature, there is a sense that humankind lives at the "mercy of nature," incapable of harnessing and developing it. The future in polytheism is varied, and probably as unknown as the gods themselves.

Hume lists a few strengths in the religious worldview of polytheism: 1) Reverence for the supernatural present in nature, 2) An affinity between humans and the divine, 3) Reverence for beauty as integral to religion, and 4) Loyalty to the superior—the soul of religion.[526]

Questions and the Truth Test in Polytheism

Belief in numerous or many gods, often associated with nature, provides little help with the "Questions That a Worldview Must Answer:"

- *God* - Many gods vie for power and supremacy to control and influence the world.
- *Sourcebook* - Myths and legends do not make good sources upon which to build your life.
- *Origins* - Most polytheistic cultures possess creator gods, but the stories of creation are usually fanciful and don't measure up to the findings of science.
- *Morality* - Standards of morality can vary from vicious headhunters to pious monks.

- *Structure* - The structure of the universe is a war of the gods (reflecting life on earth?)
- *Man* - Man is good and bad like the deities he worships.
- *Sin*—It depends on which god you consult or worship.
- *Salvation* - Consists of keeping the gods happy by sacrifice and behavior.
- *Earth* - The earth is something to be feared and appeased—not improved and developed.
- *Heaven*—There are many scenarios, but essentially, the future is unknown.

Polytheism also fails the "Truth Test." It is anything but clear and simple, and though it is reasonable to believe in supernatural powers, it is unreasonable to project them onto nature. Polytheism lacks verifiable evidence, and due to the abundance of gods, the moral standards vary greatly. Belief in many gods can boast of broad animistic acceptance, but offer little hope or encouragement for either an earthly or eternal future.

Weaknesses in the Belief in Many Gods
Hume lists numerous problems with belief in many gods including: 1) The inherent confusion and competition in polytheism, 2) Primitive animism, which is unsuited to science, 3) The many myths about deities, 4) No deity worthy of emulating, 5) Lack of clear concept of right and wrong, 6) No intrinsic value in human beings, 7) Generally no clear founders to organize and inspire, 8) Sparse history of noble human examples, 9) No magnificent goal for human society, 10) No glorious hope of a future life, 11) Not much help available from the deities, and 12) No lasting civilization-producing movements.[527]

Polytheism contains many reasons to doubt its veracity. That many civilizations, such as the Greeks and Egyptians, abandoned its tenets hundreds of years ago speaks to the primitiveness and incompleteness of the worldview. Yet, the prevalence of animism today shows its staying power and connection to the spiritual world—even if its explanation of that world is lacking.

Now let's turn to the Hindu-based religion of pantheism—that *all* is God.

ALL IS GOD - THE RELIGION OF DESPAIR
Strengths of Belief in Pantheism

Pantheism originated as a religion of India called Hinduism, and includes Gaia worship and the New Age movement in other parts of the world. Pantheists believe that everything in the universe is Brahman, an impersonal and infinite force. The Vedas, Upanishads, and other ancient Hindu writings form the basis for the teachings and rituals of Hinduism.

Hindu writings contain polytheistic creation myths as well as the assumption of a timeless and evolutionary cosmology. Man is basically good and an extension of Brahman, but the illusion and consciousness of man's self-ego keeps him from fulfillment. Sin does not really exist—only ignorance. The solution is to detach oneself from the ego and seek to be aware of one's unity with Brahman through one's own effort. "Evolving consciousness may save us."

Human beings are simply a part of all that exists, including life on earth, with no incentive to change or improve it. The future holds continuous and possibly infinite reincarnations until Oneness or Nirvana is achieved by the few.

Hume lists the following strengths in the worldview of pantheism: 1) Belief in one supreme, omnipresent, spiritual reality underlying all phenomena, 2) Belief in a knowledge of and union with the divine as life's goal, 3) Belief in the solidarity of society into which one is born which is superior to the individual, 4) Religion permeates the life of its followers, and 5) Ability to hold together so many groups for centuries by means of a common religion.[528]

Questions and the Truth Test in Pantheism

Hinduism (pantheism) gives mostly confusing or incomplete answers to the great questions of life:

- *God* - The concept of God (Brahman) is vague and undefined and contains no personal or moral nature. No one is really in charge of the universe.
- *Sourcebook* - Hinduism contains extensive ancient writings, but they lack cohesion and sometimes contradict each other. They appear to be a collection of speculations rather a source of unified truth.
- *Origins* - Pantheism reveals no theory of our origins other than creation myths. In more recent pantheistic expressions, what *is* has always been.
- *Structure* - Since the universe or divine (Brahman) is Oneness, then, no structure or order operates in the cosmos except the concept of unity.
- *Man* - Human beings are basically good, both spiritual and material beings, but ignorant of their oneness with Brahman. Man's calling is eternal oneness (Nirvana).
- *Morality* - there is no basis for right and wrong in pantheism, or a clear concept of sin.
- *Sin* - The world is a mess because of man's ignorance of his true oneness with Brahman.
- *Salvation* - Human beings overcome their ignorance and focus on the illusions of life through dying to self and merging into the divine.
- *Earth* - Life and is illusory and unimportant. Nothing should be done to change it.
- *Heaven* - There is little hope for most people—continuous reincarnations for the masses— and eventual Nirvana for the few who achieve Oneness.

Pantheism as a worldview clearly fails the Truth Test. It writings and teachings are anything but clear, and its "simplicity" lies solely in its nebulous and virtually unachievable concept of Oneness. Though Hinduism contains extensive writings, their diverse and contradictory nature bespeaks of a religion without evidence or a center. Pantheism also fails the witness of conscience test by being a "do-it-yourself" religion. There are no absolute standards of right and wrong. Hinduism points all people toward eternal conscious union with Brahman, but, by and large, its popularity is limited to India, and it contains little universal appeal.

Weaknesses in the Belief in that All is God
Hume's list of weaknesses that plague the Hindu/pantheistic worldview runs quite long: 1) No personal character or moral responsibility in the Supreme Being, 2) No permanent worth or moral ideal for the human individual, 3) No universal moral standard except social distinctions (caste system), 4) No possible improvement in person's social status until death, 5) No improvements in society as a result of the religion, 6) The dependence on empty meditation and ceremonial ritual, 7) The gross polytheistic idolatry that goes against the pantheistic teachings, 8) The castes system's inertia and divisiveness, 9) The low status of women (except in the *Bhagavad Gita*), 10) Lack of vision for the rest of the world, 11) No admirable historic figures, and 12) Lack of accessibility of the Vedas to most people.[529]

The failure of the Hindu/pantheistic worldview to inspire faith in its people, create hope for the future, and motivate people to develop and improve the earth is the greatest evidence against this ancient religion. Whereas India should be one of the most developed and progressive nations on earth, its historic poverty testifies to the dominance of this religion of despair which handcuffs its people through the caste system. Do-it-yourself morality and Oneness with an undefined Force is a tragic combination for individuals and societies. It is a blessing that Hinduism's influence remains localized—so as not to bring bondage to other peoples on earth.

Next we must turn to the strengths and weaknesses of belief in *no God.*

NO GOD - THE RELIGION OF MEN

Strengths of Belief in Atheism

Atheism/secularism is a religion due to its "binding commitment" to man being the final authority in life. The practical effect of this worldview is for strong leaders or elites to arise in the place of God to protect and provide for the masses. Atheism has the writings of scientists and philosophers in the West as its source of truth and Buddhist philosophy in the East. Western atheism exalts reason, and Buddhism, annihilates it.

Atheism believes the cosmos originated by accident through natural selection over billions of years. Everything we see is accidental and un-planned with man being the highest form of evolved animal life. It is pos-sible that space aliens began our portion of the cosmos—the theory of panspermia—at least according to Richard Dawkins and Francis Crick. [530]

There is no such thing as sin in atheism—men decide individually, or through totalitarian regimes, what is right or wrong. Morality is relative. Either self-improvement (the West) or self-extinction (Buddhism) is the means of salvation. In Western atheism "progress (especially in science) will save us." Many atheistic nations, such as those under fascist or com-munist ideologies, care little for earth's stewardship and act as consumers. Socialist nations (usually with a biblical heritage, such as Norway and Den-mark) use radical environmentalism as a means of population control and being stewards of the earth.

Death is the end of existence for atheists since all is matter, and no spirit or soul exists. The atheist version of Heaven is an earthly utopia, or a Star Wars-like planetary civilization in the future.

Robert Hume doesn't list atheism/secularism as a living religion, but I suggest the following possible strengths: 1) An appreciation for science and natural processes with a focus on empirical data for understanding the world, 2) Up-lifting the dignity and use of human reason, 3) The evidence of *micro*-evolution over time, 4) A belief in progress through human reason and invention, 5) The emphasis of the environmental movement to protect and steward the planet, 6) A focus on human rights and fair laws in secular societies, and 7) The desire for global harmony through a global world system of government.

In the West, by celebrating the dignity of human reason, atheism encourages the creative use of the mind for meeting human needs and developing the earth. The desire for world peace and prosperity through a one-world government is a laudable goal in a world scarred by war and deep poverty.

Questions and the Truth Test in Atheism

Many atheists or secularists appear to have noble ends for man's purposes on earth, but their misdiagnosis of human nature stands out as the crucial flaw that impacts atheism's solutions. It does not fare well in either the "Questions" or "Truth Test" that a valid worldview must answer.

- *God*—Without a supreme authority, powerful men usually arise as "gods" in atheistic cultures. The "God-void" must be filled. It usually creates human tyrants.
- *Sourcebook*—Atheism has no guidebook other than reason—which changes, as is often true with the progression of scientific discoveries. Human opinions are a weak foundation upon which to build a culture.
- *Origins*—Macro-evolution sounds like a good idea, but it cannot be proven by science and it goes against some of the natural laws. Primitive elements do not produce complex organisms—no matter how long the "time." In evolutionary theory, time appears to be the smokescreen that secularists hide behind. They say that given enough time, anything can happen. There is *no* evidence for this unscientific idea.
- *Structure*—There *is* none in the universe except human force. Atheism usually produces tyrannical governments that control people's lives.
- *Man*—Human beings are good, not fallen—and simply made of physical particles. Atheism has no answers for the reality of super-

natural miracles and evidence for life after death. Man should use his reason to develop and improve the world.

- *Morality*—There is no basis for right and wrong except what the tyrant or elite decide. Every person does what is right in his or her own eyes.
- *Sin*—It is completely relative to the individual or determined by the ruler. Intrinsic human rights do not exist in secular atheism-based societies.
- *Salvation*—Takes place through human improvement, science and technology.
- *Earth*—Atheists either destroy the planet (Stalin, Mao) or promote environmentalism.
- *Heaven*—It must be created on earth or in space by enlightened men or space aliens.

Atheism/secularism brings mixed results on the Truth Test. It is clear and simple in its belief that man is the measure of all things, but this clarity appears overly simplistic when dealing with supernatural phenomena. It is reasonable to use the mind for the purposes of human progress, but totally unreasonable in certain categories such as blind faith in macro-evolution and culpable credulity in the goodness of man.

Atheists rely on empirical evidence for their theories, but ignore all evidence outside of materialistic assumptions. No witness of conscience exists in atheist societies where behavior is controlled by strong rulers. Atheism is short-lived—no life is eternal. We die like dogs. As a worldview, its universality is increasing via the growing acceptance of macro-evolution and the trust in human scientific discovery to provide for the needs of man.

Weaknesses in Atheism
Atheism contains numerous weaknesses that bring its religious worldview into question: 1) A lack of evidence for its theory of macro-evolution, 2)

Its belief in man's goodness which goes against the history of mankind, 3) It is refusal to allow for the spiritual dimension of life and its evidences, 4) The lack of explanation of supernatural phenomena, and refusal to even consider it, 5) Providing no coherent basis for human morality, outside of force, 6) Its unqualified support for statism, despite the many tyrannies of history, 7) The senseless bloodshed it fomented over the past one hundred years—more than any other religion in history, 8) Its nearly universal tendency to produce despotic leaders, and 9) Its blind faith in chance, randomness, accidents, and belief in extraterrestrial life.[531]

Atheism/secularism makes a significant error by elevating human reason and power to God-status. Fallen men make very cruel taskmasters—because where human beings are concerned, power tends to corrupt, and absolute human power corrupts absolutely[532] Scorning belief in a personal God, people are left with overly optimistic trust in men, little concrete basis for hope, and no compelling reason to love.

Now we turn in our final analysis to the Muslim faith—the religion of the warring God.

WARRING GOD - THE RELIGION OF FORCE
Strengths of Belief in Islam

The Koran's monologue from God to Muhammad, his final authoritative messenger, reveals that Allah exists as the only true God and is the personal, infinite creator of the universe. Allah is a singular, distant God, with no companions, who does not need anything in creation and is unknowable by human beings. Allah demands submission from all people and belief in Muhammad as his prophet.

Human beings have dignity, possess a spiritual and physical nature, but are not made in the image of God. They were created good, and are sinless until they rebel against Allah. Human beings were created to use their free will to live in unconditional surrender to the will of Allah. Allah does nothing to deliver people from their sins—people must atone for their own sins by good works for which will be judged after they die. No one is guaranteed entrance into Paradise after death—only martyrs who will be rewarded with young virgins to sexually enjoy forever. Non-Muslims will all go to hell.

Islamic teachings show little concern for life on earth, and Muslim nations have done little to steward or improve it. What matters is submission to Allah. Since the early seventh century A.D. the Muslim faith has primarily advanced through warfare and forced tribute. Its growth today comes through high birthrates among Muslims. Islam carries a vision for world conquest and views itself as an evangelizing religion—striving (jihad) to bring the entire world under submission to Allah.

Hume lists the following strengths in the Islamic religion: 1) The theory of one supreme deity versus idolatry, 2) Its confidence in a sovereign world ruler, 3) Its teaching that God is merciful and compassionate, 4) Its principles of utter devotion to the will of God, 5) Its theory of an inescapable and just judgment day, 6) Its insistence on a continuous life of prayer, 7) The power and enthusiasm of Muhammad, 8) A worldwide outlook, 9) Strong, historic missionary aggressiveness, and 10) Unity among believers despite sects.

Islam creates an entire culture of living through the merger of church and state and the requirements of Shariah law. There is strong corporate identity in Islam as the "House of Submission" versus the rest of the world—the "House of War." The Muslim faith inspires a unique sense of devotion and fanaticism, even to the point of martyrdom for Allah.

Questions and the Truth Test in Atheism
Regarding the "Questions That Every Religious Worldview Must Answer," Islam rates high on a few aspects of the grid, and low on most others.

- *God*—Allah rules as the supreme creator God to whom all people must submit. Islam's solitary monotheism is unique among the worldviews.
- *Sourcebook*—The Koran purports to be the final revelation from God and the only sacred book among all the religions that is untainted. However, its revelations are "pure" only when read in the

Arabic language, it discourages translation into other languages, contains numerous historical errors, and it contains very little literary merit.

- *Origins*—Allah created all things including man from the dust of the earth.
- *Structure*—Allah is the supreme and arbitrary ruler of the world and Muhammad must be revered. Strict Islamic governments operate by Shariah law with very little freedom—especially for women.
- *Man*—Human beings have dignity, were created good, but were not made in God's likeness. Man has both a physical and spiritual nature, and his calling in life is submission to Allah.
- *Morality*—The Koran and Hadith give examples and teaching on right and wrong behavior that is required of all Muslims. The five pillars of Islam are the expected good works of every practicing Muslim.
- *Sin*—The concept is unclear, except that a person is considered sinless until rebelling against Allah. However, obedience to Allah can include killing in his name, slavery, multiple wives, and other sexual excesses. Sin is what Allah says it is. The world is a mess because infidels refuse to submit to Allah.
- *Salvation*—Muslims believe that "good works may save them," but there is no guarantee. World salvation will be brought about through striving (jihad) to convert the world to Islam.
- *Earth*—Muslims do not focus on caring for or stewarding the earth—only bringing people into submission to Allah. Thus, most Islamic nations are poorer and more backward than their Western counterparts (with the exception of a few oil-rich nations).
- *Heaven*—Heaven and hell exist, but only martyrs are guaranteed access to heaven and the virgins that await them. For most Muslims, especially women, there is no guarantee of paradise.

Regarding the "Truth Test," the Muslim faith comes up short. Islamic monotheism is clear and simple, but its tactics of force are barbaric or often deny human freedom. Forced submission is unreasonable to the human mind. As for evidence of validity, Islam has a well-known history and sacred book (Koran) to back up its tenets, but the lifestyle of its founder and the low quality of its scripture speak *against* its veracity. Muhammad, by any measure, was a perverse and violent despot who spoke on behalf of a warring God.

There is little witness of conscience in Islam due to its violent nature and low morals. It speaks of eternal life, but trivializes it with the absurdity of martyrs ravishing nymphs forever and the uncertainty of heaven for the masses—especially females. Islam spread as far as its violent crusades would take it during the Middle Ages (Middle East, North Africa and parts of Asia), but it lacks universal appeal due to its violent and controlling nature.

Weaknesses in Islam

Hume lists the following weakness in the Islamic religions: 1) The arbitrariness of Allah, 2) Its reliance on the method of force, 3) The excessive appeals to motives of fear and reward, 4) Its belief in fatalism (*kismet*), 5) The excessively sensuous future for martyrs in heaven, 6) Its low estimate of women, 7) The lack of great social programs, 8) Its synthesis with animism (jinn, devils, Ka-aba stone, repetitious prayers, 9) Pathetic weaknesses in Muhammad's moral character, and 10) Its denial of the theory of religious progress—Muhammad is the end of the prophetic line.

Though Islam espouses simplicity of beliefs and created a vast religious system, it appears deceptive and corrupt at its foundations. The Koran ranks as the most dubious religious text in the world. Allegiance to Muhammad seems completely unjustified based on his character and actions as a lustful, power-hungry, and violent tribal chieftain. Any religion that must operate by force instead of persuasion should be severely questioned. Its bent toward religious totalitarianism, abuse of women, and willingness to kill innocent people for the cause—in the name of Allah—reveals questionable origins that are certainly not divine.

A STRIKING SIMILARITY

We have now analyzed the message, strengths and weaknesses of the five major religious worldviews. Before I conclude our analysis, it might be interesting to point out that four of the religious worldviews—though extremely diverse in belief and ritual—are remarkably similar in their central approach and formula.

Here's the crucial insight: Four of the religious worldviews are based on *fear* and *works*.

- Polytheism—*fear* of the gods and *working* to appease them through rituals and sacrifice.
- Pantheism—*fear* of the cosmos, and *working* your way to Nirvana.
- Atheism—*fear* of scarcity and *working* to improve self and humanity.
- Islam—*fear* of a harsh deity (and prophet) and *working* to submit to him.

You'd think they were operating from the same script: Same song—just different lyrics. (Maybe a certain *liar* just isn't that creative.)

On the other hand, biblical faith is diametrically opposite of this. It doesn't operate by fear or works. Yes, there is a healthy "reverence for God" that accompanies trust in his salvation. And "good works" flow from trusting God as a natural response to his love (Galatians 5:6).

But the religion of the loving God declares that right relationship to him and others is based on *faith,* not fear—*grace*, not works. We cannot save ourselves. But the one who loves us *can*. Everyone on earth can be saved by trusting in God's provision for sin.

217

ANALYZING THE EVIDENCE

It is clear from our analysis that both polytheism and pantheism can be quickly eliminated as credible sources of truth about religion. Despite the proper awareness of supernatural powers, polytheism's worship of nature is clearly a false distributary off the River which replaced the Creator with his creation and personified demonic spirits

Pantheism is a different false stream—created by a people who were disillusioned with the chains of "caste" and needed a means of escape. Their desire for oneness with God—a noble pursuit—became perverted into an illusory unity with "Everything" which blurred moral responsibility, relationship to the Creator, and offered no concrete means of salvation and hope.

Both atheism and Islam contain attractive elements and ideas—yet are clever deviations from the truth about God. Islam *exalts* God—a proper quest—but Allah is a warring ogre who greatly afflicts people with force, control, and death. Atheism recognizes the dignity of *man*—who is made in God's image—but "puffs up" reason arrogantly so that *men* become deities. God's wonder in creation, his incredible love, and his necessary restraints on sin are lost. Harsh human regimes inevitably take their place.

Notice also this similarity between atheism and Islam. One elevates God and the other lowers him. Their goals are opposed. But the result is the same: *Violence, bloodshed,* and *controlling governments* (Nazism, Fascism, Communism, and Islamic States). Jesus' words ring true in this regard: "You will know them by their fruits" (Matthew 7:16). The greatest evidence against the truthfulness of atheism or Islam is the type of societies they produce.

That leaves us with the wondrous and liberating biblical truth of a loving God—whose grace and wisdom does *elevate individuals and nations around the world*, not through force but through compassionate moral persuasion and the blessings of freedom.

I believe that faith, hope and love will win out in the end (1 Corinthians 13:13). But the clash of the religious worldviews in the twenty-first century will be fierce.

Let's explore the looming battlefields.

Chapter Eleven

Battles

"For we do not wrestle against flesh and blood, but against
the rulers, against the authorities, against the cosmic powers over this present darkness, against the spiritual forces
of evil in the heavenly places." (Ephesians 6:12)

Many years ago, I flew into a wet-and-chilly San Francisco for a ren-
dezvous with two historians. Verna Hall and Rosalie Slater were founding
members of the Foundation for American Christian Education (FACE) and
authorities in the field of America's biblical history.

I took a taxi through historic downtown San Francisco and arrived at
their home, which also housed an expansive personal library. After a few
hours of a touring their beautiful Victorian home, coupled with "lectures"
on the history of the United States (taken from original documents from the
founding era), Verna asked me a question that would greatly impact my life.

"Ron," she asked coyly, as if the moment of tutelage had arrived, "with
all the Christian missions in Africa over the past two hundred years, why
do many of the African peoples still live in poverty and many cower under
tyrannical rulers?"

I was stunned by the question—and said, sheepishly, that I didn't know. Apparently anticipating my ignorance, she continued her well-planned homily: "I'll tell you why," she smiled, and then confidently continued: "It's because the Christian missionaries did not make *disciples* with a clearly formed worldview. They saved their souls, but didn't teach the native peoples how to apply their faith to every area of life. By not sharing the biblical worldview with the masses, they left them to live in poverty and under cruel oppression."

Following our visit, I left the city of St. Francis deeply pondering my encounter with these remarkable women. In the ensuing decades, I thought deeply about Verna's probing question and sought for answers. Many years of prayer and research brought me to the realization that religious worldviews are very important to history—both to help people improve their lives on earth, and but also to pave their way into eternity.

WORLDVIEWS SHAPE HISTORY

In the twenty-first century, worldviews just may determine the *destiny* of Planet Earth. We are engaged in a mighty worldview struggle. I believe I know which side will be the victor.

Of course, even our approach to history will be analyzed through a worldview lens. We all make assumptions about data, "what we are seeing," and draw conclusions from them. The history of the world supplies massive amounts of information about people, nations, and events, and our own religious worldview shapes how we interpret that information.

For example, if you are an atheist, you begin with the assumption that no God-given morality exists to restrain them. History is simply unplanned, accidental "survival of the fittest" on a national or global level. The ancient Incas and Aztecs died out because they weren't as strong as other societies that ended up displacing them. Western civilization came about by chance—and rose to prominence by blind "natural selection." As for the future, history will be played out by another unplanned roll of the evolutionary dice.

This is one reason why despots arise under atheism. Since man is the primary, if not the *only* intelligent force in nature, then the strongest and fittest men must rise to power to lead societies forward. They often do so with an iron fist because of no God-given restraints. Since they are the most powerful (or cunning or diabolical), then *they* must be the force that makes and shapes history.

But if you are a believer in the loving God, such as Verna Hall and Rosalie Slater, then you see the hand of God in the rise and fall of nations and the development of human civilization. God desires "all people to be saved and come to the knowledge of the truth" (1 Timothy 2:4). He commissioned His Church to "make disciples of all nations" (Matthew 28:19), which includes bringing whole societies into the freedoms and blessings of relationship to Him. History is "His Story" of changing individuals and nations.

Here are some examples of what I see through a biblical worldview lens:

- I note God's plan in dispersing Shem, Ham and Japheth and their descendants from Mesopotamia throughout the earth which gave rise to the nations of today. God directly involved himself in their times and even boundaries (Acts 17:26),
- I see the hand of God in the Middle East—the patriarch Abraham, whom atheist Richard Dawkins casually dismisses as a mythical figure,[533] fathering both the Isaac/Jewish nation and the Ishmael/Arab peoples, who remain in conflict and vie for a tiny piece of real estate called "Israel," whose only explanation for existence is God.
- I am amazed that God made Asia the continent of origins (the human family, its races, civilizations and religions), Europe the continent of development (learning, arts, and science), and America the continent of propagation (global missions).[534] Arnold Guyot, a nineteenth century geologist at Princeton University, stated it this way:

In the grand drama of man's life and development, Asia, Europe, and America play distinct parts, for which each seems to have been admirably prepared. Truly no blind force gave our Earth the forms so well adapted to perform these functions. The conclusion is irresistible—that the entire globe is a grand organism, every feature of which is the out-growth of a definite plan of the all-wise Creator for the education of the human family and the manifestation of his glory.[535]

- I view the providential hand of God guiding many aspects of the European Renaissance and Reformation movements to create modern education and science, capitalism, middle classes, republican and democratic governments, human rights, and freedom and prosperity in numerous nations.
- I glimpse God's directing the Western flow of missions—beginning with the Holy Spirit's guidance to the Apostle Paul (Acts 16:6-10)—to Europe, the Americas, the Pacific, the Far East, and now across Central Asia and back to Jerusalem.[536]
- I see the coming world clashes that the Bible describes, forming before our very eyes as described in Ezekiel 38, Revelation 16-22, and many other prophetic passages.

REMEMBER THE PLAYERS

But God is not the only moral agent who is involved in human history. As we discussed in Chapter Four, two other sources of moral suasion exist in the world: *demons and humans*. We need to constantly remind ourselves that the demonic realm remains active—what the Apostle Paul called "spiritual forces of evil in the heavenly realm" (Ephesians 6:12). These unseen malevolent beings are the driving force behind the four false distributaries of the River.

For example, it is clear from our study that diabolical spirits were involved in leading many cultures into polytheism to dim their view of the High God and enslave them spiritually. The goal of the demonic world is to "steal, kill and destroy" (John 10:10). Satan and his hordes desire humans to join in their devilish rebellion and receive their same penalty—separation from the joys of heaven. Satan wants people to go down with his ship.

It is also evident from the historical record that pantheism is a tool of destruction and despair—clearly designed by the prince of liars to keep human beings from being reconciled to God. Again, the end is clear: impoverish people and destroy hope. Bring them down with you by means of sophisticated deception.

That leaves three other worldviews to contend on the modern battlefield of history. Two of them are similar tools of demonic deception, and the third is God's expanding Kingdom. One of them— atheistic secularism—wants to counterfeit the Kingdom of God via a global secularist government. Islam, on the other hand, presents a counterfeit Messianic vision of a global caliphate. Both will use *force* (the "devilishness" behind the curtain) to achieve their ends. The Kingdom of God uses loving persuasion to bless and free individuals and nations

We have come to an amazing era in human history—dictated by the clash of three primary religious worldviews. Though two are being powered by satanic deception, maybe they will *merge* for strategic purposes one day. God only knows. The other—the Kingdom of the loving God—will have the final say in the matter, according to the Scripture (Revelation 18-22).

Here's how I view the contest. I want you to pray—and be on the winning side.

The Western Theater—Biblical Faith versus Atheism/Secularism
America and Europe fill the horizon of our first worldview battle. As the U.S. is the only remaining superpower on earth, we begin our discussion with America before moving on to Europe. A major reason for a pivotal clash of worldviews in the America nation is that for over one hundred

years, *the United States of America has been the leading nation in world evangelization*—sharing the love of Jesus around the globe. In 2015, the U.S., which contains only 5 percent of the world's population, sent out 32 percent of all missionaries engaged in proclaiming the Good News (127,000 out of 400,000). The second-largest sending nation was Brazil at 34,000.[537]

Obviously, the demonic forces want to bring America down to limit her efforts to spread God's love. The devil hates the *mission* of America— a nation founded on principles of biblical faith. Here's the background, which you might not have learned in school.

Though Richard Dawkins and other secularists dismiss, with scant evidence, the biblical foundations of the United States of America,[538] numerous original documents prove that, after Israel, America is the most biblically-based nation in the history of the world. A majority of the founding fathers were believers in Christ, and those that weren't shared God-fearing views which created a culture that assumed and promoted biblical values.[539]

America's charter—the Declaration of Independence—mentions the God of the Bible prominently and states, in the famous words of Thomas Jefferson, that "all men are created equal and are endowed by their Creator with certain unalienable rights." When the U.S. Constitution was being debated before ratification, the number one source that was quoted in Congress was the Old Testament book of Deuteronomy. [540]

Indeed, America built its very model of government on Isaiah 33:22, where God is mentioned as our judge, lawgiver, and king. From this inspiration came the executive, legislative, and judicial branches of government—meant to check and balance each other due to the fallenness of man—a uniquely biblical idea. In the 1830s, French historian Alexis de Tocqueville compared the bloody, atheist-based French Revolution with the American revolutionary experience in his book *Democracy in America.* He concluded that America's greatness lay in her faith, churches, and the power of religion that permeated every area of life.[541]

For nearly two hundred years, including three spiritual awakenings, a Civil War to end slavery, and vast immigrant waves drawn to the freedoms that faith produced, God seemed to bless America as the United States rose to become a dominant influence in the world. The United States' prestige came not from empire building and warmongering—but from the power of ideas that emanated from the Holy Scriptures.

In the twentieth century, secular/atheist/progressive thought made gains following the leads of Teddy Roosevelt and Woodrow Wilson, the Scopes-Monkey Trial (1925), and the growing assault of biblical criticism. By the 1960s, the biblical foundations had been weakened enough for a baby-boom rebellion against authority, godly values of morality, and America's biblical foundations in law, education, the media and the arts. Voluntary prayer was removed from the public schools in 1963—eventually leading to complete secularization of public education.

For many decades there has been an all-and-out cultural war in the United States as to which worldview will prevail—biblical faith that produced American greatness in its first three centuries (beginning in 1620 with the arrival of the Pilgrims in Massachusetts), or secular humanism, which gained momentum during the twentieth century until now.

Recent American presidential races have reflected this worldview tug-of-war. Jimmy Carter led the country in a decidedly secular direction.[542] Ronald Reagan's "Morning in America" revived the biblical faith foundations. Bill and Hillary Clinton brought back a secular focus. George W. Bush encouraged trust in God and American patriotism. Barack Obama promoted "Hope and Change" though a shift toward European-type social democracy. Donald Trump pointed America back to its traditional foundations under the slogan of "Make America Great Again."

Americans can't seem to decide which future they desire. Whereas biblical faith dominated American life for centuries, the nation currently stands polarized between those who want to renew the biblical principles and those who want to vanquish all vestiges of faith. America is truly a nation that is "hesitating between two opinions" (I Kings 18:21). Will its future be a spiritual renewal of the godly foundations or the triumph of secular humanism?

Quite possibly the next phase of history will be determined by America's choice of its immediate future. The jury is still out, and the nation remains torn between those who desire nanny-state social democracy or worse, and those who believe in biblical values of faith, smaller government, and individual responsibility.

The European Union occupies the other battlefield on the western front. It faces the same choice, but is much further down the road. Once a biblically-based European civilization (though never as Bible-centered as America), the EU now groans under the weight of big-government social democracies that are starting to persecute the people of biblical faith. Through low birthrates and large-scale Muslim immigration, Europe faces another worldview threat from Islam. Mark Steyn believes that "Eurabia" is a distinct possibility in the coming decades.[543]

However, I believe the European worldview wars will be fought primarily by the forces of atheism/secularism and biblical faith. The same is true in the United States of America. And at least for now, as goes America, so goes world evangelism—unless God has different plans. With all this at stake, no wonder the satanic forces are so interested in bringing down the West.

The Asian Theater—A Worldview Scrum

All *five* religious worldviews are vying for the soul of Asia—the most populous continent on the face of the earth. Even polytheistic and pantheistic influences are active here.

In numerous Asian nations, from Mongolia in the north to Indonesia in the south, folk religion "revivals" of polytheism are taking place. After breaking out of the colonial period, and following the dissolution of the USSR, many eastern countries are returning to their pagan roots in an effort to re-forge national identity. This includes a revival of Shintoism in Japan, Mahayana Buddhism in Mongolia, Tibetan Buddhism in Tibet, and tribal religions across the kaleidoscope of peoples that make up Indonesia and

Malaysia. It appears that the demonic strategy is to keep Asian peoples bound to the religious forms of the past, and especially hinder the growth of biblical faith as it expands worldwide.[544]

Indonesia is a case in point. It is currently the world's largest Muslim nation, but it will probably lose that status in the twenty-first century. A powerful biblical awakening has been growing for the past fifty years with nearly 20 percent of the population now claiming to be followers of Jesus.[545] It also hosts numerous tribal groups that still cling to their animistic ways.

India—the land of the Indus River Valley, where satanic deception created Hindu-pantheism and brings despair to hundreds of millions—is seeing a revival of Hindu nationalism in various parts of the country. Followers of Christ have been killed, and churches burned. Much of this is in reaction to the British bringing biblical ideas to India during the nineteenth century, and its significant growth since that time.

Islam also remains strong in India, but the creation of Pakistan after World War II—a post-war decision to draw a national boundary between Indian Hindus and Muslims—demonstrates the power of worldview "principalities" to impact national boundaries through religion. One million people died during those years while fleeing to one side of the fence.[546]

But the battle for India—the soon-to-be most populous nation on earth—will ultimately come down to whether faith in Jesus will overcome and liberate the caste-laden, poverty-stricken heart of Hindu pantheism. If the caste system falls—as William Carey and many other missionaries hoped and prayed—India could be in for a new day of global prominence as a leading nation in world evangelism.

Then there is China—currently the largest atheist/communist nation on earth. It has undergone the greatest biblically-based revival in the history of the world since 1949—the Church growing from three million followers of Christ when Mao Zedong came to power, to possibly 100 million today.[547] China, like the United States, is similarly embroiled in a worldview battle between atheistic communism and biblical faith. This struggle has immense ramifications for world history and the spreading of God's love to every corner of the planet.

China is a nation on the rise—one that is still firmly controlled by a communist regime, boasts the largest evangelical population in the world,[548] and the world's second largest economy which will become the first by 2025.[549] The Chinese Communists walk a delicate tightrope trying to control their society while allowing limited free enterprise to modernize and empower the people. This "opening crack" of freedom has caused an explosion of the Good News of Christ, first in the rural villages of the nation and more recently in many urban centers.

If China remains a communist nation, it could impact the world in coming decades through expansionist ambitions and deadly use of force (it has the world's largest army). However, if China becomes *free*, such as happened in the former Soviet Union, then the Good News of Jesus could explode from the Middle Kingdom to the ends of the earth. This is because Chinese believers have a vision to take the Gospel "back to Jerusalem" by "tithing" their growing Church numbers to world evangelization. At today's estimates, that would add ten million missionaries to the current global force.[550]

The Chinese-led "Back to Jerusalem" movement focuses on reaching the Muslim nations of Central Asia with the love of God and Christ's Good News. This region contains the remaining pieces of real estate in the western movement of the Gospel—now occupied by Muslim peoples. In this part of the world, Islam and disciples of the loving God will face off.

That brings us to the third worldview theater where followers of Jesus and Muhammad remain in tension. As we've stated, the battle behind the scenes involves dark, evil forces that desire to imprison people through violence and force and, on the other side, the followers of the loving God who want to offer people a choice of spiritual freedom through faith and grace.

This battle could bring down the curtain of history.

The Middle Eastern Theater—Biblical Faith versus Islam

One of the most eye-opening evidences that the God of Abraham, Isaac, and Jacob is the true God is the modern resurrection of Israel. Its re-establishment as a nation in 1949, after 2500 years of suppression and wandering, appears as a marker in the sand that God is alive and well. Hundreds of small nations have come and gone throughout the centuries. Israel alone has risen from the ashes to dominate the front pages of the newspapers of the world.

Why the vast media attention to a tiny nation? Israel is hated by jihadists who are, in turn, influenced by the demonic forces behind the Muslim religion. Both *hate* God's chosen people who brought the Messiah into the world (Jesus Christ). They also despise the God of love who will send Jesus again one day to wrap up human history and assign them their eternal fate.

Islam wants to destroy Israel for this and many other reasons. Future battles will be fought in the Middle East over this amazing strip of land that is the "apple of God's eye" (Zechariah 2:8). A few have already taken place—including the 1967 Six-Day War. By some accounts, Israel was miraculously saved—another testimony to God's covenantal protection.

This is noteworthy because Israel, today, is a secular nation—not a bastion of biblical faith. It contains a small orthodox remnant and a growing messianic church. But the majority of the Jews who returned to the land are unaware that the God of their fathers is using their renewed existence as a sign of his goodness and faithfulness. Part of the plan is Israel's "future salvation" described in Romans 11:25-27:

> I want you to understand this mystery, brothers: a partial hardening has come upon Israel, until the fullness of the Gentiles has come in. And in this way, *all Israel will be saved*, as it is written, "The Deliverer will come from Zion, he will banish ungodliness from Jacob; and this will be my covenant with them when I take away their sins.

I don't know how God will accomplish this, but he is the primary force in human history. Daily, he helps focus the eyes of the world on this insignificant piece of land called "Palestine" and arranges world events to reveal his purposes and love.

The Muslim nations surrounding Israel are also in turmoil. The Arab spring of 2011 brought the fall of cruel dictators and the rise of various extremist movements. Muslim eschatology says that an Islamic messiah, the *Mahdi* (Sunni belief) or *Twelfth Imam* (whom majority Shiites believe *is* the Mahdi)—will appear soon and that Islam will conquer the nations. [551] In keeping with the historical methods of Islam, Iran and others have vowed to "wipe the state of Israel off the map" by force—even using nuclear weapons to do so. The terrorist war launched by the now-deceased Osama bin Laden, was orchestrated to mobilize Islamic sentiments to liberate the holy land.

The United States backs Israel because it is the only democracy in the Middle East, and despite its secularism, remains God's chosen people. America wants to cooperate with God and his purposes for Israel. Because of that commitment, Islamic radicals label the United States the "Great Satan." Israel is the "Little Satan." These terms reveal demonic desperation—because the reverse is true. America and Israel hate nobody—and threaten no one. It is the Muslim world that is saber rattling, not with swords, but nuclear bombs. We know which side Satan supports because, as Jesus said: "You will know them by their fruits" (Matthew 7:16).

Conclusion

While secularism and biblical faith vie for supremacy in the West, and all the religions remain in spiritual conflict in the East, at the center of the world—in the Middle East, where it all began thousands of years ago—the stage is being set for a titanic battle between the loving God and the false gods of Islam and secularism.

The twenty-first century will be a war between three influential worldviews. There is no better explanation for the events of current history than this worldview battle to the death. Billions of people will be affected by these skirmishes, and many individuals and entire nations will have to choose—either the chains of tyranny or the blessings of faith and freedom.

As difficult as it is to predict the coming events, one thing remains clear: History is God's story. And as certain as the dawn, it is his love that will ultimately prevail.

We will preview his coming triumph in our final chapter.

Chapter Twelve

Triumph

"Then the angel showed me the river of the water of life, bright as crystal, flowing from the throne of God and of the Lamb through the middle of the street of the city; also, on either side of the river, the tree of life with its twelve kinds of fruit, yielding its fruit each month . . . No longer will there be anything accursed, but the throne of God and of the Lamb will be in it, and his servants will worship him" (Revelation 22:1-3).

We've seen that faith in a loving Creator was the first religion in history and grew in progressive revelation from man's creation to the coming of Jesus Christ. I call this revelation the River of God due to the God-created, life-giving, nourishing aspects of rivers and the use of this metaphor quite liberally in the Bible.

The biblical record begins with a river that went "out of Eden to water the garden" (Genesis 2:10) and concludes with a vision of a new heaven and earth where a "pure river of the water of life, clear as crystal proceeds from the throne of God and the Lamb" (Revelation 22:1). In these passages and many other places in Scripture, God's truth, presence, and power are associated with the life-giving benefits of rivers.

This River of God's redeeming love was present during man's ancient beginnings in the Garden of Eden, but became distorted over time, in different regions of the world, into four "false distributaries." All of these polluted religious streams are based on elements of the truth:

- Polytheism, on the wonders of nature and reality of angelic spirits.
- Pantheism, on the majestic expanse of the universe and desire for unity with God.
- Atheism, on the dignity of man who is made in God's image.
- Islam, on the reality of one God and his conquering eternal kingdom.

But instead of the true worship of God being retained, demonic influences and human reasoning distorted the truth and created false streams of religion that have held billions of people in bondage for centuries. The four distortions of understanding God are different, yet in matters of salvation, are identical: *the perversions all focus on works that are motivated by fear.* Since only one of them gives a fullness of meaningful answers to life's most important questions, aligns itself with principles of truth, and is refreshingly different from the rest, I conclude that *only one of them can be true*—humble faith in a God of love who provides atonement for and forgiveness of sins.

I also believe history is moving back toward a full manifestation of the River of God—as humankind enjoyed it in the beginning. The Creator desires all people to know him and experience his goodness and friendship. In fact, God may even use the distortions of his ways to point people to the truth. Gerald R. McDermott speculates:

> Perhaps the religions will serve this function: as providential preparations for future peoples to receive the full revelation of God in Christ. This does not mean there is a

direct continuity from the religions to Christ, but it does mean that the religions may be used by Jesus to prepare their devotees to understand and receive himself—just as the practice of animal sacrifice instituted by the Triune God (and copied by nearly every world religion thereafter) prepared the Jews to be able to understand and receive Christ as the Lamb of God who takes away their sins.[552]

This is undoubtedly God's desire because he *is* the God who sent his Son to die for all humanity. Despite the religious worldview divisions and battles that exist around the world, I believe that a wealth of indicators point to an amazing global spiritual awakening in the coming years, and that biblical faith will ultimately triumph in the world.

THE TRIUMPH OF BIBLICAL FAITH

Before we look at the signs of revival, I'd like to tell a personal story to illustrate the rising tide of biblical faith. Some years ago, I led a team to the nation of Albania—a formerly staunch communist country, which had been previously ruled by Muslims for four centuries. When we arrived in this very backward nation, we were appalled at the twisted beliefs about God that had created such poverty and despair.

For example, though Albania was a beautiful agricultural land (like southern California), the communist controls on the economy had produced a seventy-percent male unemployment rate, and you could only buy *five* items in the shops—milk, butter, bread, tomatoes, and cucumbers. We stayed in an apartment where our host had worn the same dress for twenty years.

But because the Iron Curtain had recently fallen in the early 1990s, Albania was opening up to new ideas, free enterprise, and faith in Jesus Christ. Thousands were turning to him for hope and salvation and steps were being taken to draft a new Constitution based on biblical principles of government.[553] We also noticed that missionaries were serving there from other nations that only recently had been mission fields themselves. A Brazilian team worked in one region, and when we went to serve in a different part of the country where we had been told that the people had never heard of Jesus, we arrived to find a Korean team planting a church!

In my book *The Fourth Wave: Taking Your Place in New Era of Missions,* I lay out the case for this growing global movement of biblical faith, and how the playing field has changed. I believe that the love of Jesus will touch billions of lives in the twenty-first century. Let's look at some of the amazing triumphs of faith that are taking place all over the world.

Evangelizing Nations

When William Carey, the famous missionary to India, produced the first book on global missions in 1792, he listed over one hundred countries as virtually untouched by the Good News.[554] Just two hundred years later, Todd Johnson of the Global Center for the Study of Christianity, now lists 141 countries as majority believers in Jesus, with fifty-nine others over half evangelized and only thirty-eight countries that are less than fifty percent evangelized.[555] Much of this amazing growth has taken place in the past few decades. Nations are being reached with the love of Jesus Christ.

Reaching Unreached Peoples

Mission scholars realized during the twentieth century that there were 16,000 ethnic-linguistic peoples living in the 198 countries of the world. Thousands of these groups had never had the opportunity to hear about faith in Christ. Much of biblical missions over the past few decades have focused on a concerted effort to share the love of God with them. This "Third Wave of Global Missions" successfully engaged 2,000 groups during the last century, and missionaries are now focusing on the final 2700—most of whom have less than 100,000 people.[556] Reaching all 16,000 groups with God's love is an achievable goal in the twenty-first century.

A Growing Church, South and West

There has simultaneously been an explosion of church growth in the southern hemisphere and in Asia during the past few decades. Whereas the strength of biblical faith used to reside in Europe and North America, God has been moving by his Spirit south of the equator in amazing ways. Rick Warren paints the picture well:

> The last fifty years has seen the greatest redistribution of a religion in the history of the world. For instance, in 1900, 71 percent of all "Christians" lived in Europe; by 2000 it had declined to just 28 percent who claimed to be Christian. Conversely, in 1900, only 10 percent of all people in Africa (10 million) were Christians vs. over 50 percent (360 million) today. That is a complete turnaround on a continent that's never been seen or done in history. There are by far more Christians in China than in America. There are more Presbyterians in Ghana than in Scotland. There are more Baptists in the Indian state of Nagaland than in the American South. There are more Anglicans in Uganda or Rwanda or Nigeria than in England. That is a fundamental shift. If you want to know the future of Christianity, it is the developing world. It's Africa, it's Latin America, and it's Asia.[557]

Yoido Full Gospel Church is the largest church in the world with a membership of over 800,000 believers. It is located in Seoul Korea and has planted churches in scores of nations. Seven of the eleven largest churches on earth meet in Korea, and the rest in Latin America. And speaking of Hispanics: At the beginning of the twentieth century, it is estimated that only 50,000 people in Latin America considered themselves "born again" (having a personal, evangelizing faith). One hundred years later, that number stands at 100 million.[558] Luis Bush comments,

"The spread of Christianity into the non-Western world is one of the greatest success stories of all history . . . This massive extension has been a working faith. No other cause in history has fostered such far-reaching humanitarian efforts of good will as has Christianity."[559] Followers of Jesus have truly become a loving, caring global family.

The New Face of Missions
As I mentioned in the story about our Albanian adventure, many ethno-linguistic peoples of the world, who have never before been involved in sharing God's love are becoming the new-multi-colored face of missions—like the Brazilians and Koreans we met in 1993. Though the United States remains the largest missionary sending nation in the world (127,000 missionaries), Brazil now ranks second (34,000), South Korea is sixth (20,000), and India is ninth (10,000).[560]

This represents a growing explosion of "Majority World" missionaries. In 1973 there were possibly 3400 non-Western cross-cultural missionaries in the world. That number has now erupted to over 100,000 which nearly equal the number of U.S. and Canadian missionaries.[561] Mission societies are growing too—exponentially. In 1980 there were 1,800 known evangelical missionary agencies worldwide sending out 70,000 workers. By 2010, those numbers had grown to 4,000 known evangelical missions groups sending out more than 250,000 missionaries from nearly every nation on earth.[562] Africans, Latinos, Islanders, and Asians are leading the developing Fourth Wave of Modern Missions. "The multi-colored friends of Jesus are coming."[563] For the first time in history, people from Majority World nations are leading the advance of biblical faith.

Piercing the Muslim Veil
The victory over fascism in World War II and the collapse of Soviet communism in 1989 have encouraged followers of Jesus that the Muslim world will be the next great field of harvest. The Islamic nations remain some of the poorest in the world, with oppressive governments, lack of human

rights, and a yearning for freedom. This will not be an easy task, but it appears that times are beginning to change.

Tom Doyle, a Central Asia ministry director, says: "Probably in the last ten years, more Muslims have come to faith in Christ than in the last fifteen centuries of Islam."[564] In the summer of 2010, two hundred former Muslims were baptized during a training conference in Europe. Muslims have had miraculous visitations and revelations of Jesus in a number of nations in recent years. In Iran, an underground movement of house churches has sprung up, involving thousands of believers in Jesus.[565]

Mosab Hassan Yousef is the son of one of the founders of Hamas ("Islamic Resistance Movement"), one of the most feared terrorist organizations in the Middle East. When the youthful Mosab saw the severe forms of torture used by Hamas terrorists, he began to doubt the validity of jihad, and began searching for truth in religion. In 1999, he became a follower of Jesus and is now committed to bringing peace to the Middle East through the prince of peace.[566]

Many millions of Muslims may be joining his quest in the coming years, and the people of biblical faith must be ready. Don Richardson points out: "Among the world's religions, Christianity is ethically most opposite to Islam and, as an evangelizing religion, it is the one with the keenest mettle to take Islam on in a peaceful ideological struggle—a welcome departure from pseudo-Christian crusades and inquisitions of the past."[567]

Maybe the most important jihad of the twenty-first century will be a jihad of *Jesus' love*.

TRUTH IS A PERSON

When we really unpack the meaning of the River of God, it boils down to an unequaled person who makes all the difference—Jesus of Nazareth, known as Jesus Christ. No organization is greater than its leadership. No religion is greater than its God. Jesus, the incarnate revelation of the Godhead, *is* the nourishing, communicating, revealing River of God who has made the Father known to us and provided the way back to him.

In the Old Testament Scriptures, Jesus revealed himself in various forms, possibly as the "Angel of the Lord" (e.g. Judges 13:1-22) who guided Israel out of bondage, and provided direction and salvation for a nation. In the New Testament, we meet God face-to-face in Jesus Christ— the God-man—a person who has no peer in history. He came to die for the sins of the entire world and personally demonstrated the love and grace of the living God.

Each religion rises on falls on the strength of its founder, architect, or deity. As we conclude our journey along the River of God, let's compare Jesus, the Son of the triune loving God, with the leaders of the other four false distributaries:

Jesus and Zeus—Polytheism possesses no supreme god or being, but the Greek god, Zeus, comes the closest. As with most polytheistic gods, he is a mythical figure who wars, possesses multiple wives, does good, also evil, and is certainly not worthy of emulation. Jesus lived a perfect life of sacrificial love. He has no equivalent in the pantheon of the gods.

Jesus and the Buddha—Since Hindu pantheism lists no heroes, let's compare Jesus to Siddhartha Gautama who started out as a pantheist and ended as an atheist. He abandoned his family for most of his life. He begged for bread, and did nothing to help people to change their world. Near the end of his life, he is reported as saying: "I'm still looking for truth."[568] Jesus Christ said: "I *AM* the truth" (John 14:6). There is a world of difference.

Jesus and Friedrich Nietzsche—There are numerous voices in atheism, but none thunders louder than German philosopher Nietzsche. He was a melancholy individual who called himself an "immoralist"—and eventually went insane, possibly due to contracting tertiary syphilis.[569] He gave us the phrase "God is dead." Jesus gave us *hope* through his words, "I am the resurrection and the life. He who believes in me will never die" (John 11:25).

Jesus and Muhammad—Don Richardson makes the comparison: "Jesus raised the dead; Muhammad killed the living. Jesus healed the sick; Muhammad harmed the healthy. Jesus released the oppressed; Muhammad enslaved the free. Jesus sanctified the earth with that which is heavenly;

Muhammad sullied mankind's understanding of heaven with the earthly. In fact, Muhammad could not even reach up to touch the underside of the moral standards of an average rogue."[570] The life of Jesus Christ remains the purest and greatest one ever lived. Probably the easiest way to come to the truth about religion is to compare the founders or gods of them all. There is no comparison. Jesus Christ—Son of God—Lord—Savior—is someone to whom you can truly entrust your life, your soul, and your future.

He is the River of God.

COME TO THE WATER

Thank you for taking this journey with me to the river's shore. The choice is now up to you. I believe that someone who loves you very much has been working in your life, regardless of the circumstances, or the current religious road upon which you walk. He has prepared you for this moment of discovery. William J. Abraham states:

> The activity of Christ, although crucially related to the events of his life, ministry, and death in Palestine, is not confined to that short segment of history. Jesus is the incarnate embodiment of the cosmic Christ who is at work enlightening all people. It is perfectly consistent to hold both that Jesus is the exclusive path to God and that people may genuinely encounter God outside of the Christian church without explicitly knowing about Jesus of Nazareth.[571]

If you are a seeker of the truth, you can trust the words of Jesus who said: "If you abide in my word, you are truly my disciples, and you will know the truth, and the truth will set you free" (John 8:31, 32). He also promised that, "If anyone thirsts, let him come to me and drink. Whoever believes in me, as the Scripture has said, 'Out of his heart will flow *rivers* of living water.'" I've experienced those living waters in my own life, and so have countless others.

The great Swiss reformer Ulrich Zwingli, talking about the wonders of heaven to French King Francis I in 1522, adds this encouragement to those whom are seekers:

> You will see the two Adams, the redeemed and the Redeemer, Abel, Enoch, Noah, Abraham, Isaac, Jacob, Judah, Moses, Joshua, Gideon, Samuel, Phinehas, Elijah, Elisha, Isaiah, and the Virgin Mother of God of who he prophesied, David, Hezekiah, Josiah, The Baptist, Peter, Paul; Hercules too and Theseus, Socrates, Aristides, Antigonus, Numa, Camillus, the Catos and Scipios; Louis the Pious and your predecessors the Louis, Philips, Pepins and all your ancestors who have departed this life in faith. In short, there has not been a single good man, there has not been a single pious heart or believing soul from the beginning of the world to the end, which you will not see there in the presence of God. Can you conceive of any spectacle more agreeable or indeed sublime? [572]

I have enjoyed our journey together along the vast shores of the River of God. I have pointed out the four false distributaries that contain dangerously polluted waters. They will harm you and keep you from your intended destination.

Now you're on the River's edge and great blessings await you. But the final step is yours to take. Have the courage to wade in the water. Let the refreshing streams cool your tired feet and aching legs, and bring hope to your thirsty soul.

Better yet, come up on a nearby ledge and gaze on the vast beauty of the River of God. You've been looking for it all your life—and now you have been found. My parting advice comes from the words of a song by Stephen Curtis Chapman:

"Dive"

The long-awaited rains have fallen hard upon the thirsty ground
And carved their way to where the wild and rushing river can be
found.
And like the rains I have been carried here to where the river flows;
My heart is racing and my knees are weak as I walk to the edge.
I know there is no turning back once my feet have left the ledge.
And in the rush I hear a voice. It's telling me it's time to
Take the leap of faith—So here I go . . .

CHORUS

I'm diving in, I'm going deep; in over my head I want to be.
Caught in the rush, lost in the flow; in over my head I want to go.
The river's deep, the river's wide the river's water is alive.
So sink or swim—I'm diving in.
I'm diving in.[573]

Through the revelation and love of Jesus Christ you've found the eternal,
life-changing waters that are full of truth, grace and love.

Welcome home to the River of God.

Epilogue

And **the devil, that had deceived them**, was thrown into the lake of fire and sulfur where the beast and false prophet were, and they will be tormented day and night forever.

Then I saw a great white throne and him who was seated upon it. From his presence earth and sky fled away, and no place was found for them. And I saw the dead, great and small, standing before the throne, and the books were opened. And the dead were judged by what was written in the books, according to what they had done. The Death and Hades were thrown into the lake of fire. This is the second death, the lake of fire. And if anyone's name was not found written in the book of life, he was thrown into the lake of fire.

Then I saw a new heaven and a new earth, for the first heaven and the first earth had passed away, and the sea was no more. And I saw the holy city, New Jerusalem, coming down out of heaven from God, prepared as a bride adorned for her husband. And I heard a loud voice from the throne saying, "Behold, the dwelling place of God is with man. He will dwell with them, and they will be his people, and God himself will be with them as their God. He will wipe away every tear from their eyes, and death shall be no more, neither shall there be mourning, nor crying, nor pain anymore, for the former things have passed away.

Then the angel showed me **the river of the water of life,** bright as crystal, flowing from the throne of God and of the Lamb . . . [574]

There is a River that flows from God above.
There is a fountain that's filled with His great love.
Come to this water, there is a vast supply.
There is a river that never shall run dry.

There is a River that flows from deep within,
There is a fountain that frees the soul from sin.
Come to this water, there is a vast supply.
There is a river that never shall run dry.[575]

Notes

2. Terance L. Tiessen, *Who Can Be Saved? Reassessing Salvation in Christ and World Religions* (Downers Grove, IL: Inter-Varsity Press, 2004), 297.

3. William Carey, *An Enquiry into the Obligations of Christians to Use Means for the Conversion of the Heathens* (Leicester, England: Ann Richards printer, 1792), 62.

4. http://www.religioustolerance.org/worldrel.htm, (accessed 19 January 2012).

5. Rodney Stark, *Discovering God*, (New York, NY: HarperCollins, 2007), 52.

6. Unless otherwise noted, biblical quotations in this work are from the New Living Translation.

7. Jude 1:3, KJV.

8. Thomas Cahill, *How the Irish Saved Civilization*, (New York, NY: Doubleday, 1995), 3-8.

9. Ronald Latham, translator, *The Travels of Marco Polo* (New York, NY: Penguin Classics), 1958.

10. 2 Timothy 3:16, NIV.

11. Vishal Mangalwadi, *Truth and Transformation* (Seattle: YWAM Publishing, 2009), 265.

12. Webster's First Edition of an American Dictionary of the English Language, 1967 edition.

13. A reference to John 14:6.

14. Webster's New Collegiate Dictionary, 2005 ed.

15. Dean C. Halverson, *The Compact Guide to World Religions* (Grand Rapids, MI: Bethany House, 1996), 15.

16. Pew Forum on Religion & Public Life, http://pewresearch.org/ pubs/1872/muslim-population-projections-worldwide-fast-growth (accessed 20 January 2012).

Chapter 1: Lies

17. Webster's First Edition of an American Dictionary.

18. Matthew Henry, Matthew Henry's Concise Commentary (Nashville, TN: Thomas Nelson, 2003), 46.

19. Ben Stein's popular documentary "Expelled" chronicled the extreme bias at the university level which cost many scientists their jobs when they attempted to teach any other theory than macro-evolution.

20. Michael Behe, *Darwin's Black Box* (New York: Simon & Schuster, 1996), 197.

21. Phil Saint, *Fossils That Speak Out* (Phillipsburg, NJ: P&R Publishing, 1993), 97.

22. Charles Darwin, *The Origin of the Species* (New York: Gramercy, 1995), 158.

23. The complete story of Washington For Jesus can be found in David Manuel's book *The Gathering* (Orleans, MA: Rock Harbor Press, 1980).

24. http://news.bbc.co.uk/2/hi/middle_east/4527142.stm (accessed February 8, 2012).

25. http://www.cbn.com/cbnnews/world/2009/September/Amid-Protests-Iran-President-Denies-Holocaust/ (accessed February 8, 2012).

26. R. Eng and W.T. Butler, *The Hidden Epidemic: Confronting Sexually Transmitted Diseases* (Washington, D.C.: National Academy Press, 1997), 1.

27. Centers for Disease Control, "Trends in Reportable Sexually Transmitted Diseases in the United States, 2005," Division of STD Prevention (December 2006), 1.

28. William Norman Grigg, *America's Engineered Decline* (Appleton, WI: John Birch Society, 2004), 109.

29. Francis Schaeffer, *How Should We Then Live?* (Old Tappan, NJ: Fleming H. Revell Co.,1976), 224.

30. http://familysafemedia.com/pornography_statistics.html#anchor1 (accessed February 8, 2012).

31. Sheri Girgis, Robert P. George, and Ryan T. Anderson, "What is Marriage?" in *Harvard Journal of Law and Public Policy*, Volume 34, Number 1, Winter 2011.

32. Ronald M. Deutsch, *The New Nuts Among the Berries* (Palo Alto, CA: Bull Publishing, 1977), 1.

33. Deutsch, *The New Nuts Among the Berries*, 2-4.

34. Deutsch, *The New Nuts Among the Berries*, 5.

35. Deutsch, *The New Nuts Among the Berries*, 16.

36. "There is a Sucker Born Every Minute" is the title of one of the songs in the 1980 Broadway musical *Barnum* by Jim Dale.

37. Abraham Lincoln, *His Essential Wisdom*, ed. Carol Kelly Gangi (New York: Barnes & Noble, 2007), 36.

38. Doug Simpson, *Looking for America: Rediscovering the Meaning of Freedom* (Enumclaw, WA: Winepress Publishing, 2006), 41.

39. Mark Levin, *Liberty and Tyranny* (New York: Simon & Schuster, 2009), 3.

40. Gordon Olson, *Sharing Your Faith* (Chicago: Bible Research Fellowship, 1975), W-Me-IV-7.

41. Levin, *Liberty and Tyranny*, 30.

42. Friedrich Hayek, *The Road to Serfdom* (Chicago: University of Chicago Press, 1994), 58.

43. Karl R. Popper, *The Open Society and its Enemies*, vol. 1 (New York: Image Books, 1985), 232-33.

44.   Mark Levin, *Ameritopia* (New York: Simon & Schuster, 2012), 3.

Chapter 2: Religion

45.   Walker, James B. *Philosophy of the Plan of Salvation* (New York, NY: Chautauqua Press, 1887), 26.
46.   Rodney Stark, *Discovering God*, (New York, NY: HarperCollins, 2007), 23.
47.   Walker, *The Philosophy of the Plan of Salvation*, 26.
48.   Stark, *Discovering God*, 20.
49.   Stark, *Discovering God*, 44.
50.   Stark, *Discovering God*, 20.
51.   Stark, *Discovering God*, 6.
52.   Stark, *Discovering God*, 5.
53.   Stark, *Discovering God*, 39.
54.   William Foxwell Albright, *From Stone Age to Christianity: Monotheism and the Historical Process*, (New York: Doubleday, 1957), 27.
55.   Stark, *Discovering God*, 23.
56.   Stark, *Discovering God* 24.
57.   Stark, *Discovering God*, 25.
58.   Stark, *Discovering God*, 27.
59.   Stark, *Discovering God*, 27-28.
60.   Stark, *Discovering God*, 30.
60.   Stark, *Discovering God* 25.
61.   Stark, *Discovering God*, 32.
62.   Stark, *Discovering God*, 32-33.
63.   Evans-Pritchard, *Theories of Primitive Religions* (Oxford: Cambridge University Press, 1965), 58.
64.   Stark, *Discovering God*, 33.
65.   Stark, *Discovering God*, 33.
66.   Stark, *Discovering God*, 35-36.
67.   Stark, *Discovering God*, 37.
68.   Stark, *Discovering God*, 37.
69.   See Frederich C. Crews, *Unauthorized Freud* (New York: Viking, 1998), who gives an in-depth analysis of Freud's claims, in-consistencies, and possible fraud in the development of some of his theories.
70.   Stark, *Discovering God*, 40-41.
71.   Richard Dawkins, *The Selfish Gene*, (Oxford: Oxford Univ. Press, 1976), 192.
72.   Richard Dawkins, "Is Science a Religion? *The Humanist* (Jan/Feb 1997), http:www.the humanist.org/humanist/articles/dawkins .html (accessed 2-24-12).

73. Stark, *Discovering God*, 62.

74. Andrew Lang, *The Making of Religion* (London: Longmans, Green & Co., 1898), 190-91.

75. Stark, *Discovering God*, 57.

76. Stark, *Discovering God*, 57-58.

77. Stark, *Discovering God*, 58.

78. Stark, *Discovering God*, 58.

79. Ninian Smart, *The Religious Experience of Mankind*, 3rd editor. (New York: Charles Scribner's Sons, 1984), 33.

80. Ake Hulkrantz, "The Concept of the Supernatural in Primal Religion," History of Religions 22 (1983), 231-53.

81. Stark, *Discovering God*, 60-61.

82. Wilhelm Schmidt, *The Origin and Growth of Religions: Facts and Theories*, (London: Methuen & Co.,1931), 262.

83. Stark, *Discovering God*, 62.

84. Stark, *Discovering God*, 15.

85. Julian Jaynes, *The Origin of Consciousness in the Breakdown of the Bicameral Mind* (Boston: Houghton Mifflin Co, 1976.

86. Webster's First Edition of an American Dictionary of the English Language.

87. Tiessen, *Who Can Be Saved?*, 299.

88. Tiessen, *Who Can Be Saved?*, 109.

89. Wayne House, *Charts of World Religions*, (Grand Rapids, MI: Zondervan, 2006), 1.

90. Paul G. R. Hiebert, Daniel Shaw, and Tite Tienou, *Understanding Folk Religion: A Christian Response to Popular Beliefs and Practices* (Grand Rapids, MI: Baker, 1999), 35.

91. Francis Schaeffer, *How Should We Then Live?* (Old Tappan, NJ: Fleming H. Revell Co., 1976), 19.

92. These ideas are expounded in a number of Schaeffer's books including *Escape From Reason, The God Who is There, and He is There and Is Not Silent*.

93. Vishal Mangalwadi, *Truth and Transformation* (Seattle: YWAM Publishing, 2009), 122.

Chapter 3: Truth

94. http://www.religioustolerance.org/worldrel.htm (accessed 19 January 2012).

95. Jason Mandryk, *Operation World*(Colorado Springs: Biblica Publishing, 2010), 2.

96. Mandryk, *Operation World*, 2.

97. Dr. Stephen Whatley, *Christian Encounter With World Religions*, 26-hour lecture series delivered at Faith Evangelical Seminary, Tacoma, WA, Summer of 2011.

98.   Mandryk, *Operation World*, 2.

99.   Mandryk, *Operation World*, 2.

100. Mandryk, *Operation World*, 2.

101. Harold Netland, *Encountering Religious Pluralism: The Challenge to Faith and Mission*, (Downers Grove, IL: InterVarsity Press, 2001), 33.

102. A great book on this subject is Dinesh D'Souza's *Life After Death: The Evidence* (Washington, D.C.: Regnery Publishing, 2009).

103. Stark, *Discovering God*, 5.

104. See Rodney Stark, *For the Glory of God: How Monotheism Led to Reformations, Science, Witch-Hunts, and the End of Slavery* (Princeton: Princeton University Press, 2003).

105. Mangalwadi, *Truth and Transformation*, 43.

106. Mangalwadi, *Truth and Transformation*, 39.

107. Mangalwadi, *Truth and Transformation*, 44.

108. Dinesh D'Souza, *What's So Great About Christianity* (Washington, D.C.: Regnery Publishing, 2007), 83.

109. D'Souza, *What's So Great About Christianity*, 89.

110. http://www.experiment-resources.com/history-of-the-scientific-method.html (accessed 18 February 2012).

111. Webster's First Edition of an American Dictionary of the English Language.

112. Tiessen, *Who Can Be Saved?*, 20.

113. As quoted by Josh McDowell, *More Evidence That Demands a Verdict* (Arrowhead Springs: Campus Crusade for Christ, 1975), 43.

114. McDowell, *More Evidence That Demands a Verdict*, 185.

115. McDowell, *More Evidence That Demands a Verdict*, 270.

116. Paul Little, *Know Why You Believe* (Colorado Springs: Scripture Press, 1971), 63.

117. J.M. Gundry-Volf, "Conscience," in *Dictionary of Paul and His Letters*, ed. Gerald F. Hawthorne, Ralph P. Martin, and Daniel G. Reid (Downer's Grove, IL: InterVarsity Press, 1993), 153.

118. John Calvin, *Commentary on the Gospel of John* (Edinburgh: Calvin Translation Society, 1847), 1:38, quoted in McLeod, Person of Christ, 240.

119. Madaleine L'Engle, *An Acceptable Time* (New York: Bantam Dell, 1990).

120. Bob and Cecilia Brown, "The Power of the Creation Message," *Impact*, February 1997, 1.

121. Don Richardson, *Eternity in Their Hearts* (Ventura, CA: Regal, 1984), 50.

122. Richardson, *Eternity in Their Hearts*, 50.

123. Daniel Lapin (1947 -) is a political commentator and American Orthodox rabbi living in Washington State. He is the founder of Toward Tradition, a politically conservative Jewish-Christian organization. These thoughts were shared on GBTV February 2012.

124. Stark, *Discovering God*, 39.

Chapter 4: Sources

125. Gregory Boyd, *God at War* (Downer's Grove: InterVarsity Press, 2007), 17.
126. Gordon Olson, *The Truth Will Set You Free* (Franklin Park, IL: Bible Research Fellowship, 1980), T-IV-1-2.
127. The New Book of Knowledge, vol. 7, Ursula Schoenheim, "Greek Philosophy," 355.
128. http://www.iep.utm.edu/greekphi/ "Ancient Greek Philosophy," (accessed 21 Feb 2012).
129. http://www.iep.utm.edu/greekphi/ "Ancient Greek Philosophy," (accessed 21 Feb 2012).
130. Attributed to Protagoras whose "atheism" shocked the Athenian world; in The New Book of Knowledge, vol. 7, Ursula Schoenheim, "Greek Philosophy," 353.
131. http://www.iep.utm.edu/greekphi/ "Ancient Greek Philosophy," (accessed 21 Feb 2012).
132. Levin, *Ameritopia*, 29.
133. Levin, *Ameritopia*, 23-36.
134. Levin, *Ameritopia*, 1-84.
135. Clement of Alexandria Stromata 1.28-29, in *Fathers of the Second Century*, vol. 2 of *The Ante-Nicene Fathers*, ed. Alexander Roberts and James Donaldson (Grand Rapids, MI: Eerdmans, 1962), 117.
136. *Fathers with Justin Martyr and Irenaeus*, vol. 1 of *The Ante-Nicene Fathers*, ed. Alexander Roberts and James Donaldson (reprint, Grand Rapids, MI: Eerdmans 1989).
137. Francis Schaffer, How Should We Then Live? (Old Tappan, NJ: Fleming Revell, 1976), 60.
138. Levin, *Ameritopia*, 241-48.
139. Plato *Euthryphro 3B*; and Xenophen *Memorabilia* 1.1-3.
140. Boyd, *God At War*, 1-27.
141. Boyd, *God At War*, 13.
142. Dean Sherman, *Spiritual Warfare for Every Christian* (Seattle: YWAM Publishing, 1992).
143. Sherman, Spiritual Warfare, 53.
144. Boyd, *God At War*, 99.
145. Boyd, *God At War*, 56.
146. C.S. Lewis, *The Screwtape Letters* (New York: Macmillan Co., 1970), vii.
147. Lewis, *The Screwtape Letters*, 3.
148. Cahill, *How the Irish Saved Civilization*, 82-84.

149. Phillip H. Wiebe, *Visions of Jesus: Direct Encounters from the New Testament to Today*, (New York: Oxford University Press, 1997), 44-45.
150. Tiessen, *Who Can Be Saved?* 27.
151. Tiessen, *Who Can Be Saved?* 388.
152. J.N.D. Anderson, *Christianity and World Religions: The Challenge of Pluralism* (Downers Grove, IL: Intervarsity Press, 1984), 171.
153. Lewis, *The Screwtape Letters*, 148.
154. Schaeffer, *He is There and He is Not Silent*, 18-19.
155. Schaeffer, *He is There and He is Not Silent*, 65.
156. Louis Giglio, "How Great is Our God," DVD, Passion Talk Series (Brentwood, TN: Sparrow Records, 2011).
157. Definition of conscience from Noah Webster, First Edition of an American Dictionary of the English Language.
158. James B. Walker, *Philosophy of the Plan of Salvation* (New York, NY: Chautauqua Press, 1887), 257.
159. Unless otherwise noted, these facts about the Bible are from Josh McDowell, *Evidence That Demands a Verdict* (Arrowhead Springs: Campus Crusade for Christ, 1972), 17-27.
160. See endbiblepovertynow.com led by Loren Cunningham, the founder of Youth With A Mission.
161. Bernard Ramm, *Protestant Christian Evidences* (Chicago: Moody Press, 1953), 230-31.
162. Mariasusai Dhavamony, *Christian Theology of Religions: A Systematic Reflection on the Christian Understanding of World Religions, Studies in the Intercultural History of Christianity* (New York: Peter Lang, 1998), 108:63.
163. Schaeffer, *How Should We Then Live*, 172.
164. http://www.gotquestions.org/rhema-word.html (accessed 25 Feb 2012).
165. Bible teacher Joy Dawson was a major voice within our mission for learning to hear God's voice. One of her enlightening books on the subject is *Intimate Friendship with God* (Grand Rapids, MI: Baker House, 1986).
166. Loren Cunningham, *Is That Really You, God?* (Grand Rapids, MI: Zondervan, 1984), 155-57.
167. As reported in my book, Ron Boehme, *The Fourth Wave* (Seattle: YWAM Publishing, 2011), 28.
168. Schaeffer, *He is There and He is Not Silent*, 62.
169. Walker, *Philosophy of the Plan of Salvation*, 26.

Chapter 5: Loving God—The Religion of Grace

170. An excellent book on the love of the Godhead and their desire to share love with us is William P. Young's *The Shack* (Los Angeles: Windblown Media, 2007).
171. John Micklethwait and Adrian Wooldridge, *God is Back* (New York: Penguin Press, 2009), 25.
172. Such as Sir Norman Anderson's *Christianity and World Religions* (Downer's Grove, IL: InterVarsity Press, 1984), 14.
173. Most of the information in this section is obtained from http://www.aquatic. uoguelph.ca/rivers/chintro.htm, (accessed 29 February 2012).
174. Bruce Feiler, *Where God Was Born* (New York: HarperCollins, 2005), 142-43.
175. Henry Morris, *The Genesis Flood* (Philipsburg, NJ: P& R Publishing, 1960), 47.
176. Feiler, *Where God Was Born*, 52.
177. Boehme, *The Fourth Wave*, 34.
178. James F. Lewis and William G. Travis, *The Religious Traditions of the World* (Eugene, OR: Wipf and Stock, 1999), 105.
179. Walker, *Philosophy of the Plan of Salvation*, 60.
180. Lewis and Travis, *The Religious Traditions of the World*, 105.
181. Tiessen, *Who Can Be Saved?* 170.
182. David Marshall, *Jesus and the Religions of Man* (Seattle: Kuai Mu Press, 2000), 16.
183. McDowell, *Evidence That Demands a Verdict*, 84.
184. McDowell, *Evidence That Demands a Verdict*, 84-89.
185. McDowell, *Evidence That Demands a Verdict*, 150.
186. Peter W. Stoner, *Science Speaks* (Chicago: Moody Press, 1963), 100.
187. Stoner, *Science Speaks*, 100.
188. Holy Bible, New Living Translation (Wheaton, IL: Tyndale House, 1996), 2028.
189. http://www.jesuschristsavior.net/Miracles.html (accessed 13 March 2012).
190. Philip Schaff, *History of the Christian Church* (Grand Rapids, MI: Eerdmans, 1962), 107.
191. As quoted in Frank Mead, *The Encyclopedia of Religious Quotations* (Westwood: Fleming Revell, 1965), 56.
192. Mead, *The Encyclopedia of Religious Quotations*, 53.
193. McDowell, *Evidence That Demands a Verdict* (Nashville: Thomas Nelson, 1992), 91-105.
194. Norman Geisler, *Christ: The Theme of the Bible* (Chicago: Moody Press, 1969), 48.
195. Albert Wells as quoted in William C. Robinson, *Who Say Ye That I Am?* (Grand Rapids, MI: Eerdmans, 1949), 209.
196. Ron Boehme, *If God Has A Plan for My Life, Then Why Can't I Find It?* (Seattle: YWAM Publishing, 1992), 115.

197. Olson, *The Truth Shall Make You Free*, T-VIII-1.

198. Olson, *The Truth Shall Make You Free*, T-VIII-1.

199. McDowell, *Evidence That Demands a Verdict*, 185-270.

200. McDowell, *Evidence That Demands a Verdict*, 107-114.

201. G.B. Hardy, *Countdown* (Chicago: Moody Press, 1970), 87.

202. Micklethwait and Wooldridge, *God is Back*, 354-355.

203. That is the focus of my book *The Fourth Wave*.

204. Quoted in Sidney Collette, *All About the Bible* (Old Tappan, NJ: Revell, 1989), 314-315.

205. His personal journey to faith is found in Hugh Ross, *The Creator and the Cosmos* (Colorado Springs: NavPress, 1995).

206. Winfried Corduan, *A Tapestry of Faiths: The Common Threads Between Christianity and World* (Eugene, OR: Wipf & Stock), 77.

207. Frank Hugh Foster, *The Genetic History of New England Theology* (New York: Russell & Russell, 1963), 1ff.

208. Much of this perspective is taken from Gordon Olson, *The Truth Will Set You Free*, T-IV-7.

209. Frank Hugh Foster, *The Genetic History of New England Theology* (New York: Russell & Russell, 1963), 97.

210. Olson, *Sharing Your Faith*, W-Me-III-5-6.

211. Millard J. Erickson, *How Shall They Be Saved? The Destiny of Those Who Do Not Hear of Jesus* Grand Rapids, MI: Baker, 1996), 191-92.

212. Tiessen, *Who Can Be Saved?* 27.

213. An excellent book on the dominion mandate containing essays from many different authors is *His Kingdom Come*, Jim Stier, general editor (Seattle: YWAM Publishing, 2008).

214. See Todd Burpo, *Heaven is For Real* (Nashville, TN: Thomas Nelson, 2010), Dinesh D'Souza, *Life After Death: The Evidence* (Washington, D.C.: Regnery Publishing, 2009), and Don Piper, *90 Minutes in Heaven* (Ada, IL: Revell, 2004).

215. Vishal Mangalwadi, *The Book That Made Your World*, Chapter Thirteen "Science: What is its Source" (Nashville: Thomas Nelson, 2001), 220-245.

216. Mangalwadi, *The Book That Made Your World*, 241.

217. Mangalwadi, *The Book That Made Your World*, 245.

218. Mandryk, *Operation World*, 2.

219. Mandryk, *Operation World*, 3.

220. Mandryk, *Operation World*, 3.

221. Tiessen, *Who Can Be Saved?*, 383.

222. Tiessen, *Who Can Be Saved?*, 403.

223. C.S. Lewis, *The Weight of Glory* (New York: HarperOne, 2001), 47.

Chapter 6: Many Gods—The Religion of Fear

224. Julian Jaynes, *The origin of Consciousness in the Breakdown of the Bicameral Mind* (Boston: Houghton Mifflin Company, 1976).
225. Stark, *Discovering God*, 24.
226. Stark, *Discovering God*, 96.
227. Stark, *Discovering God*, 164.
228. Stark, *Discovering God*, 77.
229. Stark, *Discovering God*, 96.
230. Samuel Noah Kramer, *History Begins at Sumer* (Philadelphia: Univ. of Pennsylvania Press, 1956, 1981).
231. Feiler, *Where God Was Born*, 166-167.
232. Albert Hyma and Mary Stanton, *Streams of Civilization, vol. 1* (Arlington Heights, IL: Creation-Life Publishers, 1978), 34.
233. Hyma and Stanton, *Streams of Civilization, vol. 1*, 34.
234. Lewis and Travis, *Religious Traditions of the World*, 52-53.
235. Lewis and Travis, *Religious Traditions of the World*, 52.
236. Lewis and Travis, *Religious Traditions of the World*, 53.
237. John B. Noss, *Man's Religions* (New York: Macmillan Publishing, 1980), 33.
238. Noss, *Man's Religions*, 35.
239. Lewis and Travis, *Religious Traditions of the World*, 54-55.
240. Lewis and Travis, *Religious Traditions of the World*, 56.
241. R. W. Rogers, *The Religion of Babylonia and Assyria* (New York: Easton and Mains, 1908), 204.
242. Lewis and Travis, *Religious Traditions of the World*, 56.
243. Noss, *Man's Religions*, 39.
244. Noss, *Man's Religions*, 39-40.
245. Stark, *Discovering God*, 3.
246. Lewis and Travis, *Religious Traditions of the World*, 56-57.
247. Stark, *Discovering God*, 165.
248. Lewis and Travis, *Religious Traditions of the World*, 57.
249. Richard H. Wilkinson, *The Complete Gods and Goddesses of Ancient Egypt* (New York: Thames and Hudson, 2003), 147.
250. Lewis and Travis, *Religious Traditions of the World*, 60.
251. Lewis and Travis, *Religious Traditions of the World*, 60.
252. Lewis and Travis, *Religious Traditions of the World*, 61.
253. J. Gwyn Griffiths, "The Orders of Gods in Greece and Egypt (According to Herodotus)." *The Journal of Hellenic Studies* 75 (1955), 21-23.
254. C. Kerenyi, *The Gods of the Greeks* (New York: Thames and Hudson, re-print 2004).

255. C. Kerenyi, *The Gods of the Greeks*, 16.

256. C. Kerenyi, *The Gods of the Greeks*, 15-18.

257. C. Kerenyi, *The Gods of the Greeks*, see "Zeus and His Spouses," 91-100.

258. C. Kerenyi, *The Gods of the Greeks*, 24.

259. C. Kerenyi, *The Gods of the Greeks* 72-75.

260. House, *World Religions*, 14-17.

261. Stark, *Discovering God*, 82-83.

262. Stark, *Discovering God*, 108-110.

263. Stark, *Discovering God*, 108.

264. Halverson, *The Compact Guide to World Religions*, 37.

265. Halverson, *The Compact Guide to World Religions*, 37.

266. Most of the material in this section is taken Stephen Whatley, *Christian Encounter With World Religions*.

267. Halverson, *The Compact Guide to World Religions*, 88.

268. Noss, *Man's Religions*, 194.

269. House, *World Religions*, 67-68.

270. Halverson, *The Compact Guide to World Religions*, 56, 63.

271. House, *World Religions*, 67-69.

272. House, *World Religions*, 67-69.

273. House, *World Religions*, 69.

274. Halverson, *The Compact Guide to World Religions*, 60.

275. Halverson, *The Compact Guide to World Religions*, 60 61.

276. Halverson, *The Compact Guide to World Religions*, 58.

277. House, *World Religions*, 69.

278. House, *World Religions*, 69.

279. House, *World Religions* 69.

280. Huston Smith, *The World's Religions* (New York: Harper Collins, 1991), 372.

281. House, *World Religions*, 69.

282. The Lewis quote is found in William Luther White, *The Image of Man in C.S. Lewis* (Nashville: Abingdon, 1969), 37.

Chapter 7: All is God—The Religion of Despair

283. R.E. Hume, translator, *The Thirteen Principal* Upanishads (London: Oxford University Press, 1934), 209.

284. Arvind Sharma, editor, *Our Religions* (New York: HarperCollins, 1993), 7.

285. Halverson, *The Compact Guide to World Religions*, 87.

286. Sharma, *Our Religions*, 35.

287. Sudhakar Chattopadhyaya, *Evolution of Hindu Sects* (New Delhi: Munshiram Manoharlal, 2000), 1.

288. Chattopadhyaya, *Evolution of Hindu Sects*, 72.

289. Sharma, *Our Religions*, 3.

290. Noss, *Man's Religions*, 72.

291. Noss, *Man's Religions*, 72-73.

292. Stark, *Discovering God*, 229.

293. See House, *World Religions*, Noss, *Man's Religions*, and Lewis and Travis, *Religious Traditions of the World*.

294. Lewis and Travis, *Religious Traditions of the World*, 58.

295. Stark, *Discovering God*, 211.

296. Hyma and Stanton, *Streams of Civilization*, 41.

297. Hyma and Stanton, *Streams of Civilization*, 39-40.

298. Hyma and Stanton, *Streams of Civilization*, 40.

299. Noss, *Man's Religions*, 75.

300. Hume, *The World's Living Religions*, 22.

301. Ralph T.H. Griffith, translator, *The Hymns of the Rig Veda*, Benares: E.J. Lazarus & Company, 1896), VI. 23.6.

302. Arthur Berriedale Keith, *The Religion and Philosophy of the Veda Upanishads* (Delhi: Motilal Banarsidass Publishers, 1925, 1998), 279.

303. Lewis and Travis, *Religious Traditions of the World*, 229.

304. Stark, *Discovering God*, 217-218.

305. Lewis and Travis, *Religious Traditions of the World*, 237.

306. Noss, *Man's Religions*, 84.

307. Noss, *Man's Religions*, 92.

308. Noss, *Man's Religions*, 80.

309. Noss, *Man's Religions* (New York: Macmillan Publishing, 1980), 92.

310. Hume, *The Thirteen Principal Upanishads*, Chand 5.10.7, 233.

311. Hume, *The Thirteen Principal Upanishads*, 76-81.

312. Hume, *The Thirteen Principal Upanishads*, 84.

313. Noss, *Man's Religions*, 85.

314. Noss, *Man's Religions*, 86.

315. Stark, *Discovering God*, 228.

316. Lewis and Travis, *Religious Traditions of the World*, 234.

317. Lewis and Travis, *Religious Traditions of the World*, 235.

318. Lewis and Travis, *Religious Traditions of the World*, 235.

319. Stark, *Discovering God*, 228.

320. Stark, *Discovering God*, 228.

321. Lewis and Travis, *Religious Traditions of the World*, 240-42.

322. Hume, *The World's Living Religions*, 34.

323 Robert E. Noss, "Jainism: A Study in Asceticism," *Man's Religions*, 94-105.

324. Hume, *The World's Living Religions*, 34.

325. Sharma, *Our Religions*, 38.

326. Priya Hemneway, *Hindu Gods: The Spirit of the Divine* (San Francisco: Chronicle Books, 2003), 28.

327. Stark, *Discovering God*, 231.

328. House, *World Religions*, 58.

329. Stark, *Discovering God*, 232.

330. Stark, *Discovering God*, 233.

331. House, *World Religions*, 58.

332. Sharma, *Our Religions*, 52.

333. Sharma, *Our Religions*, 5.

334. Sharma, *Our Religions*, 5.

335. Sharma, *Our Religions*, 13.

336. House, *World Religions*, 85, and Halverson, *The Compact Guide to World Religions*, 15.

337. House, *World Religions*, 85.

338. Sharma, *Our Religions*, 64.

339. House, *World Religions*, 58.

340. Hume, *The World's Living Religions*, 26.

341. Stark, *Discovering God*, 233.

342. Stark, *Discovering God*, 216.

343. Hume, *The World's Living Religions*, 24.

344. Hume, *The World's Living Religions*, 28-29.

345. Stark, *Discovering God*, 223.

346. Lewis and Travis, *Religious Traditions of the World*, 276.

347. Noss, *Man's Religions*, 80-84.

348. Sharma, *Our Religions*, 20.

349. Sharma, *Our Religions*, 56-57.

350. Hume, *The World's Living Religions*, 39.

351. Sharma, *Our Religions* 13.

352. House, *World Religions*, 58.

353. Sharma, *Our Religions*, 13.

354. Sharma, *Our Religions*, 45.

355. Hume, *The World's Living Religions*, 27.

356. Sharma, *Our Religions*, 48.

357. Sharma, *Our Religions*, 57.

358. Noss, *Man's Religions*, 70.

359. Noss, *Man's Religions*, 86.

360. Hume, *The World's Living Religions*, 27-28.

361. Sharma, *Our Religions*, 21.

362. See Vishal Mangalwadi, *The Book That Made Your World*, for a brilliant analysis from an Indian thinker on how a biblical view of the material world is essential for progress.

363. Bibhuti S Yadav, as cited in Klaus Klostermaier, *A Survey of Hinduism* (Albany: State University of New York Press, 1989), 4.

364. Mangalwadi, *Truth and Transformation*, 44-45.

365. Sharma, *Our Religions*, 36.

366. Sharma, *Our Religions*, 63.

Chapter 8: No God—The Religion of Men

367. Ignace Lepp, *Atheism in Our Time* (New York: The MacMillan Co., 1963), 168.

368. http://www.huffingtonpost.com/2012/03/24/atheist-rally_n_1377443.html (accessed 3 April 2012).

369. House, *World Religions*, 54.

370. *Webster's First Edition of an American Dictionary of the English Language.*

371. Mandryk, *Operation World*, 2.

372. Most the details for this section are taken from Halverson, *A Compact Guide to World Religions*, 53-60.

373. Sharma, Arvind, ed., Masao Abe, "Buddhism," in *Our Religions*, 101-102.

374. House, *World Religions*, 67.

375. Christmas Humphreys, *Buddhism* (Baltimore: Penguin, 1951), 41.

376. Eugene Burnouf as quoted by Rodney Stark, *Discovering God* (New York: HarperCollins, 2007), 241.

377. Stark, *Discovering God*, 241.

378. Mostly taken from House, *World Religions*, 67.

379. Sharma, Arvind, ed., Masao Abe, "Buddhism," in *Our Religions*, 115.

380. Sharma, Arvind, ed., Masao Abe, "Buddhism," in *Our Religions*, 86.

381. House, *World Religions*, 68.

382. Sharma, Tu Wei Ming, "Confucianism," in *Our Religions*, 147.

383. Halverson, *A Compact Guide to World Religions*, 71-72.

384. Sharma, Tu Wei Ming, "Confucianism," in *Our Religions*, 200.

385. Stark, *Discovering God*, 266.

386. *Analects* 12:1.

387. Sharma, Tu Wei Ming, "Confucianism," in *Our Religions*,184.

388. Halverson, *A Compact Guide to World Religions*, 72-73.

389. House, *World Religions*, 83.

390. Stark, *Discovering God*, 148.

391. Halverson, *A Compact Guide to World Religions*, 219.

392. Sharma, Liu Xiaogan, "Taoism," in *Our Religions*, 225.

393. Halverson, *A Compact Guide to World Religions*, 220.

394. Halverson, *A Compact Guide to World Religions*, 221.

395. Sharma, Arvind, ed., Liu Xiaogan, "Taoism," in *Our Religions*, 242.

396. Sharma, Arvind, ed., Liu Xiaogan, "Taoism," in *Our Religions*, 282.

397. House, *World Religions*, 75.

398. Hanns Lilje, *Atheism, Humanism and Christianity* Minneapolis: Augsburg Publishing House, 1964), 11-27.

399. Ignace Lepp, *Atheism in Our Time* (New York: The MacMillan Co., 1963), 6.

400. Thomas F. O'Dea, *Alienation. Atheism, and the Religious Crisis* (New York, Sheed and Ward, 1969), 104.

401. Halverson, *A Compact Guide to World Religions*, 183.

402. Charles Hummel, *The Galileo Connection: Resolving Conflicts Between Science and the Bible* (Downers Grove, IL: InterVarsity Press, 1986), 91-94.

403. Rodney Stark, "God's Handiwork: The Religious Origins of Science" (*For the Glory of God*. Princeton, NJ: Princeton University Press, 2003), 121-200.

404. See Halverson, 183-184, and Rodney Stark, "God's Handiwork: The Religious Origins of Science," *For the Glory of God*, 121-200.

405. Vishal Mangalwadi, "Science," *The Book That Made Your World*, 220-245.

406. Colin Brown, *Christianity and Western Thought: A History of Philosophers, Ideas and Movements, vol. 1* (Downers Grove, IL: InterVarsity Press, 1990), 184.

407. Colin Brown, *Christianity and Western Thought*, 105-106.

408. David Hume, *Dialogues Concerning Natural Religion*, ed. Norman Kemp Smith, Nelson, 1935; (New York: T. Nelson, 1997), 146.

409. A. N. Wilson, *God's Funeral*. New York: W. W. Norton & Co., 1999.

410. David Hume, Stanford Encyclopedia of Philosophy, http://plato.stanford.edu/entries/hume/, (accessed 24 April, 2012).

411. Allen W. Wood, "Rational Theology, Moral Faith and Religion," in *The Cambridge Companion to Kant* (London: Cambridge University Press, 1992), 414.

412. Wilson, *God's Funeral*, 36.

413. Kant's Philosophy of Religion, Stanford Encyclopedia of Philosophy, http://plato.stanford.edu/entries/kant-religion/#3, (accessed 24 April 2012).

414. Wilson, *God's Funeral*, 38.

415. Wilson, *God's Funeral*, vii-viii.

416. House, *World Religions*, 54.

417. Thomas Hardy, *The Collected Poems of Thomas Hardy* (New York: MacMillan, 1974).

418. Wilson, *God's Funeral*, 188.

419. Richard Dawkins, *The Blind Watchmaker* (New York: Norton, 1986), 6.

420. Charles Darwin, *The Origin of the Species* (New York: Gramercy Publishing, 1995), 171.

421. Michael Behe, *Darwin's Black Box*, 252.

422. House, *World Religions*, 54.

423. Friedrich Nietzsche, *The Gay Science*, Section 125, tr. Walter Kaufman.

424. Orlo Strunk, Jr., *The Choice Called Atheism* (Nashville: Abingdon Press, 1968), 30.

425. Strunk, The Choice Called Atheism, 31-32.

426. http://www.americanhumanist.org/Humanism/Humanist_Manifesto_I, (accessed 4 April 2012).

427. Thomas F. O'Dea, *Alienation, Atheism, and the Religious Crisis*, 113.

428. Hanns Lilje, *Atheism, Humanism and Christianity*, 42-43.

429. A.N. Wilson, *God's Funeral*, 83.

430. Wilson, *God's Funeral*, 83.

431. Karl Marx, "A Contribution to the Critique of Hegel's Philosophy of Right," Paris, *Deutsch-Franzosische Jahrbucher*, 10 February, 1844.

432. Wilson, *God's Funeral*, 92.

433. Strunk, *The Choice Called Atheism*, 62-67

434. See Mark Kramer, ed. *The Black Book of Communism: Crimes, Terror, Repression* (Boston: Harvard University Press, 1999).

435. Life News, http://www.lifenews.com/2011/04/21/earth-day-abortion-has-killed-1-2-billion-worldwide-in-50-years/ (accessed 24 April 2012).

436. Halverson, *The Compact Guide to World Religions*, 187.

437. House, *World Religions*, 54.

438. House, *World Religions*, 54.

439. Hanns Lilje, *Atheism, Humanism and Christianity*, 35-36.

440. Halverson, *The Compact Guide to World Religions*, 187.

441. Thomas F. O'Dea, *Alienation, Atheism, and the Religious Crisis*, 148.

442. House, *World Religions*, 54.

443. Halverson, *The Compact Guide to World Religions*, 187.

444. House, *World Religions*, 54.

445. House, *World Religions*, 187.

446. O'Dea, *Alienation, Atheism, and the Religious Crisis*, 114.

447. Levin, *Ameritopia*, 3-8.

448. D'Souza, *Life After Death, and Josh McDowell, Evidence That Demands a Verdict*.

449. Mark Kramer, *The Black Book of Communism: Crimes, Terror, Repression* (Boston: Harvard University Press, 1999).

450. Strunk, *The Choice Called Atheism*, 37.

451. Hegel, George Wilhelm, *Lectures on the Philosophy of Religion*, ed. P. Hodgson (Berkeley: Univ. of California Press, 1995), 40.

Chapter 9: Warring God—The Religion of Force

452. Sharma, Seyyed Hossein Nasr, "Islam," in *Our Religions*, 428.
453. House, *World Religions*, 44.
454. Don Richardson, *Secrets of the Koran* (Ventura, CA: Regal Books, 2003), 27.
455. Don Richardson, *Secrets of the Koran*, 143.
456. Sharma, Seyyed Hossein Nasr, "Islam," in *Our Religions*, 429.
457. Sharma, Seyyed Hossein Nasr, "Islam," in *Our Religions*, 432.
458. Reza Safa, *Inside Islam* (Lake Mary, FL: Charisma House, 1996), 25.
459. Ibn Warraq, *Why I Am Not a Muslim* (Amherst, NY: Prometheus Books, 1995), 92.
460. Richardson, *Secrets of the Koran*, 41.
461. Safa, *Inside Islam*, 28-29.
462. Safa, *Inside Islam*, 28.
463. Safa, *Inside Islam*, 30.
464. Safa, *Inside Islam*, 36.
465. Sharma, Seyyed Hossein Nasr, "Islam," in *Our Religions*, 464.
466. Halverson, *World Religions*, 105.
467. Richardson, *Secrets of the Koran*, 50.
468. Richardson, *Secrets of the Koran*, 145.
469. Richardson, *Secrets of the Koran*, 129.
470. Safa, *Inside Islam*, 47.
471. Richardson, *Secrets of the Koran*, 37.
472. Maxime Rodinson, *Muhammad* (New York: Pantheon Books, 1971), 196.
473. Maxime Rodinson, *Muhammad*, 167.
474. Richardson, *Secrets of the Koran*, 77.
475. Safa, *Inside Islam*, 81.
476. Ibn Warraq, *Why I Am Not a Muslim* (Amherst, NY: Prometheus Books, 1995), 93.
477. Richardson, *Secrets of the Koran*, 47.
478. Rodinson, *Muhammad*, 96.
479. Warraq, *Why I Am Not a Muslim*, 95.
480. Raheel Raza, "Muslim Women Struggling for their Basic Human Rights," March 8, 2007, http://www.thestar.com/opinion/article/189406—muslim-women-struggling-for-their-basic-human-rights (accessed 12 April 2012).
481. Mona Eltahawy, "Abusing Women and Islam," *The New York Times*, August 14, 2009, http://www.nytimes.com/2009/08/15/opinion/15iht-edeltahawy.html (accessed 11 April 2012).

482. Jean Sasson, *Daughters of Arabia* (London: Bantam Books, 1994), 207.

483. Rodney Stark, *For the Glory of God: How Monotheism Led to Reformations, Science, Witchhunts, and the End of Slavery*, "God's Justice: The Sin of Slavery,"291-366.

484. Richardson, *Secrets of the Koran*, 210-211.

485. They are all listed in Appendix B of Don Richardson, *Secrets of the Koran*, 254.

486. Bat Ye'or, *Islam and Dhimmitude: Where Civilizations Collide* (Cranbury, NJ: Associated University Presses, 2002), 48.

487. Bat Ye'or, *Islam and Dhimmitude: Where Civilizations Collide*, 41.

488. Sharma, Seyyed Hossein Nasr, "Islam," in *Our Religions*, 450, 453.

489. Sharma, Seyyed Hossein Nasr, "Islam," in *Our Religions*, 435.

490. House, *World Religions*, 44.

491. Halverson, *World Religions*, 107.

492. Halverson, *World Religions*, 107.

493. Halverson, *World Religions*, 107.

494. Halverson, *World Religions*, 107.

495. Richardson, *Secrets of the Koran*, 226.

496. Sharma, Seyyed Hossein Nasr, "Islam," in *Our Religions*, 456-457.

497. House, *World Religions*, 44.

498. Richardson, *Secrets of the Koran*, 27.

499. Edward Gibbon, *The Decline and Fall of the Roman Empire*, vol. 5 (New York: Random House, 1994), n.p.

500. Safa, *Inside Islam*, 83.

501. House, *World Religions*, 44.

502. Sharma, Seyyed Hossein Nasr, "Islam," in *Our Religions*, 444.

503. Safa, *Inside Islam*, 19.

504. Halverson, *World Religions*, 106.

505. Halverson, *World Religions*, 107.

506. Sharma Seyyed Hossein Nasr, "Islam," in *Our Religions*, 460.

507. House, *World Religions*, 44.

508. Halverson, *World Religions*, 106.

509. Sharma, Seyyed Hossein Nasr, "Islam," in *Our Religions*, 439, 442.

510. Sharma, Seyyed Hossein Nasr, "Islam," in *Our Religions*, 464.

511. Sharma, Seyyed Hossein Nasr, "Islam," in *Our Religions*, 460.

512. Sharma, Seyyed Hossein Nasr, "Islam," in *Our Religion*, 44.

513. Halverson, *World Religions*, 108.

514. David Pryce-Jones, *The Closed Circle: An Interpretation of the Arabs* (New York: Harper Collins, 1991), n.p.

515. Noss, *World Religions*, 535.

516. House, *World Religions*, 46.

517. Richardson, *Secrets of the Koran*, 38.

518. Richardson, *Secrets of the Koran*, 92-93

519. House, *World Religions*, 47.

520. Toby Lester, "What is the Koran? For People Who Understand," January 1999, *The Atlantic Monthly*.

521. Richardson, *Secrets of the Koran*, 18.

522. Richardson, *Secrets of the Koran*, 79.

523. Sharma, Seyyed Hossein Nasr, "Islam," in *Our Religions*, 429.

Chapter 10: Comparisons

524. Tiessen, *Who Can Be Saved?* 313.

525. Hume, *The World's Living Religions*, 268-269.

526. Hume, *The World's Living Religions*, 269.

527. Richard Dawkins, *The God Delusion* (New York: Houghton Mifflin, 2006), 85-90.

528. Hume, *The World's Living Religions*, 175-176.

529. Hume, *The World's Living Religions*, 175.

530. Hume, *The World's Living Religions*, 41.

531. Hume, *The World's Living Religions*, 42.

532. The Richard Dawkins Foundation, "New Evidence for Panspermia in the News," http://richarddawkins.net/discussions/597670-new-evidence-for-panspermia-in-the-news, (accessed 30 April 2012).

533. See Pier Luigi Luisi, *The Emergence of Life:From Chemical Origins to Synthetic Biology* (London: Cambridge Univ. Press, 2006), 1-14.

534. Attributed to Lord Acton, *Letter to Bishop Mandell Creighton*, 1887,http://www.quotationspage.com/quote/27321.html (accessed 17 April 2012).

535. Dawkins, *The God Delusion*, 57.

Chapter 11: Battles

536. Arnold Guyot, taken from Ron Boehme, *The Fourth Wave* (Seattle: YWAM Publishing, 2011), 60.

537. Arnold Guyot, *Physical Geography* (Princeton: Princeton Press, 1873), 5.

538. Ruth Tucker, *From Jerusalem to Irian Jaya: A Biographical History of Christian Missions* (Grand Rapids, MI: Zondervan, 1983).

539. Gordon Conwell Seminary, Center for the Study of Global Christianity, http://thechurchreport.com/index.cfm?fuseaction=siteContent.default&objectID=148026, (accessed 20 April 2012).

540. Dawkins, *The God Delusion*, 60-68.

541. Verna M. Hall, *The Christian History of the Constitution of the United States of America* (San Francisco: Foundation for American Christian Education, 1966).

542. Rosalie Slater, *Teaching and Learning America's Christian History* (San Francisco: Foundation for American Christian Education, 1965), 240.

543. Alexis de Tocqueville, *Democracy in America* (New York: Bantam Classic, 2000), 35-363.

Chapter 12: Triumph

544. I wrote my first book on the Carter election of 1976 and his secular worldview in *What About Jimmy Carter* (Washington, D.C., Third Century Publishers, 1976).

545. Mark Steyn, *America Alone* (Washington, D.C.: Regnery Press, 2006), 125-127.

546. Micklethwait and Wooldridge, *God is Back*, 5.

547. Mel Tari, *Like A Mighty Win* (Houston: New Leaf Publishing, 2001).

548. Sharma, Seyyed Hossein Nasr, "Islam," in *Our Religions*, 502.

549. David Aikman, *Jesus in Beijing: How Christianity is Transforming China and Changing the Global Balance of Power* (Washington, D.C.: Regnery Press, 2006), 47.

550. Micklethwait and Wooldridge, God is Back, 5.

551. Christian Zibreg, China is now the World's Second Largest Economy, Will Pass the U.S. by 2025." http://www.geek.com/articles/ news/china-is-now-the-world's-largest-economy-2010082/ (accessed 14 April 210120.

552. http://backtojerusalem.com/ (accessed 20 April 2012).

553. Sharma, Seyyed Hossein Nasr, "Islam," in *Our Religions*, 464.

554. Gerald R. McDermott, "What If Paul Had Been from China? Reflections on the Possibility of Revelation in Non-Christian Religions," in *No Other Gods Before Me: Evangelicals and the Challenge of World Religions*, ed. John G. Stackhouse Jr. (Grand Rapids, MI: Baker, 2001), 32.

555. I am a friend of American attorney Roger Sherrard who has taken over thirty trips to Albania and is a primary drafter of the new national Constitution.

556. Carey, *An Inquiry into the Obligation of Christians*, 38-61.

557. Todd Johnson, "Status of Global Missions," Center for the Study of Global Christianity, www.globalchristianity.org (accessed 10April 2012).

558. Johnstone, *The Church is Bigger Than You Think*, 105.

559. Rick Warren, "The Future of Evangelicalism," *Pew Forum Newsletter*, November 20, 2009, 3.

560. Johnson, *The Atlas of Global Christianity*, 311.

561. Bush, *Funding World Missions*, 480.

562. Johnson, *The Atlas of Global Christianity*, 310.

563. Rob Moll, "Missions Incredible," Christianity Today, March 2006, 36.

564. David Taylor, "Envisioning a Global Network of Mission Structures," Mission Frontiers, March/April 2010, 16.

565. Ron Boehme, *The Fourth Wave*, 162.

566. Sarah Stegall, "Evangelists Say Muslims Coming to Christ at Historic Rate," Charisma news on-line, August 20, 2010.

567. "Dreams and Visions of Jesus," The 30-Days Prayer Network, http://www.30-days.net, (accessed 10 April 2012).

568. Mosab Hassan Yousef, *Son of Hamas: A Gripping Account of Terror, Betrayal, Political Intrigue, and Unthinkable Choice* (Carol Stream, IL: Salt-River, 2010).

569. Richardson, *Secrets of the Koran*, 183.

570. Journey to Buddhism quotes, http://www.tumblr.com/tagged/buddha?before=1296998165, (accessed 24 April, 2012).

571. Magnus Bernd, "Nietzsche, Friedrich" (Britannica Biographies 1, History Reference Center, 2010).

572. Don Richardson, *Secrets of the Koran*, 81-82.

573. William J. Abraham, *The Logic of Evangelism* (Grand Rapids, MI: Eerdmans, 1989), 219-20.

574. Ulrich Zwingli, "An Exposition of the Faith," in *Zwingli and Bullinger*, ed. Geoffrey Bromiley (Philadelphia: Westminster Press, 1953), 275-76.

575. "Dive" by Stephen Curtis Chapman. Used by permission.

Epilogue

576. Revelation 20:10-15, 21:1-4, and 22:1 (English Standard Version)

577. "There is a River," Words and Music by Max and David Sapp, © 1969 (Used by permission).

Bibliography

Abraham, William J. *The Logic of Evangelism.* Grand Rapids, MI: Eerdmans, 1989.

Aikman, David. *Jesus in Beijing.* Washington, D.C.: Regnery, 2006.

Albright, William Foxwell. *From Stone Age to Christianity: Monotheism and the Historical Process.* New York: Doubleday, 1957.

Allen, E.L. *Christianity Among the Religions.* London: G. Allen & Unwin, 1960.

Anderson, J.N.D. *Christianity and World Religions: The Challenge of Pluralism.* Downers Grove, IL: InterVarsity, 1984.

Anderson, Sir Norman. *Christianity and World Religions.* Leicester, England: Inter-Varsity, 1970.

Barrett, David B. *World Christian Encyclopedia.* New York: Oxford University Press, 1982.

Behe, Michael. *Darwin's Black Box.* New York: Simon & Schuster, 1996.

Boehme, Ron. *Leadership for the -21st Century.* Seattle: YWAM Publishing, 1989.

_____. *The Fourth Wave.* Seattle: YWAM Publishing, 2011.

_____. *What About Jimmy Carter?* Washington, D.C.: Third Century Publishers, 1976.

Boyd, Gregory. *God At War.* Downer's Grove, IL: Inter-Varsity, 1997.

_____. *Satan and the Problem of Evil.* Downer's Grove, IL: Inter-Varsity, 2001.

Brown, Colin. *Christianity and Western Thought: A History of Philosophers, Ideas and Movements,* vol. 1. Downers Grove, IL: InterVarsity, 1990.

Burpo, Todd. *Heaven is For Real.* Nashville: Thomas Nelson, 2010.

Cahill, Thomas. *How the Irish Saved Civilization.* New York: Doubleday, 1995.

_____. *Mysteries of the Middle Ages.* New York: Random House, 2006.

Carey, William. *An Enquiry in the Obligation of Christians to Use means for the Conversion of the Heathen.* Leicester, England: Ann Richards (printer), 1792.

Chattopadhyaya, Sudhakar. *Evolution of Hindu Sects.* New Delhi: Munshiram Manoharlal, 2000.

Chopra, Deepak and Mlodinow, Leonard, *War of the Worldviews.* New York: Harmony Books, 2011.

Collette, Sidney. *All About the Bible.* Old Tappan, NJ: Revell, 1989.

Cook, Harold R. *Highlights of Christian Missions.* Chicago: Moody, 1967.

Corduan, Winfried. *A Tapestry of Faiths: The Common Threads Between Christianity and World.* Eugene, OR: Wipf & Stock Publishers, 2009.

Cunningham, Loren. *Is That Really You, God?* Grand Rapids, MI: Chosen Books, 1984.

_____. *The Book That Transforms Nations.* Seattle: YWAM Publishing, 2007.

Dawkins, Richard. *The God Delusion.* Boston: Houghton Mifflin, 2006.

_____. *The Selfish Gene.* Oxford: Oxford University Press, 1976.

_____. *The Blind Watchmaker.* New York: Norton, 1986.

Dawson, Joy. *Intimate Friendship With God.* Grand Rapids, MI: Baker, 1986.

Dhavamony, Mariasusai. *Christian Theology of Religions: A Systematic Reflection on the Christian Understanding of World Religions.* Studies in the Intercultural History of Christianity. New York: Peter Lang, 1998.

De Tocqueville, Alexis. *Democracy in America.* New York: Bantam Classic, 2000.

De Vries, Jan. *The Study of Religion.* New York, NY: Harcourt, Brace & World, 1967.

Deutsch, Ronald M. *The New Nuts Among the Berries.* Palo Alto, CA: Bull Publishing, 1977.

D'Souza, Dinesh. *Life After Death: The Evidence.* Washington, D.C.: Regnery, 2009.

Edwards, Gene. *A Tale of Three Kings.* Chicago: Tyndale House, 1992.

Eng, R. and Butler, W.T. *The Hidden Epidemic: Confronting Sexually Transmitted Diseases.* Washington, D.C.: National Academy Press, 1997.

Erickson, Millard J. *How Shall They Be Saved? The Destiny of Those Who Do Not Hear of Jesus.* Grand Rapids, MI: Baker, 1996.

Evans-Pritchard, E.E. *Theories of Primitive Religions.* Oxford: Cambridge University Press, 1965.

Feiler, Bruce. *Where God Was Born.* New York: Harper Perennial, 2005.

Foster, Frank Hugh. *The Genetic History of New England Theology.* New York: Russell & Russell, 1963.

Geisler, Norman. *Christ: The Theme of the Bible.* Chicago: Moody, 1969.

Gibbon, Edward. *The Decline and Fall of the Roman Empire,* vol. 5. New York: Random House, 1994.

Griffith, Ralph T.H.translator. *The Hymns of the Rig Veda.* Benares: E.J. Lazarus & Company, 1896.

Griffiths, J. Gwyn. "The Orders of Gods in Greece and Egypt (According to Herodotus)." *The Journal of Hellenic Studies 75,*1955.

Guinness, Os and Seel, John. *No God But God.* Chicago: Moody, 1992.

Guyot, Arnold. *Physical Geography.* Princeton, NJ: Princeton Press, 1873.

Hall, Verna M. *The Christian History of the Constitution of the United*

States of America. San Francisco: Foundation for American Christian Education, 1966.

Halverson, Dean C. *The Compact Guide to World Religions.* Minneapolis: Bethany House, 1996.

Hardy, G.B. *Countdown.* Chicago: Moody Press, 1970.

Hardy, Thomas. T*he Collected Poems of Thomas Hardy.* New York: MacMillan, 1974.

Hegel, George Wilhelm. *Lectures on the Philosophy of Religion.* ed. P. Hodgson. Berkeley: Univ. of California Press, 1995.

Hemneway, Priya. *Hindu Gods: The Spirit of the Divine.* San Francisco: Chronicle Books, 2003.

Henry, Matthew. *Matthew Henry's Concise Commentary.* Nashville: Thomas Nelson, 2003.

Hiebert, Paul G. R., Shaw, Daniel and Tienou, Tite. *Understanding Folk Religion: A Christian Response to Popular Beliefs and Practices.* Grand Rapids, MI: Baker, 1999.

Hinson, E. Glenn. *The Evangelization of the Roman Empire.* Macon, GA: Mercer University Press, 1981.

House, H. Wayne. *Charts of World Religions.* Grand Rapids, MI: Zondervan, 2006.

Hume, David. *Dialogues Concerning Natural Religion.* ed. Norman Kemp Smith Nelson, 1935. New York: Thomas Nelson, 1997.

Robert E. Hume. *The World's Living Religions.* New York, NY: Charles Scribner's Sons, 1959.

Hummel, Charles. *The Galileo Connection: Resolving Conflicts Between Science and the Bible.* Downers Grove, IL: InterVarsity, 1986.

Humphreys, Christmas. *Buddhism.* Baltimore: Penguin, 1951.

Hyma, Albert and Mary Stanton. *Streams of Civilization.* Arlington Heights, IL: Creation-Life Publishers, 1992.

Jaynes, Julian. *The Origin of Consciousness in the Breakdown of the Bicameral Mind.* Boston: Houghton Mifflin, 1976.

Johnson, Todd. *The Atlas of Global Christianity.* Edinburgh, Scotland: Edinburgh University Press, 2009.

Johnstone, Patrick. *The Church is Bigger Than You Think.* Pasadena, CA: William Carey Library Publishers, 1998.

____. *Operation World.* Bromley, U.K: Send the Light Publishers, 2007.

Keith, Arthur Berriedale. *The Religion and Philosophy of the Veda Upanishads.* Delhi: Motilal Banarsidass Publishers, 1925, 1998.

Keller, Timothy. *The Reason for God.* New York: Riverhead Books, 2008.

C. Kerenyi. *The Gods of the Greeks.* New York, NY: Thames and Hudson, 2004.

Kim, Djun Kil. *The History of Korea.* Westport, CT: Greenwood Publishing Group, 2005.

Klostermaier, Klaus. *A Survey of Hinduism.* Albany: State University of New York Press, 1989.

Kramer, Mark, ed. *The Black Book of Communism: Crimes, Terror, Repression.* Boston: Harvard University Press, 1999).

Kramer, Samuel Noah. *History Begins at Sumer.* Philadelphia: Univ. of Pennsylvania Press, 1956, 1981.

Lang, Andrew. *The Making of Religion.* London: Longmans, Green & Co., 1898.

Latham, Ronald, trans. *The Travels of Marco Polo.* New York, NY: Penguin Classics, 1958.

Latourette, Kenneth Scott. *A History of Christianity, Volume 1: to A.D. 1500.* New York: Harper & Row, 1975.

____. *A History of Christianity, Volume 2: A.D. 1500—A.D. 1975.* New York: Harper & Row, 1975.

Lawrence, Carl. *The Coming Influence of China.* Gresham, OR: Vision House, 1996.

Lepp, Ignace. *Atheism in Our Time.* New York: MacMillan, 1963.

Lewis, C.S. *The Screwtape Letters.* New York: MacMillan, 1970.

Lewis, James and William G. Travis. *Religious Traditions of the World.*

Eugene, OR: Wipf and Stock Publishers, 1999.

Lilje, Hanns. *Atheism, Humanism and Christianity.* Minneapolis: Augsburg, 1964.

Mangalwadi, Vishal. *Truth and Transformation.* Seattle: YWAM Publishing, 2009.

_____. *The Book That Made Your World.* Nashville: Thomas Nelson, 2011.

Mandryk, Jason. *Operation World.* Colorado Springs: Biblica, 2010.

Marshall, David. *Jesus and the Religions of Man.* Seattle: Kuai Mu Press, 2000.

Martyr, Justin. *The Apostolic Fathers with Justin Martyr and Irenaeus*, vol. 1 of *The Ante-Nicene Fathers,* ed. Alexander Roberts and James Donaldson (reprint). Grand Rapids, MI: Eerdmans, 1989.

Marx, Karl. "A Contribution to the Critique of Hegel's Philosophy of Right." Paris, *Deutsch-Franzosische Jahrbucher.* 10 February, 1844.

McDowell, Josh. *Evidence That Demands a Verdict.* Nashville: Thomas Nelson, 1992.

_____. *New Evidence That Demands a Verdict.* Nashville: Thomas Nelson, 1999.

Mead, Frank. *The Encyclopedia of Religious Quotations.* Westwood: Fleming Revell, 1965.

Medlycott, A.E., *India and the Apostle Thomas.* London: Cambridge Publishers, 1905.

Menzies, Gavin. *1421: The Year China Discovered America.* New York: HarperCollins, 2003.

Micklethwait, John and Adrian Wooldridge. *God is Back.* New York: Penguin, 2009.

Miller, Darrow. *Discipling Nations*. Seattle: YWAM Publishing, 2001.

____. *Life Work*. Seattle: YWAM Publishing, 2009.

Morris, Henry. *The Genesis Flood.* Philipsburg. NJ: P& R Publishing, 1960.

Neill, Stephen. *A History of Christianity in India.* Cambridge: Cambridge University Press, 2002.

Netland, Harold. *Encountering Religious Pluralism: The Challenge to Faith and Mission,* Downers Grove, IL: InterVarsity, 2001.

Noss, John B. *Man's Religions.* New York: MacMillan, 1980.

Newbigin, Lesslie. *The Gospel in a Pluralistic Society.* Grand Rapids: Eerdmans, 1989.

O'Dea, Thomas F. *Alienation. Atheism, and the Religious Crisis.* New York: Sheed and Ward, 1963.

Parrinder, Geoffrey. *Encountering World Religions.* New York: Crossroad Publishing, 1987.

Piper, Don. *90 Minutes in Heaven.* Ada, IL: Revell, 2004.

Popper, Karl R. *The Open Society and its Enemies,* vol. 1. New York: Image Books, 1985.

Pryce-Jones, David. *The Closed Circle: An Interpretation of the Arabs.* New York: Harper Collins, 1991.

Ramm, Bernard. *Protestant Christian Evidences.* Chicago: Moody, 1953.

Richardson, Don. *The Secrets of the Koran.* Ventura, CA: Regal, 2003.

_____. *Eternity in Their Hearts.* Ventura, CA: Regal, 1984.

Robinson, William C. *Who Say Ye That I Am?* Grand Rapids, MI: Eerdmans, 1949.

Rodinson, Maxime. *Muhammad.* New York: Pantheon Books, 1971.

Rogers, R.W. *The Religion of Babylonia and Assyria.* New York: Easton and Mains, 1908.

Ross, Hugh. *The Creator and the Cosmos.* Colorado Springs: NavPress, 1995.

Safa, Reza. *Inside Islam.* Lake Mary, FL: Charisma House, 1996.

Saint Phil. *Fossils That Speak Out.* Phillipsburg, NJ: P&R Publishing, 1993.

Sasson, Jean. *Daughters of Arabia.* London: Bantam Books, 1994.

Schaff, Philip. *History of the Christian Church.* Grand Rapids, MI: Eerdmans, 1962.

Schmidt, Wilhelm. *The Origin and Growth of Religions: Facts and Theories,* London: Methuen & Co. 1931.

Sharma, Arvind. *Our Religions.* New York: HarperCollins, 1993.

Shakir, M.H., trans. *The Qur'an.* Elmhurst, NY: Tahrike Tarsile Qur'an Inc., 2006.

Schaeffer, Francis. *How Should We Then Live?* Old Tappan, NJ: Revell, 1976.

_____. *The God Who Is There.* Downers Grove, IL: Inter-Varsity, 1998.

_____. *He is There and He is Not Silent.* Carol Stream, IL: Tyndale, 1972.

Schaff, Philip. *History of the Christian Church.* Grand Rapids, MI: Eerdmans, 1962.

Dean Sherman, *Spiritual Warfare for Every Christian* (Seattle: YWAM Publishing, 1992).

Slater, Rosalie. *Teaching and Learning America's Christian History.* San Francisco: Foundation for American Christian Education, 1965, 240.

Smart, Ninian. *The Religious Experience of Mankind,* 3rd edit. New York: Charles Scribner's Sons, 1984.

Smith, Huston. *The World's Religions.* San Francisco: HarperCollins, 1991.

Stackhouse, John G. ed. *No Other Gods Before Me: Evangelicals and the Challenge of World Religions.* Grand Rapids, MI: Baker, 2001.

Stark, Rodney. *Discovering God.* New York: Harper Collins, 2007.

_____. *For the Glory of God.* Princeton, NJ: Princeton University Press, 2003.

Steyn, Mark. *America Alone: The End of the World as We Know It.* Washington, D.C.: Regnery, 2006.

Stier, Jim, Richlyn Poor and Lisa Orvis. *His Kingdom Come.* Seattle: YWAM Publishing, 2008.

Stoner, Peter W. *Science Speaks.* Chicago: Moody, 1963.

Strunk, Orlo Jr. *The Choice Called Atheism.* Nashville: Abingdon, 1968.

Tari, Mel. *Like A Mighty Wind.* Houston: New Leaf Publishing, 2001.

Tiessen, Terance L. *Who Can Be Saved? Reassessing Salvation in Christ and World Religions.* Downers Grove, IL: Inter-Varsity, 2004.

Tucker, Ruth A. *From Jerusalem to Irian Jaya.* Grand Rapids, MI: Zondervan, 1983.

Walker, James B. *Philosophy of the Plan of Salvation.* New York: Chautauqua Press, 1887.

Warraq, Ibn. *Why I Am Not a Muslim.* Amherst: Prometheus Books, 1995.

White, William Luther. *The Image of Man in C.S. Lewis.* Nashville: Abingdon, 1969.

Wiebe, Phillip H. *Visions of Jesus: Direct Encounters from the New Testament to Today.* New York: Oxford University Press, 1997.

Wilkinson, Richard H. *The Complete Gods and Goddesses of Ancient Egypt* .New York: Thames and Hudson, 2003.

Wilson, A.N. *God's Funeral.* New York: W. W. Norton & Co., 1999.

Wood, Allen W. "Rational Theology, Moral Faith and Religion." *The Cambridge Companion to Kant.* London: Cambridge University Press, 1992.

Ye'or, Bat. *Islam and Dhimmitude: Where Civilizations Collide.* Cranbury, NJ: Associated University Presses, 2002.

Young, William P. *The Shack.* Los Angeles: Windblown Media, 2007.

Youself, Mosab Hassan. *Son of Ham*as. Chicago: Tyndale, 2010.

Zwingli, Ulrich. "An Exposition of the Faith," in *Zwingli and Bullinger.* ed. Geoffrey Bromiley. Philadelphia: Westminster, 1953.

REFERENCE WORKS

Britannica Biographies 1. History Reference Center, 2010.

The New Book of Knowledge, vol.16. Danbury, CT: Grolier Inc., 1988.

Webster's New Collegiate Dictionary, 2005 ed.

Webster's First Edition of an American Dictionary of the English Language. New York: Iversen Associates, 1967 ed.

OTHER SOURCES

Major Religions of the World.
http://www.adherents.com/Religions_By_Adherents.html.

Religions of the World. http://www.religioustolerance.org/var_rel.htm

Stephen Whatley, *Christian Encounter With World Religions.* 26-hour lecture series delivered at Faith Evangelical Seminary, Tacoma, WA, Summer of 2011.

The Major World Religions. http://www.omsakthi.org/religions.html

About the Author

Dr. Ron Boehme (pronounced BAY-mee) is a career missionary with Youth With A Mission who founded YWAM works in Washington, D.C., and the states of Virginia and Washington. He's ministered in over 60 nations around the world and is in frequent demand as a speaker on revival, personal discipleship, world missions, and current events.

He also serves as a professor of Leadership and Inter-Cultural Studies at Faith International University & Seminary in Tacoma, Washington.

His books include including *Leadership for the -21st Century: Changing Nations Through the Power of Serving*, If *God Has Plan for My Life, Why Can't I Find It?*, *Restoring America's Conscience,* and *The Fourth Wave: Taking Your Place in the New Era of Missions.*

Visit the author on-line at www.usrenewal.org.